NOT JUST CHALK

AND TALK

Copyright Dick Abram and Patrick Binks ©2014

First Edition
Issued on DVD in December 2012

Second Edition 2013
Produced by Blaisdon Publishing
3 Park Chase, Hornby, Bedale
North Yorkshire DL8 1PR
bruce@blaisdon.force9.co.uk

in conjunction with Book Empire

ISBN 978 1902838 52 6

All rights reserved. No part of this publication may be reproduced,
stored in a retrieval system, or transmitted in any way,
or by any means without the prior permission of the copyright holders.

Acknowledgements

Our contributors include those who have helped provide photographs and ships' badges; we are most grateful to Richard Porter from Britannia Royal Naval College, Dartmouth, Trevor Muston from Navy News, Stephen Courtney from the National Museum of the Royal Navy, Jenny Wraight from the Naval Historical Branch, Debbie Corner from the Royal Navy Submarine Museum and Barbara Gilbert from the Fleet Air Arm Museum. Our publisher, Bruce Webb of Blaisdon Publishing, is sincerely thanked for his sterling efforts on our behalf.

The photographs which have not been accredited belong to the authors or the editors; the ships' badges and posters are Crown copyright © and are used with permission.
If there are any photographs with copyright that inadvertently have not been acknowledged, accreditation will be made when requested.

Front and back covers: All photos by permission of Navy News (MOD)

CONTENTS

FOREWORD v
PREFACE vii
PART ONE – SETTING THE SCENE
   Chapter 1
      Over Three Centuries 1
      The Naval Instructors 1
      The Naval Schoolmasters 6
      The Royal Marines Schoolmasters 11
      One Branch 11
      After the Demise 16
PART TWO – STORIES BY INDIVIDUALS
   Chapter 2
      We Joined the Navy 19
   Chapter 3
      Down to Business 44
      HMS Ganges 45
      Royal Marines School of Music, Deal 50
      HMS Raleigh 53
      HMS Sultan 56
      HMS Dryad 59
      HMS Dolphin 62
      HMS Daedalus 65
      HMS Collingwood 67
      Naval Home Command 71
   Chapter 4
      We Saw the Sea 75
      During the Second World War 75
      During the 1950s 83
      During the 1960s 96

    During the 1970s 103

    During the 1980s 130

    During the 1990s 135

    During the 2000s 140

Chapter 5

    '… and Women may Apply.' 144

Chapter 6

    Up the Ramparts 155

    Meteorology and Oceanography 156

    Royal Naval College Greenwich 167

    Royal Naval Engineering College, Manadon 173

    Service and Dockyard Schools and Colleges 186

    Work Study and Management Services 202

    Information Systems 205

    RN School of Educational and Training Technology 221

    Submarine Service 236

    The Royal Marines 248

ANNEXES

    Annex 1 – Chronology of the Instructor Branch and Specialisation 259

    Annex 2 – Number of Instructor Officers in the Royal Navy 1920 to 1995 262

    Annex 3 – Heads of Naval Education 263

    Annex 4 – Deans of the Royal Naval College, Greenwich 264

    Annex 5 – Deans of the Royal Naval Engineering College, Manadon 265

    Annex 6 – Heads of Meteorology & Oceanography 266

    Annex 7 – Officers-in-Charge of the RN School for Meteorology and Oceanography ... 267

    Annex 8 – Royal Naval Training Establishments in 1955 269

    Annex 9 – Heads of RN Service Schools and RN Dockyard Schools and Colleges 271

    Annex 10 – Instructor Officers in Information Systems (SACLANT and OPCON) 273

GLOSSARY 274

FOREWORD

Rear Admiral John Bellamy CB CBE

As a senior member of the Instructor Branch, I was honoured to be asked to write this foreword although, some 41 years into retirement, it is not easy to comprehend all that has happened to the branch and then the specialisation during the intervening years.

One thing that has not changed is that, when I joined the Service in 1939, King's Regulations and Admiralty Instructions specified that the duty of the Instructor Officer, as the only graduate other than a Medical Officer, was to assist the Command by using his scientific knowledge to solve any problems that might arise.

As the Instructor Officer Appointer and Recruiter during the early 1960s there was pressure to meet demands in the newly developing fields of oceanography, information systems, work study and management services and there were also those individuals, some of them seen as mavericks, who developed their own sub-specialisations to the lasting benefit of the Service.

My first three months of training was at the beginning of the war, mostly in navigation at the Royal Naval College, Greenwich, and then at sea in the Far East in an old D class cruiser whose officers were a mixture of active service, some having been long-retired, several RNR and RNVR and an Australian Captain. Nobody quite knew what to make of the Warrant Schoolmaster and myself, and to a great extent we developed our own roles. We ran the Action Plot based on the information from a bundle of signals, giving just a verbal report to the Captain when anything interesting such as an enemy raider came up. It was a far cry from the Ops Rooms of today. My own task was to prepare Midshipmen for their celestial navigation examinations. Generally one was accepted as a useful member of the team with a part to play despite the blue distinctive cloth, and not just thought of as the wine caterer or auditor of the mess accounts.

My next seagoing job with added responsibility for meteorology was in *Glasgow*, the flagship of the America and West Indies Station, from which I was promoted Commander in 1948. Then in 1954 I went to *Ark Royal*, during which commission the distinctive blue cloth disappeared and one was accepted as a fully paid-up member of the 'Sergeant's' team, of about ten strong, with regular access to the Command. That this integration of Instructor Officers into wider aspects of the Royal Navy continued is greatly to the credit of all those concerned.

I congratulate everyone who has contributed to this much-needed record.

John Bellamy
Kington Magna, Dorset

PREFACE

One day in the Royal Naval Club in Old Portsmouth the two of us reflected that 2011 marked 15 years since the demise of the Royal Navy's Instructor Specialisation. We noted that many people probably knew only of the Instructors' primary role in education and training while remaining unaware of the many other areas – sometimes referred to as Ramparts – in which Schoolies had been involved. Recognising that much of this knowledge might soon be forgotten, or may already have been lost, we agreed that something needed to be done to preserve those memories lest the stories be lost forever.

It's now or never, we thought, and agreed to get started. In the beginning we contacted those who would contribute their own stories, and also those whom we thought would take the lead and produce an article by reaching out and coordinating the contributions of others. We have been delighted with the incredibly enthusiastic and cooperative responses.

The basic structure of the book is in three parts: the first sets the scene; then there are several chapters by individuals joining the Royal Navy, jobs in education and training, and more; in the last part there are several chapters on the individual Ramparts. The basic contents have remained pretty well as first planned with one major addition. We originally thought that most people would know about the activities of Instructor Officers in education and training and we had not included these topics. However, feedback from our colleagues made us realise this error and a chapter covering those tasks was added.

We invited more than 100 Instructor Officers to suggest a book title and received numerous responses. The title we thought best summed up our Instructor heritage as described in the book was: Not Just Chalk and Talk.

Except for the earlier part of the first chapter, 'Over Three Centuries', and two stories in the chapter, 'We Saw the Sea', all the articles have been written specifically for this book. We are delighted that two colleagues, who had joined the Royal Navy as Instructor Officers before the Second World War, agreed to contribute and so the personal stories begin in 1937. Understandably the stories finish in 1996, when the Specialisation was disbanded.

Sadly, whilst we have been collecting the stories, then editing the book, seven contributors have died: Admiral John Bellamy, Ken Bowell, Terry Le Manquais, Ken Langley, Peter Poll, Alan Robertson and Mary Talbot.

We want to acknowledge that the book is the work of more than 80 people, all of whom tried hard to avoid errors in their articles by circulating them amongst their peers. We, too, have done our best to double-check everything. However, if any errors have crept in, please excuse us and blame our fallibility. We also requested photographs from all our contributors, but sadly, very few personal ones seem to exist.

Our role has been to pull the compilation together. In trying to achieve a common style 'Instructor' has normally been omitted throughout from the rank title of individuals and we really have tried to minimise acronyms.

There will inevitably be areas of Instructor Officer activity that others will think should have been included in this work whether cultural or professional. Instructor Officers have played sport at all levels up to representing their nations. There have been appointments as Executive Officers and Commanding Officers, Directing Staff on a wide range of senior courses, and as interpreters and attachés. We have tried to maintain an overall balance between topics whilst at the same time taking on board most of the suggestions proffered by our contributors. If some topics do not appear it is probably because no one offered to write about them.

Finally, we would like to thank our friends Dolores York, John Galley and Roger Porteous, who gave us guidance on designing and editing the book, and all of our contributors. We appreciate the considerable effort that so many people made in honouring their commitments. You will see for yourself the tremendous work that has gone into these articles. Without the efforts of so many people, these stories might never have been told.

We hope you enjoy reading the result.

Dick Abram and Patrick Binks
Portsmouth
July 2013

PART ONE – SETTING THE SCENE

Chapter 1

Over Three Centuries

The Instructors of the Royal Navy and the Schoolmasters of the Royal Navy and of the Royal Marines were originally composed of people whose prime role was to teach. Each branch had its own history and evolved on its own lines. Although they were listed separately in the Navy List until 1946, they were complementary.

The story that follows relies heavily on a 'History of the Branch' and one on Schoolmasters, thought to have been written in the 1920s. Rear Admiral Brinley Morgan provided both of these papers and despite many enquiries, it has not proved possible to identify the authors. Further information has also been extracted from documents provided by the Naval Historical Branch and The National Archives and, where appropriate, a reference is quoted.

Developments leading to officers being employed outside the core requirement of Education and Training are expanded on when they occur, as is the further widening of opportunity once the branch becomes part of the General List. The final section relating to the demise of the Specialisation is written by an officer personally involved in those changes.

This is the story of Instructors over a period of more than 300 years.

The Naval Instructors

In this first section the history of Instructors is covered, from their beginning until they were amalgamated with the Schoolmasters to form one branch in 1946.

From the 1600s to the First World War

Although persons were employed in ships of war to teach navigation to young gentlemen since the 17th Century, a definite Instructor Branch with status and conditions of service did not become established until 200 years later. The earliest Schoolmasters were employed by the ship's Captain, who paid them a private allowance out of the funds provided by the parents of the young gentlemen he took to sea. In smaller ships this allowance was insufficient to attract suitable men, and in 1702 an Order in Council of Queen Anne confirmed on the teachers the rank and pay of Midshipmen and also authorised the payment from public funds of a bounty of £20 a year to 'ingenious persons' who should 'enter themselves on board Her Majesty's Ships of the 3rd, 4th, and 5th rates to instruct the youth in the Art of

Seamanship'. The Corporation of Trinity House of Deptford Strond made the test of ingenuity. In larger ships matters were left entirely in the hands of the Captain. The duties of these teachers were carefully spelt out in 1731 in the first printed 'Regulations and Instructions Relating to His Majesty's Service at Sea'.

At the beginning of the 19th Century, the whole question of the early training of officers was reviewed and the Royal Navy wanted to make conditions of service more attractive and encourage recruitment. The training of officers called for Schoolmasters of correspondingly higher scholastic qualification than previously, and this resulted in a long series of minor changes that marked the initial development of the branch.

The title of Schoolmaster was altered to Naval Instructor in 1842 to avoid confusion with that of the Schoolmaster of Seamen. Appointment by commission began in 1861, and in the same year the branch was allocated the distinctive blue stripe, although wearing a uniform remained optional until 1891. From 1864 Naval Instructors were advanced in rank according to seniority, their rank on entry being that of Lieutenant with promotion to Commander after 15 years' service. They could enter at age 22 and were retired at 60, until 1869; entries after that date were retired at 55.

The evangelical movement in England, which included many senior RN officers, wanted to improve the lot of seagoing clergy and these changes in status of Instructors helped, as many Chaplains also doubled up as an Instructor in a ship. In spite of these improvements in pay and position, suitable men were difficult to attract. The number of men graduating each year with honours in mathematics or science and who were physically fit, wished to teach, and who wanted to go to sea was never large, even when compared with the small number of entries required.

After 1862 one Naval Instructor was appointed to all the boy seamen training ships to act as the headmaster. The Naval Instructor taught navigation, mathematics, mechanics, physics, and French in accordance with the syllabus laid down in the regulations to prepare for the examination for the rank of Lieutenant. The Naval Instructor was also responsible for supervising the navigation sight-taking required of Midshipmen by the regulations, and he was expected to be present whenever such sights were taken. The examinations, held at the Royal Naval College, Greenwich, ultimately controlled the whole of the teaching with regard to both style and content. The Naval Instructor had no official place in the fighting organisation of the ship, although he was usually employed unofficially in connection with gunnery and torpedo control, when these developed in later years.

During this time there was no titular head of the branch. Joseph Woolley was appointed Director of Education for the Admiralty in 1864, but he was a civilian, not a Naval Instructor, and he had an office in the Admiralty. The post was abolished in 1874 when its functions were divided between a civilian Director of Studies at Greenwich, which had been opened the previous year, and an Inspector of Schools at the Admiralty, where the first incumbent in this post was the Reverend John Harboard, RN who was a Chaplain and a Naval Instructor.

Royal Naval College, Greenwich
by permission of NMRN

The number of Naval Instructors on the active list varied depending on the number of ships carrying Midshipmen, since this determined the requirement. In January 1900, for example, there were 76 Naval Instructors, 43 of whom were also Chaplains, carrying out a dual role of religious duties and instructing; 43 of the Instructors were in ships with Midshipmen and 24 in training ships and shore establishments.

In 1902, after a gap of nearly 30 years, the office of Director of Education was revived, and that of Director of Studies at Greenwich was absorbed into it. The new Director, Professor Ewing, an eminent physicist and engineer, later becoming Sir Alfred Ewing, had an office at Greenwich as well as one at the Admiralty, and he remained in that post until 1916. He was assisted by a Deputy Superintendent of Examinations and a Deputy Inspector of Naval Schools, both of whom were Naval Instructors.

In 1903 and 1904, the whole system of entry and training of young officers was radically altered. It was decided to abolish the training ship *Britannia* and instead to enter Cadets through the Naval Colleges at Osborne and Dartmouth, sending them to sea as Midshipmen at 17 to 18 years of age, approximately two years older than before. Reducing the need for schooling at sea meant that Naval Instructors were no longer required at sea, and the whole branch might eventually have been allowed to die out but those already serving were allowed to continue. They were employed at sea when available and until the last of the *Britannia* entry of Cadets had become Sub Lieutenants. Generally they were not appointed to the new colleges of Osborne and Dartmouth, which were staffed by civilians, except to teach the rudiments of navigation. Several were, however, appointed to the training cruisers attached to the two colleges.

After Professor Ewing joined the Admiralty, drastic changes were made in the examinations for the rank of Lieutenant. The syllabus was widened in scope, new standards were defined and teaching methods similar to those of the Mechanical Science Tripos at Cambridge were introduced. These alterations called for a change in the scope and style of the teaching, both at sea as well as at Greenwich. As most Naval Instructors at the time had taken honours degrees in mathematics, few experienced much difficulty in adapting themselves to the new requirements.

During the First World War

In July 1914, there were 32 Naval Instructors on the active list, not including Chaplains acting in a dual capacity. Of these, five were in ships with Midshipmen, the remainder being in training ships or shore establishments. In October 1914, two months after the outbreak of war, the Navy List showed that in addition to those afloat and ashore in training establishments or at the Admiralty, there were six employed in the Intelligence Division, since they were qualified foreign language interpreters. This distribution altered as the war went on, when more officers of experience were required for the training establishments and for the Royal Naval Air Service.

In 1915, the Cadets at Osborne, Dartmouth and the training cruisers numbered about 550, and they were sent to ships of the Grand Fleet to continue their training under war conditions. It was decided to make good on the loss of schooling that these young officers had incurred. To this end a considerable number of Naval Instructors were entered for temporary service and, after a preliminary course at Greenwich, were sent to ships of the Grand Fleet in which there were Midshipmen and Cadets. During the next three years many more Instructors entered in this way. Most of these men were already members of the scholastic profession, and very few had any desire or intention to make a career in the Royal Navy. Consequently, of the 57 serving at the end of the war, only 14 stayed on.

In 1916, Sir Alfred Ewing relinquished the post of Director of Naval Education. After a short hiatus, a civilian Adviser on Education, Alexander P McMullen MA, who held similar responsibility, replaced him, but his Office at Greenwich was transferred to the Admiralty. The Deputy Inspector of Naval Schools and the Deputy Superintendent of Naval Examinations, both Instructor Captains, were also moved from Greenwich to the Admiralty.

Royal Naval College, Osborne, Isle of Wight circa 1890
by permission of NMRN

The post of Director of Studies at Greenwich was discontinued, but his responsibilities were entrusted to a Board comprising the Captain of the College and the Professors; the Senior Instructor Officer, an Instructor Captain, who was appointed Professor of Navigation and Dean of the College, was the ex-officio Chairman.

An early view of Britannia Royal Naval College, Dartmouth circa 1910
by permission of NMRN

Instructors between the Wars

In 1919, the conditions of service, pay and training of the entire Royal Navy were again reviewed and revised. The use of Chaplains in the dual capacity was discontinued; because the roles of Instructor and Chaplain had changed, one individual could no longer perform both efficiently. The title of Naval Instructor was abolished in favour of those of Instructor Lieutenant, Instructor Lieutenant Commander, Instructor Commander and Instructor Captain, similar to that adopted for the Accountant/Supply and Medical branches.

Under the regulations, candidates for entry had to be less than 30 years of age and graduates with honours in mathematics, mechanical sciences or natural sciences. On entry, they went through a six-month course at Greenwich, principally to learn the principles of navigation, and this was followed by shorter courses at the technical establishments at Portsmouth and at the Compass Observatory. After that they were sent to sea. Since no ship, other than a Training Ship, carried more than one Instructor Officer, they had no shipmate of their own cloth on whom to lean and they had to trust to the regulations and their own good sense.

In the Navy List for October 1932, there were 70 Instructor Officers on the Active List, of whom 2 were Instructor Captains; half of them were in ships with Midshipmen and half were ashore in educational establishments. It had become the practice to alternate sea and shore appointments as far as service requirements permitted.

In 1936, Captain Arthur Hall, previously Deputy Inspector of Naval Schools, was appointed Director of the Education Department of the Admiralty. He continued to hold this post after being promoted in 1941 until he retired in 1945 as Rear Admiral Sir Arthur Hall KBE CB, becoming the civilian Director of Studies and Dean of the Royal Naval College, Greenwich.

The duties at sea had altered and the Instructor Officer was now responsible to the Captain for all the scholastic work of the ship, including that of the Schoolmaster teaching the seamen. The success of the joint efforts of the two officers depended on personality, adaptability and co-operation.

In each fleet, the Senior Instructor Officer was appointed as Fleet Education Officer on the staff of the Commander-in-Chief, to whom he was the adviser on scholastic matters. He was responsible for the scholastic work of all the ships in the fleet, each of which he visited during the Admiral's Inspections. In the Mediterranean he was also in charge of the Fleet and Vocational Training Centre in Malta.

Instructors and Meteorology

Although there had earlier been an Admiralty Section of the Meteorological Office of the Air Ministry, the Naval Meteorological Branch was formed in 1937 and announced in Admiralty Fleet Order 2033. From the beginning some Instructor Officers were sent for Met training and then filled appointments both ashore and afloat.

This is a particular example of an important general development that sprang from a new responsibility in the 1930s: that the Instructor Officer was 'to assist the Commanding Officer with his scientific knowledge in solving any problems that might arise'. This simple statement had considerable and important ramifications later for Instructors.

The Naval Schoolmasters

In this section, the history of Schoolmasters is covered from their beginning until they were amalgamated with the Instructors to form one branch in 1946.

Trinity House records show that, prior to 1700, James Nicholson and Henry Knight were employed as teachers in the warships *Kingfisher* and *Dorsetshire*; but it was by an Order in Council in 1702 that the appointment of Schoolmasters to serve in operational warships was authorised. They would be required to teach arithmetic and navigation; in 1731 reading and writing were added, 'not only for the young gentlemen but also for other youths in the ship'. In 1733 under a further brief Order in Council, the Schoolmaster became an authorised member of the ship's complement. The names of Schoolmasters serving afloat in the 18th and 19th Centuries are recorded in Ships' Records at The National Archives in Kew.

From 1837 to the First World War

The need for seamen to be educated and prepared for the higher ratings and eventually for warrant rank was first officially recognised in 1837. In that year the rate of Seaman's Schoolmaster, Petty Officer First Class, was established to hold voluntary school on board and to teach seamen reading, writing, arithmetic, plane trigonometry, the use of logarithms and some navigation. The Seaman's Schoolmaster was tested to be fit to carry out his role by the Naval Instructor of the Flagship.

In 1862 the title Seaman Schoolmaster was altered to that of Naval Schoolmaster, and from that date a certificate from the Committee of the Council on Education was required; in training ships the senior Naval Schoolmaster held the title of Head Naval Schoolmaster.

Naval Instructors in the training ship HMS *Exmouth* circa 1860
by permission of NMRN

To make the Service more attractive and to obtain the Schoolmasters needed for the Royal Navy, Naval Schoolmasters were rated Chief Petty Officer in 1867, ranking with Masters-at-Arms and with the same pay. They wore a round jacket with three buttons on the cuff.

In the training ship the Head Naval Schoolmaster was given acting Warrant Rank and received an extra two shillings a day. He also received £20 a year for training pupil teachers who, after passing through a normal training college ashore, could be rated Naval Schoolmaster. A Head Naval Schoolmaster wore black braid on his sleeve.

School in operational seagoing ships was never very successful and, therefore, in 1889 Naval Schoolmasters were withdrawn from all seagoing ships and employed only in training ships and in the school ships for gunnery and torpedo. At the same time, Head Schoolmasters were given the substantive rank of Warrant Officer, ranking with Carpenters and wearing the same uniform. Their duties remained as before, however, their basic pay was increased but their training ship allowances had been abolished.

Some provision for school at sea was made by granting Captains the power to appoint any rating who was considered suitable as an 'acting' Schoolmaster to conduct school and to be paid for doing so.

No alterations in the conditions of service were made for some years, but the demands made upon Naval Schoolmasters continued to increase. The standard of general education and of technical knowledge was rising, and because more and more was being required of Naval Schoolmasters, in 1904 it became necessary again to raise their pay and improve their position. In that same year the difficulty of obtaining suitable candidates led to an Order in Council establishing the commissioned rank of Chief Schoolmaster, equivalent to that of Chief Carpenter, and to an increase in the number of Head Schoolmasters. Requirements continued to change, and the wider use of electricity and the introduction of wireless telegraphy called for teachers at Naval technical schools with considerable scientific knowledge and experience.

HMS *Dreadnought*
by permission of NMRN

In 1912, the Hood Committee was appointed to consider the whole question of the training and advancement of ratings and eventual promotion to Warrant Officer. It recommended, among other things, establishing scholastic examinations as qualifying tests for advancement and promotion. These recommendations were approved by the Admiralty, but not actioned until 1918 because of the war.

During the First World War

After a year of war, the Commander-in-Chief, Grand Fleet recommended that Schoolmasters should be appointed to all ships of his fleet down to and including light cruisers. He intended that this should give both the men and the boys some of the schooling they would normally have received at the training establishments ashore and also something to do to relieve the tedium of long evenings on board in harbour.

As a result, some 240 Schoolmasters were entered for temporary war service and sent to the Grand Fleet, where they found large numbers of willing pupils. Many of these Schoolmasters were experienced and successful teachers at the public and other schools, to which most returned at the end of the war. Their influence and the excellent work they did afloat demonstrated the importance of Naval Schoolmasters at sea and, in 1916, all were given Warrant Rank. Two years later, the opportunity for promotion to Senior Master and subsequently to Headmaster was added.

Schoolmasters between the Wars

After the war, it was decided to carry out the full recommendations of the Hood Committee. Educational Certificates that were recognised both afloat and ashore were given on the results of the Higher Educational Test; many men wanted them as evidence of their standard of general education. To provide teachers for all these examinations at sea, in the depots and the training establishments, as well as to continue the work in the Naval technical schools, it was necessary to enter a large number of Schoolmasters for permanent service.

Competent and suitable men proved somewhat difficult to recruit and, consequently, the branch was gradually reorganised; candidates had to be between 21 and 30 years of age and qualified to teach mathematics and science in a secondary school.

The majority were certified teachers and 25% held university degrees. On entry they were on probation and sent to *Defiance,* the torpedo training ship at Devonport, where, like new entry Instructor Officers at Greenwich, they received six months of preparation for their future work. They started with the rank of Warrant Officer and after 15 years of service were promoted, if recommended, to Commissioned Officer from Warrant Rank. Some of them were selected much earlier for promotion to Senior Master with higher pay and increased prestige.

A few were subsequently promoted to Headmaster, with the rank of Lieutenant, and after eight years to that of Lieutenant Commander. A very select few of these were promoted to Commander.

Where possible, Schoolmasters were sent to Greenwich for a six-month advanced course in mechanics, physics and navigation. Selection for Senior Master was made from officers who had been through this course successfully. The distinctive blue stripe of officers of the Instructor Branch was worn on the sleeve, and the retirement age was 55.

At sea, Schoolmasters taught boys in the forenoon and afternoon; in the evening they held a variety of classes at which attendance was voluntary. There was an Instructor Officer to help and advise them in ships that carried Midshipmen, and the Fleet Education Officer saw them from time to time; but normally, particularly in smaller ships, they were alone.

Schoolmasters were responsible for the school reference library, a limited collection of standard works on technical subjects, and for books on history, geography and other subjects that they issued to ratings preparing for examinations. Another important part of their duties at sea was managing the ship's general library, consisting mainly of works of fiction, supplied by the Admiralty for the use of the ship's company.

Employment ashore was in *Ganges* and *St Vincent,* where boys were trained and schooled on entry, in the depots and RN barracks; the schoolmasters were also at the technical schools and the mechanical training establishments where ratings had specialist training. For some 30 years a specially selected senior member of the branch was employed in the Education Department at the Admiralty.

Instructors and Schoolmasters in the Second World War

With the onset of the Second World War, both Instructor Officers and Schoolmasters were very much involved.

Large numbers of Instructor Officers carried out meteorological duties both at sea and at Naval Air Stations in the UK and abroad. The records show that 264 officers completed the Met course at the Royal Naval College, Greenwich between 1939 and 1945; a further 115 were trained on the IO's **general** course in the same period.

Royal Naval College, Greenwich – staff and students in the early 1940s
by permission of the Fleet Air Arm Museum

Both Instructor Officers and Schoolmasters borne for educational duties became more involved as key members of the Action Information Organisation in their ships. Their roles were in gunnery transmitting stations, Ops Rooms or bridge plotting rooms and here they kept an up-to-date chart of all known movements of friendly and enemy ships, based upon several hundred signals and messages. Additionally at sea as part of the cypher staff, they were responsible for decyphering all incoming signals and encyphering any signals that the Commanding Officer wanted to send.

Ashore, they were increasingly employed in teaching officers and ratings the principles, operation and maintenance of the new scientific devices, including radar and sonar, that were being rapidly developed and fitted in ships.

The Royal Marines Schoolmasters

From the late 18th Century the Royal Marines established a separate Schoolmaster Branch to provide education for the marines and to teach their sons and daughters in 15 schools that were established in the Portsmouth, Plymouth and Chatham commands. Those in the branch were dressed as Royal Marines and shown separately in the Navy Lists as part of the Royal Marines.

In the 1930s, a review of the Royal Navy and the Royal Marines Schoolmaster branches decided not to recruit to fill any RM vacancies but to fill them using RN Schoolmasters on temporary appointments.

By the end of the Second World War, there were ten RM Schoolmasters remaining, including a Chief Schoolmaster (ranked as a Captain Royal Marines), a few Head Schoolmasters and the rest were Schoolmasters Royal Marines (all Commissioned Warrant Officers).

One noteworthy person who entered via this route was John Bell who was initially a Corporal in the Royal Marines; became a Royal Marines Schoolmaster; an Instructor Officer; found time to take a London External degree in Science; qualified and served for several years as a Met officer; qualified as a French interpreter and in 1975 became head of the Instructor Branch.

One Branch

This next section of the chapter describes the period of 50 years from after the Second World War, when the branches amalgamated, until the demise of the Instructors in 1996.

Amalgamating the Three Branches

By 1946, the duties of the separate branches of Instructor Officers and Royal Naval and Royal Marines Schoolmasters had become so interrelated that they were amalgamated, and all Schoolmasters became Instructor Officers. Those with First or Second Class degrees were later designated as 'dagger' officers in the Navy List and those without that level of qualification, referred to as 'non-dagger', had no 'dagger' symbol in the Navy List.

Following the Second World War, much wider use was made of Instructor Officers in shore establishments. They were employed at the RN Colleges at Greenwich and Dartmouth, in the Cadet training ship, at the Admiralty Compass Observatory, the RN Signal School and Boys' training establishments. All Instructor Officers were expected to keep themselves ready to lecture on navigation, mathematics and mechanics up to the standard required of Sub Lieutenants at Greenwich.

Loan Appointments

From the mid-19th Century until about 1950, many Naval Instructors, Naval Schoolmasters, and then Instructor Officers enjoyed loan appointments with the Commonwealth navies.

The Royal Naval Engineering College

Since 1879, Keyham College, on the outskirts of Devonport Dockyard, had been the focus of training of Engineering Officers for the Royal Navy. In 1937, the Manadon estate to the north of Plymouth was bought with plans to move all engineering students there. This did not happen fully until after the war, but from 1940 Keyham and Manadon became one unit named *Thunderer*. Keyham closed in 1958. Instructor Officers played a significant role in training at Keyham College and at Manadon.

Schools and Technical Colleges Abroad

In 1948, the Admiralty, together with the War Office and the Air Ministry, undertook to provide educational facilities for children of statutory school age for RN and Dockyard personnel serving overseas. Schools were set up in Malta, Singapore and Mauritius; facilities were provided also in Gibraltar. In addition there were colleges for apprentices in the Dockyards at Gibraltar, Malta, Singapore and Bermuda. Instructor Officers held the posts of headmaster or principal in all these schools and colleges as well as occupying other positions.

Broadening Roles and Losing the Blue Stripe

Returning to the wider canvas of the Royal Navy generally, the officer branches were Executive, Engineering, Instructor, Supply, Medical, Dental and Chaplain with virtually all authority afloat and ashore residing in the hands of the Executive Officers. By 1955 it was clear that the Royal Navy was not making best use of its available talent, particularly at the senior officer level. The concept of the General List was therefore introduced in January 1956 by Admiralty Fleet Order (AFO) 1/56 from which two paragraphs are quoted:

> 'Their Lordships have fully considered the role of the Instructor Branch in the Royal Navy of the future. The contribution of the Instructor Branch to the efficiency of the Naval Service, and the general effectiveness of the branch, have greatly increased over recent years as a result of the wider part taken by the branch in the life, organisation, and work of ships and establishments, over and above their particular functions in connection with education and instruction, and their responsibilities in connection with Action Information Organisation and Meteorology. It is considered that this tendency to broaden the role of the Instructor Officer should continue; and Commanding Officers should make full use of their powers to delegate responsibilities for general duties in ships and establishments to Instructor Officers.
>
> It is considered, however, that the special responsibilities and role of the Instructor Branch set it apart from the main officer structure and preclude it from forming part of the new General List. It will in consequence continue to form a separate list, and the title 'Instructor' will continue to be used as part of the officer's title of rank. Instructor Officers will, however, wear the same uniform as General List Officers and will reckon for all purposes except that of command as the equivalent by rank and seniority, of General List Officers.'

This meant that Instructor Officers lost the distinctive blue stripe between the gold lace.

Instructor Officers continued to provide for the educational requirements of the Royal Navy afloat and ashore, with officers employed in the training establishments and the three RN Colleges at Manadon, Greenwich and Dartmouth.

Increasingly giving 'Scientific Advice to the Command' was interpreted more widely after the Second World War and AFO 1/56. The appearance of a new technology in the Service frequently resulted in Instructor Officers fielding it to some degree for a number of years until it could be completely supported by one of the other specialisations.

This policy had advantages both for the Service and for Instructor Officers. For the Service, the right person could be provided quickly because of the diversity of disciplines available in the Instructor Branch and because of the relative speed with which Instructor Officers could be produced due to the Short Service entry system and its associated brief initial training. For an Instructor Officer it could mean a widening of career opportunities.

AFO 630/62 entitled 'Officers - Future of the Instructor Branch' resulted from a working party set up in 1960. The Director of the Naval Education Service, Rear Admiral Charles Darlington, sent a letter to all Instructor Officers and included the following main points:

- Separate Branch. The Instructor Branch will remain as a separate branch of the Royal Navy, and its title will be unchanged.

- Wider Responsibilities. The tendency to broaden the role of the Instructor Officer should continue. The revised definition of Command in AFO 633/62 will enable Instructor Officers in future to carry out these duties as of right without the need for any power of Command to be specifically conferred on them in each instance.

- Employment in General List Posts. This practice should continue wherever and whenever the interest of the Service requires it.

- Meteorology. The Instructor Branch will continue to man the weather service.

- Structure. The eventual size of the Permanent List will be smaller, and methods of entry and transfer have been made more flexible. Officers not selected for the Permanent List will have the opportunity to apply for a 16-year Pensionable Commission or to extend their 5-year Short Service Commission for a further period of 5 years.

Overall the areas in which Instructor Officers were employed over the years as a result of these policies have included:

- Meteorology and Oceanography, from 1935.

- Management Services, which were called Works Study at the time, from 1957.

- Operational and Administrative Information Systems, from early 1960s.

- Surveying, from 1964.

- Submarine Service, from mid-1960s.
- Royal Marines, from mid-1960s.

Although the numbers involved have varied, at times more than 140 Instructor Officers were in complement billets in the activities listed above.

Throughout this time and during the future moves towards including Instructor Officers in the General List, the core role of Instructor Officers continued to be education and training. Enhancements were being made in these areas, however, with the development of programmed learning, the setting up in *Collingwood* of the Royal Naval Programme Instruction Unit, which moved to *Nelson* and then expanded to become the Royal Naval School of Educational and Training Technology (RNSETT). Other new aids to training were provided by Service and commercial video production units and by computer-based training.

Joining the General List

During the period 1973-74, Captain John Franklin sat on a small committee under Rear Admiral Frank Hearn, set up by the Director General Naval Manpower and Training, to look into the structure of Officers in the Royal Navy. Their report included a recommendation for the extension of the General List to include Instructor Officers. The Second Sea Lord sent this report to the Admiralty Board, and it was approved. As a consequence, therefore, the following message was promulgated in AFO 704/77:

> 'From 1 January 1978, the General List of Naval Officers will be extended to include the Permanent List of Instructor Officers with IOs losing the 'Instructor' from their rank; the Permanent List of the Instructor Branch becoming the fourth Specialisation 'I'. IOs not on the Permanent List become part of the Supplementary List in both cases an 'I' denoting their Specialisation.'

Director Naval Education Service (Rear Admiral John Bell) visiting RNAS Culdrose in 1976
Officers include Lieutenant Commander Colin Cameron and Commanders Mike Lilley and Mike O'Reilly

This may sound like a radical change, but, in fact, it was the result of evolution. This process continued with Instructor Officers filling an increasing number of General List 'Pool' appointments.

However, in the Ministry of Defence, the two-star post specific to the Director of the Naval Education Service disappeared, and the most senior Instructor Officer, in addition to his normal appointment, also became Chief Naval Instructor Officer. This brought the Instructors in line with the other specialisations and what had previously been an 'I' two-star post could then be used elsewhere.

The Number of Instructor Officers

Before 1950 the number of Instructor Officers was less than 220, even during the Second World War. After that time, however, the education, training and other requirements of the Royal Navy meant that many more Instructors were needed, particularly for the new technologies.

The numbers of Instructor Officers rapidly increased, reaching a peak of 773 in 1955; the number continued at around 600 until the end in 1996.

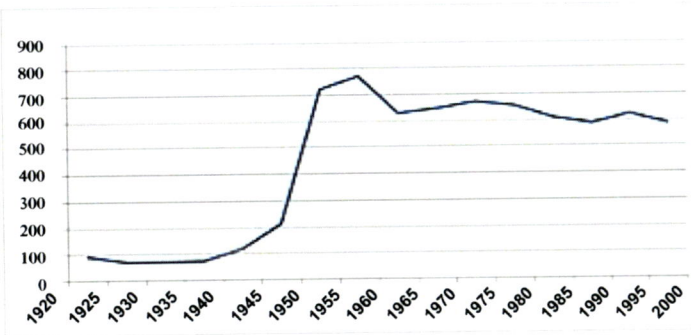

Number of Instructor Officers from 1920 until 1995

The number of IOs by rank are shown in detail for each five years in Annex 2; the Heads of Naval Education throughout the 20th Century are listed in Annex 3.

WRNS Officers Working as Instructor Officers

Suitably qualified officers in the Women's Royal Naval Service (WRNS) had been undertaking Instructor appointments from the 1930s, initially in education, training and meteorology, and then in other areas. The numbers involved were relatively small, but their contribution to the work of the Instructors was significant.

Throughout this time the WRNS Officers were separate, and this included their promotions, titles and terms and conditions. It was not until 1985, however, that the first WRNS Officers specifically recruited as Instructors passed out of Dartmouth. Finally, in the early 1990s, the WRNS Officers became integrated with the Royal Navy and lost their old rank titles and blue lace stripes.

The Beginning of the End

In December 1994 following the recommendations of the Officer Study Group (OSG), the Navy Board took the decision to disband the Instructor Specialisation in pursuit of a Platform Derived Structure (PDS). The OSG considered that the platform specialisations (Seaman, Engineer and Supply) would be able and willing to absorb the essential skills provided by non–platform-derived officers, such as Instructors.

The PDS sought to establish a uniformed manpower requirement based on operational posts and was a response to several imperatives from the Defence Cost Study: the need to achieve already assumed cost savings and the work of the Requirement Evaluation Team. This response affirmed that the OSG's philosophy of increased use of civilians and greater use of PDS officers in training was sound and that most of the Instructor requirement could thus be met by these means.

At the time of the OSG, the Director of the Naval Oceanography and Meteorology (DNOM), Captain Alex Morrice, argued that the future of the Officer Structure needed careful study, and that the study should understand what the Instructors had brought to the Service. The entry route for Instructor Officers allowed the Royal Navy to recruit quickly a mature graduate stream to do jobs that needed doing. The Short Service Commission entry gave manpower planners the ability to respond rapidly to changes in the skills needed by the Service and to evaluate and retain those who had the potential to deliver value for money in the long term. DNOM's input to the OSG was that the name of the group and where it was positioned in the Officers' Structure was not important; provided the entry mechanism was preserved and there was a reasonable career structure with prospects, the Royal Navy could continue to benefit from a quality, mature, graduate entry.

There was a hiatus between the decision to disband the Instructor Specialisation and setting up the detailed work to develop the proposal into a workable strategy; rumours spread that the specialisation had been reprieved. In parallel, there was some disquiet amongst some senior officers with regard to the efficacy of the decision. There is no doubt that the Instructor Specialisation was highly valued and that the requirement for its skills had not magically disappeared. To scotch any misapprehension that it was to continue in its present form, the Navy Board confirmed the decision to disband the specialisation and required the transitional arrangements be put in place.

In early 1995, the Naval Secretary summoned Captain Simon Goodall and asked him to form a project team, as part of the Naval Secretary's department, to deliver a plan for the rebranding of 'I' skills by June 1996, together with the transition arrangements for serving officers. This was achieved and the Instructor Specialisation, which had existed in one form or another since the 17th Century, ceased on 6 July 1996.

After the Demise

This final section covers the period just after the demise and includes a reflection on how successful was the changeover to the new arrangements.

What Happened Next

At the outset, it was recognised that the OSG conclusion about the willingness and capacity of platform branches to absorb all the Instructor skill sets was flawed; it was also thought that the longer term aspirations for developing 'I' skills were suspect.

A strategy was developed that reduced over 580 Instructor Officers to a Training Management (TM) Specialisation of about 200 within the Engineering Specialisation; the remaining 380 posts were civilianised, deleted or transferred to other specialisations.

The key outcomes were that:

- The IOs who had specialised in Meteorology and Oceanography, the I(METOC)s, were absorbed into the Seaman Specialisation, initially as a self-sustaining specialisation of around 100. These officers had preserved conditions of service pending the development of a new type of Warfare Officer, the Seaman (Hydrographic, Meteorological, Oceanographic) or X(HM), through the coming together of the Hydrographic and METOC specialisations.

- The specialist training management function that had served the Royal Navy so well did not fit readily into a PDS career, so a self-sustaining Engineering (Training Management), or E(TM), Specialisation of about 200 strong was maintained. Some operational posts and some training execution posts were included; these were expected to be reduced with the advent of the RN training partnerships with outside companies.

- The aim was to develop Information Systems (IS) skills in the PDS officers and their recruiting targets were raised; however, since Instructors occupied 44% of the IS posts across the Naval Service, there was concern that the rate of development would lag behind an increasing need. Instructor Officers in this field were transferred to the Engineering (IS) specialisation, and it was accepted that numbers would gradually shrink. E(IS) Officers had the same career prospects as E(TM)s, and the recruitment of a few officers with IS skills through the E(TM) route continued until the picture became clearer.

Afterthoughts

The outcomes have been remarkably robust and officers in all the groups have competed well in promotions to one-star posts.

- The X(HM) concept has reached full maturity.
- The E(TM) focus on training has sharpened core professionalism, which had been dissipated

somewhat as a result of many capable Instructor Officers being sent to appointments outside the Instructor mainstream. E(TM)s retained some of those wider opportunities, but the development of core skills improved as a result of the narrower focus.

- The E(TM) Specialisation has been sustained at about 200.
- The IS role is now more widely distributed across the Royal Navy.

Rear Admiral Simon Goodall CBE, reflecting on the changes, comments as follows:-

"I always believed the PDS concept was flawed in that it did not recognise the difficulty of developing skills above and beyond those needed on operations. Complex organisations need to be more agile in recruiting and developing skills than PDS allowed, and I believe that the Branch Structure Development Project did its bit to ensure the continuance of a vital element of the Officer Structure against the unremitting pressure for conformity to a particular model. In short, we retained the flexibility of a sideways entry mechanism to the Officer Corps, and I still believe that it is one of the greatest gifts that the Instructor Specialisation and, latterly, the E(TM) Specialisation gives to the Service. The Royal Navy should think twice and then think again if it ever considers giving up that capability in the future."

PART TWO – STORIES BY INDIVIDUALS

Chapter 2

We Joined the Navy

Until 1963, the route that Instructor Officers followed for their initial training in the Royal Navy varied. Instructors could join through several establishments, including the Royal Naval College, Greenwich and the RN Barracks, Portsmouth. In 1963 it became the norm for all Instructors, along with their fellow Seamen, Engineer and Supply Officers, to join through the Britannia Royal Naval College, Dartmouth, although for a time those officers over about 25 years of age continued to join through RN Barracks, Portsmouth.

The personal stories that follow relate the recollections of some of those who joined via these various routes, letting you share the flavour of the training regime for these officers during their first few months in the Service.

Joining through the Royal Naval College, Greenwich in 1937

Ken Bowell

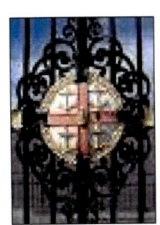

For me, joining the Instructor Branch ultimately depended on a cancelled squash match that gave me the opportunity to attend a talk given by Instructor Captain Saxton in the lecture room of New College, Oxford, in the early summer of 1937; this talk had been brought to my attention by the University Appointments Board.

I had at that time become unwilling to see my future as a Schoolmaster, and the Second World War was seen as inevitable. The branch, therefore, offered a reasonable alternative.

I resolved to make an application for a temporary commission, and this application was successful. Consequently, in September, I joined the Royal Naval College, Greenwich with the barest minimum of uniform – having spent at least twice the Admiralty uniform allowance.

Following my introductory training, I was appointed to *Erebus* in Portsmouth to join the staff providing the initial harbour training for the 18-year-old entry. This was in September 1938; however, before Christmas, *Erebus* was sold to South Africa in anticipation of the war, and the whole training organisation was transferred over Christmas to *Frobisher*. She also had to be prepared for war and so, during Easter 1939, the training organisation was again moved, this time to Dartmouth to occupy some very old huts in the grounds.

This entry of Cadets included Prince Philip, later Duke of Edinburgh. It was during this term that the Royal Family visited the College in the Royal Yacht, and Cadet Philip officially met Princess Elizabeth for the first time at a private tea party in the Captain's house.

This reminds me of an incident that happened some 15 years and 4 ships later when I was again on the staff at Dartmouth as a Commander. The Duke of Edinburgh came to the College to distribute the prizes and attend the Passing Out Parade. Afterwards, as usual, the rest of the College staff was introduced to the Duke. On this occasion, the normal handshake and formal salute were upset when he came to me and threw up his hands with the exclamation, 'Good God, you're not still here, are you?'

Joining through the Royal Naval College, Greenwich in 1939

Brin Morgan

Early in 1939, I applied to join the Instructor Branch of the Royal Navy and in February was interviewed by Instructor Captain A H Saunders in a small office in the Peter Jones Building in Sloane Square. The interview lasted all of about 15 minutes, during which the Director, Instructor Captain A Hall (later to become Instructor Rear Admiral Sir Arthur Hall), burst in, saw that I was being interviewed, shook my hand warmly, said, 'How nice to see you'. He bounced out again, remarking as he left, 'Come and see me later Archie'. The most important question I was asked was, 'Do you dance?'

I left the interview with no great hopes of success and heard nothing until, answering a knock at the door of my home in South Wales, I faced a man who said he had come from Gieves to measure me for my uniform. He assured me that I had been accepted, measured me and said the uniform would be sent. There was no question of payment, since I would have an account at Gieves.

Sometime later, I received confirmation of my acceptance from the Admiralty with instructions to acknowledge my appointment to the Royal Naval College at Greenwich in the approved manner with, 'I have the honour to be, Sir, your obedient Servant ...' I duly joined Greenwich with four other New Entry Instructor Officers in May 1939.

The course was run by an Instructor Commander and consisted mainly of astro-navigation with no opportunities to take a sight, lots of chart work and a few lectures in mechanics. There was no drill; in fact, I never set foot on a parade ground until I was a Captain. A proposed visit to the swimming baths at Woolwich was cancelled, which was probably just as well, as it would have exposed my inability at that time to swim anything more than one width of the baths. Our duties at sea and Naval customs were explained to us during lengthy stand easy periods, and we were warned that we were likely to be made responsible for the Wardroom Officers' mess bills and the wine accounts.

Royal Naval College, Greenwich in the early 1980s

Little was said about cyphering and the hazards of Evening Quarters, nor strangely about meteorology. All meals were taken in the newly renovated Painted Hall, and early on I misguidedly said, 'Good Morning' at breakfast to a Commander who sat opposite. He looked up, stared at me and rapped out, 'Good Morning, Good Morning, Good Morning', and said he hoped that would suffice for the rest of my stay.

Early in the course, I bought a second-hand sword from Moss Bros for £3 and, at some stage, added 'tin pants' which spent the war wrapped in black tissue paper at my home. I also acquired some white kid gloves, which I still have, and an uncomfortable pair of half Wellingtons.

The most memorable occasion during the course was the Dinner attended by His Majesty King George VI on 11 July, held to celebrate the reopening of the Painted Hall as the College mess after extensive redecoration.

Joining at HMS Royal Arthur as a Seaman Officer in 1945

Peter Poll

I joined as a Midshipman (Special) (Science) Royal Navy Volunteer Reserve in August 1945 and an old pay book reveals that I was on a monthly pay rate of £10! New entry training consisted of two weeks of purgatory at *Royal Arthur,* Skegness (aka Billy Butlin's Holiday Camp), where overnight we became 'men dressed as seamen' but distinguished from real sailors by a white band round our caps instead of a name tally.

We were in the tender care of a sadistic Chief Gunnery Instructor, who insisted he was sane as he had the certificate to prove it.

We moved then to *Raleigh* at Torpoint, where we were given six weeks of basic training, spent mostly on the parade ground either marching or doubling round it, cradling a 6-inch projectile in our arms.

This was followed by time at sea in *Diomede*, a 6-inch gun cruiser, where we enjoyed, and I really mean enjoyed, ten weeks at sea slinging and learning the facts of life from the Leading Hand of our mess. In those days, Leading Seamen were really important and experienced people.

Finally, we went to *King Alfred* in Hove, near Brighton (aka the municipal swimming baths) where we completed our training and passed out as Midshipman or Sub Lieutenant RNVR depending on age.

After these periods of initial training, I was appointed to Newcastle as Deputy Port Wireless Telegraphy Officer, where I was responsible for fitting ship/shore communication sets in new construction ships.

After about a year, I was promoted to Acting Sub Lieutenant RNVR and returned to *Mercury* for a spot of leave. During the high jinks after a dinner, I noticed some officers with light blue between their stripes; on enquiry I was told that they were clever blokes with degrees. My comments resulted in my seeing the Instructor Commander the next day and having an interview soon afterwards with Instructor Captain John Fleming, who would later be Instructor Rear Admiral Sir John Fleming, the head of the branch. The outcome was my transfer to the Instructor Branch.

Joining at HMS Royal Arthur as a Seaman Officer in 1945

Stewart Burrows

I joined the Royal Navy in February 1945 at *Royal Arthur* under the Y Scheme, passing out at the end of the year as a Midshipman Royal Navy Volunteer Reserve. During the next seven years, I went through an unbroken succession of sea appointments until, as an Extended Service Lieutenant with a Bridge Watchkeeping Certificate and four years' seniority, I applied to join the Instructor Branch in 1952.

I was accepted as an Instructor Lieutenant with four years' seniority and at the same time given clearly to understand that, if I was to entertain any hope of a future in the branch, I had to get a degree. This I did externally through evening classes at Portsmouth Polytechnic during my first appointment as an Instructor Officer at *Dolphin* where I taught submariners the rapid sight reduction tables that were new at the time.

Joining through Royal Naval College, Greenwich in 1945

Trevor Spraggs

I completed my engineering degree at Imperial College of Science and Technology, where my professor was very friendly with the then head of the branch, Instructor Rear Admiral Hall. Hence, I was interviewed and duly joined the Royal Navy in October 1945.

After completing a course in navigation at the Royal Naval College, Greenwich, my next appointment was to learn the ropes for a short time at *King Alfred*, a training establishment, then in Hove, near Brighton. The Royal Navy had taken over the swimming baths and converted them into classrooms.

Terrestrial navigation was taught there, and the staff marked out a field with buoys, and the students used Wall's Ice Cream barrows, complete with compasses and azimuth rings, in place of ships.

Then *King Alfred* moved as a whole from Hove to Exbury near Lymington, Hampshire (becoming *Mastodon*) and I went there for a short time to teach navigation. After that I was sent to *Cabbala*, a Signal School for ratings and WRNS at Warrington where I spent two weeks on courses on Instructional Technique and Resettlement. This was followed, in 1946, by a three-month course on terrestrial and celestial navigation and ship construction.

Joining through Royal Naval Barracks, Portsmouth in 1947

Robin Budgett

I was deferred under the National Service Act until after I had graduated and was destined for the Royal Engineers having passed the War Office Selection Board.

However, peace being declared, I had the choice of a possible commission in the Royal Engineers after six months as a sapper, or an immediate commission as an Instructor Sub Lieutenant.

The difference between 2/6 and 11/- per day resulted in my joining the Royal Navy at R.N. Barracks, Portsmouth (*Victory*).

After the issue of pay books, some 'slops' and being measured for uniforms our group was sent on leave until our uniforms were ready!

In February, we joined *Vernon II* which comprised *Ramillies* and *Royalist* for our initial training followed in my case by *Collingwood* and then appointed to the staff at *Ariel,* the Air Electrical School near Warrington in Lancashire. The instruction was strictly divided into theory classes taught by

Instructor Officers in the School Block and practice taught by senior ratings in the Laboratory Block; there was no collaboration between the two groups!

Two years later I was appointed to the battleship *King George V* and together with *Anson* and *Victorious* they formed the Fleet Training Squadron based at Portland Harbour. Because of the need to conserve money, fuel was scarce and we were not permitted to steam further than Torbay although once we did visit the Channel Islands, when flying the flag of Commander-in-Chief, Portsmouth. *Victorious* then took over the role of *KGV* which was paid off and I became the Instructor Officer for a group of specially selected stokers as part of a scheme to increase the number of mechanicians in the Navy.

Shortly afterwards, steaming restrictions were relaxed and we went to Gibraltar where a regatta was held for the Fleet 'Cock' Trophy which *Victorious* won. This resulted in the XO leading a run ashore across the border into Spain to La Linea; the next day the Senior Instructor Officer on board persuaded me to apply for a Permanent Commission to which I was transferred in November 1949. I never regretted that decision.

Joining through Royal Naval Barracks, Portsmouth in 1951

John Franklin

I had just completed a postgraduate year at Imperial College and had enrolled for a PhD when the thought came to me that I might prefer to get my National Service over with first. Looking at the possibilities, I discovered that there was a choice of options. I could perhaps do two years as a National Serviceman in the ranks or apply for a three-year Short Service Commission as an Instructor Officer.

For me this was an easy choice, and I quickly applied to join the Royal Navy, leaving the PhD to be resumed later on, something I never did!

The interview was brief, and I was asked to demonstrate my potential for teaching; I did this by explaining how to play chess! This seemed to satisfy the Interview Board, and I received a phone call the next day telling me I had been accepted.

Upon querying when I was required to start, I was told that I could choose any one of many dates. This was not what I had anticipated, since I had imagined the Royal Navy to be a highly doctrinaire setup, so I was even more convinced I had done the right thing.

Whilst at University, I had joined the Territorial Army; upon being told that I had been accepted into the Royal Navy, I sent in my resignation immediately. This was duly lost at the Territorial Army Headquarters, and so I found myself a private in the Army at the same time as I was a Lieutenant in the Royal Navy – a court-martial offence!

Royal Naval Barracks, Portsmouth circa 1950
by permission of Navy News (MOD)

Having kitted myself out at Gieves, I joined *Victory* and *Phoenix* for a New Entry Course that lasted just three weeks. Fortunately, I had been in the Sea Cadet Corps during the war, so I knew my knots and could play the part of the old sea dog without giving too much away! From Portsmouth, I was sent to the Royal Naval College, Greenwich, ostensibly to do the Navigation Course.

However, after one day on the course, the Dean sent for me. Heavens, I thought, have they seen through me already? I was asked first if I was enjoying the course – to which I naturally replied in the affirmative. Then I was asked how would I like to join the staff? This is a strange setup, I thought. How did they expect me to teach navigation after only one day of instruction? But it wasn't that, of course.

'Report to the head of the Applied Mechanics Department', I was told, 'and he will let you know what he has in store for you'.

I can see that venerable gentleman now, dressed in pinstriped trousers and black coat and sitting on a swivel chair in front of his desk. Turning to me as I entered, he said, 'Have you done any mechanics?' I replied that I had done something of this in my degree.

'Right', he said 'You'll do'.

'When do you want me to start?' I asked.

Turning back in his swivel chair towards a timetable pinned to the wall, he said: 'I see your first class is in half an hour!' And with that, the interview was over.

Rushing out, I recounted my experience in the staff room. A kind staff member said he would take the class, which was on the theory of gyroscopes, giving me until the next day to prepare lesson two. Thus it was that I encountered my first experience of what every Instructor Officer has often had to endure –

being, at most, some 24 hours ahead of one's students! It was forcefully impressed upon me that an Instructor Officer's watchword was 'adaptability' — an opinion that was to be continually reinforced as the years rolled by.

Joining through the Royal Naval College, Greenwich in 1953

Ken Healey

I joined in September 1953 and, with nine other new entries, was appointed to Royal Naval College, Greenwich. There were similar-sized cohorts who started at *Vernon* and *Collingwood* at the same time. My group comprised graduates with mathematics, chemistry and physics; I think the *Collingwood* group was all engineers, while *Vernon* included largely arts graduates.

We joined up with many of these other IOs in the Training Squadron, the carriers *Implacable* and *Indefatigable,* for the next stage of our training in January 1954.

The Greenwich group was a mixed bunch, with graduates from Oxford, Cambridge, Birmingham and Bristol and three from the University of Wales, including Glyn Thomas, who, like me, was also from University College Cardiff. We Welsh used to joke that we had been sent to Greenwich to make sure we could use a knife and fork.

Our course as such was a mixture of naval history, radio communication theory, a detailed exposition on the Sperry gyro, metallurgy, and general naval subjects, the latter enjoyably expounded by our Course Officer, Lieutenant Commander 'Tom' Pearce. Probably much of the content was determined by which Greenwich staff members were available at the time. Several of these were retired Instructor Officers. The gyroscope lecturer, for example, had spent several years at Sperry; during his lectures the Cambridge mathematician could often be heard commenting on the mathematics involved!

Our Course Officer prepared us for our first Guest Night, and we had a list of proscribed subjects for conversation: no politics, no swearing and no mentioning of women by name. We sat together in the upper section of the magnificent Painted Hall, whereupon the efforts of the Course Officer were undermined by a colleague who had joined us, Lieutenant Commander Ralph Maddison Pounder, who broke every carefully instilled rule in a loud voice.

There was no marching or parade drill, but sport, particularly rugby, was encouraged. The Captain of the College was a formidable sportsman and fearsome submariner who was eventually to become Rear Admiral Sir Anthony Miers VC KBE CB DSO*, known throughout the Navy as 'Crap' Miers; he was always the last to leave on Guest Nights. He never missed a home rugby game that was played on Blackheath Common and was loudly critical if a person made a mistake on the field; anyone who had a poor match could expect to be called to his office the following day.

Painted Hall in Royal Naval College, Greenwich

Looking back, it was a very enjoyable three months. The camaraderie of the course was excellent and stood us in good stead when we joined the Training Squadron after Christmas. There we faced such joys as parade drill on the flight deck, pulling whalers in Portland Harbour during a particularly harsh winter and early morning runs around Portland Bill. This was a bit of a culture shock after our first three months and, compared with Greenwich, the food was awful! The plus side was a three-week cruise to Gibraltar, where we called at Lisbon for three days on the passage south. As we stood on the flight deck sailing up the Tagus on a fine, warm, spring morning, somebody said, 'This is what we joined for!'

Joining through HMS Collingwood in 1954

Ken Cropper

 Having obtained some uniform from a prescribed Naval tailor and joined *Collingwood*, arrivals were issued with their remaining kit and told to appear the next day dressed in No 5s at a location on the far side of the vast parade ground: on the face of it a not unreasonable order except for the collar problem. The white shirts were starched, the collars were without points and seemed to be made of recycled marble, and the buttonholes impenetrable.

After this struggle, the crossing of the parade ground still remained — and no one had yet been taught how to salute. How each individual coped is the stuff of grandparents' boasts. I remember this time for learning about 'Out Pipes', 'Going Ashore', being told to 'Excuse One's Rig' to the most senior officer in uniform and finding I was addressing the Commander himself, who, for some strange reason said, 'Yes, please', leaving me standing agape!

The 18 Instructor Officers in my entry then went to sea in the carrier *Ocean* for three months of really punishing work, particularly the watchkeeping spent in the Ops Room and the unbearably hot engine rooms. But, apart from our cutter having to be towed back to the ship from outside Weymouth harbour, we acquitted ourselves well as the senior course under training, and we were lucky to have as our Course Officer the ebullient Lieutenant Commander Harry Brierley, who represented us loyally in an occasionally cynical Wardroom.

Original Wardroom in HMS *Collingwood* in early 1960s

Joining through HMS Collingwood in 1955

Alan Burdis

I might have been able to escape National Service but, in any case, I wanted to join the Royal Navy. I joined *Collingwood,* and the first problem was walking into an RN establishment under an unaccustomed brown trilby and somehow getting past *Collingwood's* guard without arrest.

Next, we went to the carrier *Theseus* for three months in the Training Squadron, which included six weeks in dry dock.

As the acting Duty Officer on the afternoon of departure, I was left alone on the bridge and told I was in charge of the ship as we lay at anchor off Portsmouth; I never found out where the responsible officer was hiding. That same evening as the Commander's understudy, I was informed that dinner was ready to be served. I duly banged on the anteroom door, made the announcement and led the way, only to be called back; notifying the Commander was a part of the drill that hadn't registered. Fortunately, Commander Godfrey Place VC forgave enthusiasm and allowed me to creep back into my shell.

Later, on passage at night in the North Sea, on a crowded and relatively silent bridge, I called out, 'White light flash at green ten'. Silence continued for a long minute until the radar plot confirmed. The Captain, who happened to be on the bridge at the time, eventually announced, 'You've got bloody good eyes, Schoolie'. Sadly, our cruise to Hamburg was cut short by Suez and the recall to Portsmouth.

HMS *Collingwood* Main Gate in 1960s

Joining through Royal Naval Barracks, Portsmouth in 1955

Peter Rogers

At the end of our last lecture at University, all females and those who had completed National Service before going to University were dismissed. The remainder, including me, were detailed to listen to a recruiter speak about alternatives to National Service; basically, to apply for a Short Service Commission in any of the three services in some specialist field, for example, the Royal Army Medical Corps, or the Electrical Engineering branch in the RAF.

I opted for the Instructor Branch of the Royal Navy, but the chap said I wouldn't have a cat in hell's chance, unless I had a relative already serving, or had a family history of Naval Service. However, I took an application form, filled it in and sent it off. Four weeks later, I was interviewed in Queen Anne's Mansions and some six weeks after that, in September 1955, I reported to the RN Barracks, Portsmouth *(Victory)* for Naval training with 23 other young bloods.

Our training comprised two weeks of Divisional Officers' course, followed by three months at sea in the carriers *Ocean* or *Theseus;* 12 Instructor Officers were sent to each ship. However, *Ocean* had already sailed for Cyprus with soldiers and equipment, so we had a two-week wait for her return. Instead, we deployed to RNAS Bramcote (*Gamecock*), near Nuneaton in Warwickshire, for a two-week Instructional Technique course.

HMS *Theseus* – one of two carriers used for training
by permission of NMRN

Ocean duly returned, and we embarked at Portsmouth, sailing to the Mediterranean for Cyprus with more soldiers and Army equipment. During the next two months, our training was interspersed with short visits for runs ashore in Malta, Tangier and Gibraltar, followed by a week at Portland, before disembarking at Portsmouth for Christmas leave.

After Christmas, our original group of 24 was again split, with some going to Greenwich, a few to *Vernon* and the rest, including me, to *Collingwood*. The first three months of 1956 were very cold and not conducive to parade training, which was interspersed with our electrical training. However, for three of us, early relief was at hand. As the dates of Fleet Air Arm leave were not identical to those for General Service, we were sent on Easter leave early, prior to our appointment to the Air Electrical School at Worthy Down *(Ariel)*. The remainder stayed at *Collingwood* to complete the course and take up appointments there.

Joining through Royal Naval Barracks, Portsmouth in 1956

Terry Lillicrap, Bill Norrie, Frank Feest and Dick Abram

After Admiralty interviews in Queen Anne's Mansions, mainly by Commander Charles Darlington (later to become Rear Admiral Sir Charles Darlington, Director Naval Education Service) and Lieutenant Commander Peter Poll, successful candidates arrived a few weeks later at the RN Barracks, Portsmouth (*Victory*) in August 1956.

Following our joining instructions and Admiralty Fleet Order 1/56, we had, with difficulty in some cases, to ensure that our gold lace rank had no blue stripe. Additionally, we were told to have appropriate civilian headgear. A few of the 24 had chosen a trilby; most had chosen flat caps, but one had chosen to wear a silver grey homburg!

As new Instructor Officers we had first to be taught to salute; this was even before we crossed the road from the Wardroom to 'slops' to get kitted out. After being issued with tin trunks, some items of uniform, gas masks and other pieces of kit, we did basic parade training. This should have been followed with two weeks of Divisional and Leadership courses, then joining our ships: half the course with their Course Officers Harry Brierley and Brian Drinkall going to *Ocean*, and the others with Course Officer Ron Curry joining *Theseus*, light fleet carriers of the Home Fleet Training Squadron. In fact, none of that happened because the Barracks had started summer leave the previous Friday, and these courses were not available; neither were the carriers, since they were already involved in carrying troops to Malta and Cyprus.

After hasty phone calls between the Course Officers and the Admiralty, we received new appointments. Although we were still appointed to the carriers, we were to first join *Vanguard*, which at that time was partly mothballed and moored in the Hamoaze area to the north of Devonport Dockyard. We made the journey from Portsmouth to Plymouth by train with all our gear and it was not long before the bar had run dry.

Having been rushing around for three days not knowing what we were doing, the first time we appeared in uniform was at Divisions on the Quarterdeck of *Vanguard* at 0800 the next day. This was when it was discovered that one of our number had purchased his uniform from a tailor who had produced a set of No 5s in a colour between that of RN and RAF uniforms. This officer was not popular with the Course Officers, Training Commander, Executive Officer or Captain, so he was sent by boat to Gieves to come back properly dressed!

Whilst in *Vanguard*, we seemed always to be changing our rig. For example, we started the day by wearing No 8s for boat work, then No 5s for breakfast, battledress for course work, No 5s for lunch, battledress for more course work or sports gear for physical activities, No 5s for tea and Mess Undress for dinner! That experience was a very useful training for later life.

As we were at anchor, we had to go ashore by boat and so we became aware of boat times and routines. Additionally, we played various team games on the *Fisgard* sports grounds, frequently against the Royal Marines Young Officers, who were also due to go to the Home Fleet Training Squadron.

HMS *Vanguard* – last RN battleship, later used for training
by permission of NMRN

We attended the ABCD (Atomic, Biological and Chemical Defence) Course at *Defiance*. On the first day the Course Officer there described ABCD as 'Absolute Bl--dy Chaos Daily' and this was taken as an indication that the course need not be taken seriously. At the end we were shocked to discover that there was an exam and several weeks later we were informed that our course had scored the lowest marks ever.

After about six weeks in *Vanguard,* the carriers became available and we eventually joined them; there we slung our hammocks in the Gunroom and rapidly learned the benefits of spreaders. Continuing our training, we spent time in all parts of the carriers, including the bridge and the Ops Room, witnessing amongst other things the RN and RAF helicopter pilots practising mass take-off and landing of helicopters as we cruised between Plymouth and the Solent – with hindsight pre-Suez practice. Another place that we visited was Portland, where some went out in frigates doing workups with Flag Officer Sea Training and some had a day in a submarine.

Eventually, whilst in Portsmouth, those in *Ocean* were told that the ship was returning to Plymouth for stores prior to returning to its training role and we would head for the Mediterranean with a visit to Malta. We did get to Plymouth, but the Suez Operation was then underway and all trainees were disembarked at short notice.

The 16 of us with Science or Engineering qualifications were appointed to join *Collingwood* in November for a six-month Electrical and Electronic Engineering course, with Lieutenant Commander

Philip D'Authreau as the Course Officer. The other eight were appointed to *Vernon* for a three-month Science Conversion course with Lieutenant Commander Peter Hockley as Course Officer.

Following these courses, all of us were sent to our first full appointments.

Joining through Royal Naval Barracks, Portsmouth in 1957

Peter Colson

I believe my entry, New Entry Instructor Officer Course 11, was the first or second group to miss going to the training carriers, which had been decommissioned in early 1957.

After one week at the RN Barracks, Portsmouth, we went to *Collingwood* as a group of 12 for a four-month course. The 13th member of our group was an arts graduate who went to *St Vincent*.

After this initial training, the Appointer tried to get everyone to a ship for six to eight weeks as a trainee, if there were a spare cabin. I went to the navigation training ship *Redpole* and the deep-diving and submarine rescue vessel *Reclaim*, but was 'bumped' because my cabin was required for officers involved with a staff visit to a European port. This happened also to some others because it was really difficult for the Appointer to obtain six to eight weeks in one ship.

Then in September, approximately six months after joining, I went to *Ariel* at Worthy Down for my first appointment.

Joining through Royal Naval Barracks, Portsmouth in 1959

John Foot

I applied to join the Instructor Branch during my last year at University. I remember having an interview in Queen Anne's Mansions in the spring of 1959 with Captain Bill Watts; it lasted no more than an hour.

Then there was silence. It was at the end of October 1959 when I received my formal acceptance letter, which I still have, together with a copy of 'Hints for Officers Joining the New Entry Divisional Courses'.

I entered through the RN Barracks, Portsmouth, starting initial training at the Royal Naval Divisional School in November 1959, having had to join on the previous Thursday to make sure we had the correct uniform. The course lasted for four weeks and was followed by Christmas leave.

After that, I joined Greenwich for the New Entry Instructor Officers' course, which lasted for the whole of the spring term. During this time, as well as undertaking an Instructional Techniques course, we attended lectures on the work of the Instructor Branch, Naval History and Navigation. In mid-April 1960 I flew to Malta to join the submarine depot ship *Forth* for training.

I undertook sea training in the diving tender *Miner VI* during a visit by the Fleet Clearance Diving Team to Syracuse and later went to the Battle class destroyer *Dunkirk*. On my return to the UK from Gibraltar, I started my first appointment at the Air Electrical School *(Ariel)*, which had by then moved to RNAS Lee-on-Solent *(Daedalus)*.

Joining through Britannia Royal Naval College, Dartmouth in 1960

Alan Walker

I joined the Royal Navy at *Fisgard* as an Artificer Apprentice in January 1960. After 16 months at Torpoint and a term at *Collingwood*, I was sent to Dartmouth as an Upper Yardman Candidate on the Temeraire 1960 Scheme. The first term went well, and I looked forward to that second term at Dartmouth in the rank of Upper Yardman Cadet; sadly that time turned into a nightmare as I kept going blind in one eye

Britannia Royal Naval College, Dartmouth in 1981
by permission of NMRN

Towards the end of March, I received the bad news. An operation, which I had had to correct a squint when I was eight years old, had left me with monocular vision, producing a tendency to see double. This was not good news for watchkeeping! I was left with the choice of leaving the Royal Navy or going back to being a 'Tiff'.

I completed my apprenticeship in September 1964 after the statutory four years plus the additional eight months at Dartmouth and joined my first ship, the commando carrier *Albion,* as a leading hand. In March 1965, we sailed for the Far East for 18 months where the ship was involved in Indonesia's confrontation with Borneo and Malaysia. By the end of 1965, I was a Petty Officer, the captain of the ship's hockey team and improving my educational qualifications via the correspondence courses run by Instructor Officers in *Collingwood.*

I was in touch with many Instructor Officers, through training and sport, and made aware that there was an opportunity for one rating each year to apply for the Instructor Branch. My application for a one-year Certificate in Education course at Garnett College in Roehampton was helped by having passed the City and Guilds examinations in Telecommunications. After an interview at the Directorate Naval Education Services, I was accepted as a serving rating candidate for a 16-year Medium Career Commission.

Still a Chief Petty Officer, I was sent to RNSETT to help out whilst awaiting my college exam results. In July I was told that I had passed and was to report to the Senior Instructor Officer (SIO) *Sultan* on the Monday morning, dressed as a Sub Lieutenant. It had been 11 years and 3 months since I had left Dartmouth as an Officer Under Training.

I discovered later that the SIO, Commander Ken Harper, had asked for me because I was a hockey player; I would become the secretary of the RN Under-22 Hockey team, when that team was formed.

In my Instructor Officer role, I would be teaching steam to Stoker Petty Officers, but there was little point in saying, 'I am a Greenie by background'. Three years later, I was appointed to the staff at Dartmouth, teaching astro-navigation to Iranians, which was another even steeper learning curve. Never did I get to teach anything remotely electrical. Welcome to being a Schoolie!

Joining through Britannia Royal Naval College, Dartmouth in 1963

Iain Sidford

The winter of 1962–63 was particularly hard and prolonged, so swopping the never-ending journeys on the London underground for life in the grey funnel line as an Instructor Officer seemed a good change. The interview, which was carried out in rooms above Admiralty Arch, reinforced that view; it was a very gentlemanly procedure, nothing at all like the three-day rigorous selection procedure for the RAF at Biggin Hill – for the RAF had been a close second choice.

My father favoured the RAF, having been a wartime Lancaster pilot, but my grandfather wanted me to join the Royal Navy because he had been a stoker at Jutland, when they really did stoke coal. The RAF offer came by post soon after the selection procedure, leaving a difficult period whilst waiting to hear from the Navy, but eventually an offer came, too.

The offer was a Short Service Commission with the opportunity to apply for a Permanent Commission after three years. Entry to Dartmouth was in September 1963, preceded by visits to Gieves for uniform fitting and the purchase of a brown trilby, a hat then being more or less *de rigueur* for going ashore!

Dartmouth was a life changer in many ways. We Instructor Officers Under Training (IOUTs) were the first to join the Royal Navy through Dartmouth, alongside our colleagues from the other specialisations, Seaman, Engineer and Supply. We were allocated to the various divisions of Hawke, Blake, Grenville, Drake, St Vincent and Exmouth, where we spent the first six weeks with the Cadets in the junior division before moving to join the Sub Lieutenants in the senior division. The IOUTs trained together as a class, including parade training.

Doubling everywhere was obligatory, including up and down the steps to Sandquay. The Physical Education made me fitter than I had ever been before and, through exercise, I cannot remember having eaten so much and so regularly at any other time in my life. A full-cooked breakfast was followed by hearty 'elevenses' before a three-course lunch. A mid-afternoon tea, complete with cake and kedgeree, was followed by a formal dinner in the Gunroom.

The training was extensive, covering the history and customs of the Royal Navy, the Naval Discipline Act, exercising command, seamanship and navigation, how to handle small boats and basically everything necessary to be a Naval Officer. There were opportunities to learn foreign languages, sing Verdi's Requiem, learn ballroom dancing and, for those who lacked social skills, etiquette training.

Britannia Royal Naval College, Dartmouth in 2004
by permission of BRNC

The latter was done so skilfully that nobody could have felt embarrassed at his lack of knowledge. There was also a film that explained how we could catch venereal disease, which left us rolling around in laughter! This was not to be regarded as encouragement, as we learned that if we caught this disease we would find ourselves subject to the Naval Discipline Act.

There was opportunity for going on the river; dinghy sailing and yacht sailing were encouraged and were enhanced by the presence in our senior division of Rodney Pattison, the future Olympic gold medal sailor. The enthusiasm for hard work did not extend to the dreaded Early Morning Activities (EMAs). Standing in our junior division on the first morning at 0615, Mike Roscoe and I discovered that our names had not been included in the roll call. We interpreted this as meaning that our presence was not required, and we felt that it would be unsportsmanlike to reveal our presence to the Sub Lieutenant doing the roll call. Needless to say, we did not advertise our situation and did not attend again for the rest of the term. This later led to some tricky moments when, for example, we needed to take and pass the signals exam, never having attended 'early morning flashing'.

To my surprise, parade training was actually enjoyable, even though I remember running around the ramparts of the parade ground quite regularly with a Lee Enfield rifle held above my head as a punishment. The Gunnery staff regularly offered terms of endearment, and it was quite difficult to keep a straight face, especially when they explained how easy it was to remember how to get one's finger into the trigger guard of a Lee Enfield. The Royal Navy was by then thoroughly modern, and sword drill was absolutely essential. We took great pride in our parade skills at divisions and eventually at the Passing Out Parade, where we wore our Lieutenants' uniforms for the first time.

Joining through Britannia Royal Naval College, Dartmouth in 1964

John Dobson

I was in the early days of the branch at Dartmouth. I recall that when I was preparing to join the Royal Navy, the Junior Officers' Appointer, Brian Drinkall, told me that the choice was either to join at the RN Barracks, Portsmouth in June 1964 or Dartmouth in September 1964. He strongly recommended waiting for the latter, and he was correct in my opinion.

We were a group of 21 IOUTs. I still have the mug shots of a strange-looking group of criminal faces, taken during those first few days when we were still in shock at what we had let ourselves in for. I retrieved the photos later, when I was a Naval Appointer, and had been asked by Captain Willie Waddell to do some spring-cleaning to make space in the cupboards.

The problem was that Dartmouth had hardly advanced from the 14-year-old entry to taking in 18-year-olds, certainly not old men of 20-something years. The result was that we were treated like children, which some in our group actually had. I still recall several of us being instructed to 'eat up our greens' by the person in charge of the Catering Department, the formidable Miss Bulla. We were deeply suspicious of the lime juice drink at meals, which we were convinced was designed to lower any sexual feelings, although we were far too busy to have any!

Much of the time was spent knocking us into shape, which for some was a serious challenge. This involved getting up for parade training at 0600, some being detained for 'Backward Marching', which I always found to be an odd term to use! Memorising the flags of the world's countries was not easy and we passed only by bribing one of the Gunnery Instructors to tell us the answers in advance. In fact, the bribe was very small as he was really in fear for his job, trying to teach what he considered to be a group of morons. The problem was on the day of the test there was a dead calm, and the flags hung limply. The examining officer was hugely impressed, and probably a little suspicious, at our brilliance in identifying them.

INSTRUCTOR OFFICERS UNDER TRAINING
Course Officer ... Instr. Lieut.-Cdr. D. C. Blacker

Name	Division	Name	Division
Beanland, A. E.	D	McGrath, A.	E
Davis, A. M.	E	Moore, J. D. S.	V
De Brunner, N. G. W.	E	Moxon, J. D.	B
Dobson, J. M.	G	Newberry, D.	B
Gregory, J. B.	H	North, M. K.	V
James, D.	D	Onyett, R. M.	H
Johnson, M. C.	G	Poole, A. J.	H
Lane, R. T.	V	Swift, B.	E
Leaworthy, J. C.	D	Thomas, R.	G
Macken, A. L. G.	B	Warner, G. C.	H
McGeorge, J. E.	G		Total 21

Britannia Royal Naval College, Dartmouth – 1964 Blue Book entries for Instructor Officers
by permission of BRNC

We spent a few days at sea, in *Cachalot,* an extremely aged diesel submarine, and the inshore mine-sweeper *Brearley,* which was attached to the college. The former persuaded some of the team subsequently to join the Submarine Service, although for me it did exactly the opposite. The course lasted from September to December 1964 and we 'passed out' after the Christmas Ball, some quite literally, having had rather a lot of champagne. To go from some rather hairy and uncomfortable, undistinguished uniforms, with no insignia, to smooth doeskin No 5s with two gold stripes, was particularly gratifying. This was even more so as those on the Murray Scheme, which was the current four-year course for the 18-year-old entry, was deemed to be superior to ours, and they graduated with only one stripe. I recall that they found themselves doing rather a lot of saluting in the days following the ball!

In all it was an exhausting but valuable four months, which I am convinced equipped us well for the years ahead. I was particularly friendly with Sub Lieutenants Brigstocke and Gretton, to mention just two who rose to great heights. Such friendships, which would not have been made at the RN Barracks, Portsmouth, lasted throughout my 32 years of service.

Joining through Britannia Royal Naval College, Dartmouth in 1971

Tony Mizen

Married with a second child on the way, the decision to join the Royal Navy was a big step for the Mizen household. As the postal strike meant that mail was not getting through. Lieutenant Commander 'Jock' Ambrose, the Appointer, rang me to say that I should hand in my notice at the school, where I was teaching in Derbyshire, and join Dartmouth in September 1971.

A grant for my uniform was forthcoming, and Gieves in Leicester did their very best to kit me out with their finest No 5s and Mess Undress.

On that day in September 1971, 27 other budding Instructor Officers and I arrived at Newton Abbot station, loaded our baggage onto a lorry and boarded the Pusser's bus, which would soon become a very familiar mode of transport.

Over the next 48 hours, we were shorn, kitted out with various items of Naval attire, including that very itchy battle dress, allotted to a Division – mine was Jellicoe – taken on a tour of the establishment, given introductory lectures in Casper John Hall and initiated in the wonders of the parade ground. Our mentor throughout the term was Lieutenant Commander Dermot Dorrian; he and his wife were charming hosts and, more importantly, his door was always open for a friendly chat when any of us felt the need.

I suppose the most indelible memory embraces all those Early Morning Activities and how they impinged on an otherwise pleasant timetable of events. It was during the morse and flashing classes that we teamed up with the Graduate Entry, which included Prince Charles amongst its number.

I soon made friends with fellow members of Jellicoe Division, one of whom said it was sensible to fail the swimming test and spend the rest of the term preparing for a last-gasp success in a warm pool instead of freezing on the autumn cross-country runs. These were wise words that I, along with a few other wiseacres, gladly put into practice. Come the end of term, we had all passed the swimming test, somehow. For our parade training we enjoyed the direction of Colour Sergeant Smith, whose best line was, 'Don't call me Colours as I am not an 'effing' rainbow'. He was certainly talented, and our time on the parade ground became reasonably pleasant, even for the long-suffering, clockwork oranges amongst us.

Having joined the Royal Navy, our expectations about sea time were, not surprisingly, on the high side. However, after the seemingly endless 'river tests' and our three days in the Ton class minesweeper *Walkerton*, I am not so sure that everyone still hankered after a life at sea. My sea trip was to Saint Malo, but my memory of the voyage is restricted to the confines of my bunk and the close-to-hand bucket, as a howling gale kept most of us off the bridge. Our second trip was to Jersey, and for one

Instructor Officer it became a great success as, at the cocktail party, he met his future wife. Another trip involved us being thrown around the skies in the BRNC Wasp helicopter, so much so that one IOUT grabbed the 'don't touch' black and yellow chord and fell out with the door onto the landing strip.

Britannia Royal Naval College, Dartmouth – the Gunroom in 1960s
by permission of BRNC

I recall many other occasions when we were tested and, amongst these, I should mention the Dartmoor Leadership exercise; this appeared to involve us getting very wet, with little sleep and feeling somewhat downhearted at our lack of ingenuity when faced with a simple task of traversing from A to B. Nobody failed, so we must have made the right sounds when it was our turn to take charge. Relaxation for me came in the form of sports activities and, soon after joining, I found myself captaining the college basketball team under the guidance of Lieutenant Commander J J Hogan III US Navy. It does seem strange now to think that the Dartmouth team included three Iranian Naval Officers under training.

Mess life was always on a grand scale, as we ate our way through the generous portions on offer and kept the Gunroom bar in profit. Formal mess dinners were especially memorable events; at one of the dinners, the racing driver Graham Hill, still bearing the scars of a recent accident, not only spoke well, but joined in the after-dinner mess games. On another occasion, we listened to Lord Carrington for 20 minutes and, to this day, I still have no idea what he was talking about; no doubt a politician doing what he does best.

The Christmas Ball was a phenomenal event, one that allowed us to show off our second stripe in the company of our wives and girlfriends on the Passing Out Parade weekend.

Like many IOUTs before us, we then bomb-burst onto the Naval training world at *Ganges, Collingwood, Sultan, Daedalus, Fisgard* and *Caledonia*. Fit as a fiddle and raring to go, I had planned to stay for a Short Career Commission, but stayed the course for 28 wonderfully fulfilling and challenging years.

Joining through Britannia Royal Naval College, Dartmouth in 1979

Andrew Trevithick

I remember how quickly the transition was between deciding to join the Royal Navy, being interviewed in London by two imposing Instructor Officers and a headmaster and then being on the train to Totnes, arriving with a multitude of other youths and piling onto a bus bound for several months of incarceration!.

I was 25, recently married, and the prospect of three months away from my bride and having to enjoy a boarding school monastic existence, did not fill me with great humour.

Britannia Royal Naval College, Dartmouth – the Parade Ground
by permission of BRNC

There were ten of us, and I remember well those first few days of belonging to an imposing institution and that long drive in a cold RN bus down to somewhere near Plymouth to be fitted out with battle dress worn with no insignia of rank. EMAs were punishing – it was freezing cold, dark and unsocial. My 32-year-old cabin mate in Hawke Division often had a sense of humour failure, grumbling about the younger officers under training and wincing every time the Senior Sub Lieutenant tasked him with some urbane activity. But looking back, it did seem like fun, although marching classes were typically manic as eight out of the ten Schoolies were hopeless marchers, and most of the academic studies were of little use to a mostly mature and learned group, even if the lessons were enlivened by the odd naked lady thrown up on the overhead Vu-graphs!

River work was cold! I had sailed before, knew the Hurley 22 sailing yacht well, and was put in charge of the Hawke sailing team where we conquered all. The sailing got me out of other more painful activities. We had flights up to 2,000 feet in the college Wasp helicopter, we went to Plymouth to join the submarine *Dreadnought* for what I now know was her last dive, but none of us volunteered for submarines. We sailed from Dartmouth in a Ton class minesweeper for navigation training when everyone was ill, including the Lieutenant Commander instructing us.

There were grandiose lectures, plays and discussions held in Casper John Hall, but still some of the group would fall asleep, incurring the wrath of some eagle-eyed officer! The swimming test was dreadful: Hawke Division was due for inoculations to be swiftly followed by the test. I lost all energy and could not get out of the pool on my own until sometime later after everyone had left. Had I known that remedial swimming took place during EMAs, I would not have tried so hard.

At the end of all this was the dreaded three-day Dartmoor Leadership Exercise. What a shambles! We thought that we showed commendable common sense and initiative in tackling our task, but the staff thought otherwise. The Royal Marines woke us at 0200 to move our tarpaulins. I couldn't see colleagues through the driving snow and I had a complete sense of humour failure! But we succeeded, and nine out of ten got through the ordeal.

Our time in the Dartmouth Training ship arrived quite quickly; we flew to Naples and joined *Hermes*. Nobody on board seemed to know who we were and what we were to do. *Hermes* had suffered a fire the previous month so, newly striped up as officers, we were allocated aircrew officer accommodation and basically hid for three weeks. I do, however, recall spending at least seven days painting the flight deck crane yellow.

We disembarked at Falmouth and returned to Dartmouth for the final effort – the fitting of our two sets of No 5 uniforms: a posh set from Gieves and a contract set for our future daily work. Then the staff set about preparing us for the big occasion of the Passing Out Parade. At one stage, the ten of us were threatened with not taking part – but we rallied and, I think, produced a decent show of marching and not crashing into the end wall, which had been the case on numerous other practice occasions! On completion, our hats went into the air and all breathed a sigh of relief.

Dartmouth to me was merely a three-month hurdle to get over. Hand on heart I couldn't say I enjoyed the experience, but age and further maturity play odd tunes with the mind, and I look back with gratitude on my time there.

With initial training over, our Appointer had sent down ten envelopes with our initial futures enclosed. The main buzz, of course, was that the place called '*Collingrad*' was the establishment to be avoided at all costs…six of us had *Collingwood* including myself – gulps! First though, we went to *Nelson* for three weeks for an Instructional Techniques course to learn how to teach RN style

Britannia Royal Naval College, Dartmouth – Passing Out Parade
by permission of BRNC

Interestingly, my time in the Royal Navy ended nearly 30 years later and included being in command of *Collingwood* that once feared first establishment, but the one that actually set me up for a fulfilling career.

Chapter 3

Down to Business

After initial training the majority of Instructors went to training establishments to begin their careers in their prime roles of education and training. The Appointers sent these new Instructors to establishments where they could be under the wing of other more experienced Instructor Officers and where there were several others in their first appointments.

Many went to establishments like *Collingwood, Daedalus* and *Ganges* that were well set up to look after the new Instructors. In these establishments, Instructors could gain experience in their teaching, in their divisional roles looking after sailors, in adventurous training and in a wide range of sporting activities. This gave them all the greatest range of experience within a structured, well-established set-up with senior Instructor Officers (Commanders or Captains) to assist and support them during this formative period.

For those continuing to a longer commission, the Instructor Officers could progress from instructing to training design, training planning, managing training groups or schools as they were promoted. They worked in the training establishments and in the three colleges of Dartmouth, Manadon and Greenwich, with the Royal Navy and the Royal Marines.

In this chapter, the aim is to show the role of Instructors in every rank, beginning as a Sub Lieutenant, then Lieutenant and through the ranks to Rear Admiral, but always within the training environment.

Many establishments have been chosen to show the variety of places where Instructors served, although sadly many of these are now closed.

HMS GANGES

Background: *Ganges* was a shore training establishment from 1905, having taken over from the wooden ship *Ganges* previously anchored out in the harbour.

The 1944 Education Act had raised the compulsory school leaving age to 15 years in 1947 and this meant that the young men were at least 15 years 3 months old when they started as boy ratings.

Where: *Ganges* was based at Shotley Gate, Harwich, Suffolk on the peninsula formed by the rivers Stour and Orwell. The tip of the peninsula is aptly named Bloody Point!

What they did there: *Ganges* was a shore training establishment for boy entrants into the Royal Navy. The other new-entry training establishment for young sailors was *St Vincent* at Gosport, Hampshire.

As a Sub Lieutenant and Lieutenant from 1957 to 1960

Frank Feest

I joined the Instructor Branch of the Royal Navy straight out of university in August 1956 as a non-dagger officer in the rank of Instructor Sub Lieutenant. After completing five and a half months of new entry training and Christmas leave, I took up my first full appointment at *Ganges* in February 1957. When I joined, I was a bachelor like most of the other young Short Service IOs who were serving there at that time. Much of my time was taken up with learning the job, carrying out any necessary duties – and planning my wedding for the summer leave period! I was promoted to Instructor Lieutenant a year after entering the Royal Navy. Just four days later, with the Captain's permission, I was married during my first summer leave from *Ganges*. As I was only 23 years old, I was not entitled to an officer's married quarter and so rented a small flat in Ipswich.

At that time, about 1,800 boy ratings each year entered for at least a year of training, but their 12-year engagement in the Royal Navy only began on their 18th birthday.

For the young man fresh from school who joined at *Ganges* in the early 1950s, life was still hard. They began their transformation from schoolboy to boy rating in the *Ganges* Annexe, which was housed in a group of buildings across the Shotley Road from the main establishment. The Annexe training was primarily an induction into the service with kitting out, including the newly introduced zip-up jumpers, trousers with zips and plastic caps, parade training, finding out how to wash and iron their kit and learning about service traditions. Of course, there was also physical training and this included a three-minute session of voluntary boxing to test the lads' guts and was held in front of an audience of both staff and boys. The new entries, known as 'nozzers', had some basic schooling from the two Instructor Officers attached to the Annexe to pass an educational test for Able Seaman.

Successful completion of the initial training meant that the nozzers were put into classes in one of the Divisions according to their specialization: seaman, communications, engineering mechanic and naval airman. They were then marched across the road to the main establishment to join their divisions, all named after famous admirals – Anson, Blake, Collingwood, Drake, Exmouth, Frobisher, Grenville, Hawke, Keppel and Rodney.

HMS *Ganges* – the original training ship based at Shotley Gate in 1900
by permission of Navy News (MOD)

The training that was given in the main establishment appeared to be non-stop. After breakfast, there was the daily parade, where all the boys would fall in by divisions. On Sundays, there were Ceremonial Divisions. Each Instructor Officer was attached to a division and was expected either to parade with his division or fall in with the unattached officers alongside the dais.

Punishments were frequent and strictly administered. Many boys had to run up and down Laundry Hill and the area known as Faith, Hope and Charity. The worst offenders were still being beaten, although it did not happen very often. I sometimes thought that the offending boy's anticipation during the formal ceremonial of the punishment administered by the Establishment Master-at-Arms might perhaps have been worse than the actual cuts!

A much gentler part of the trainee's day was spent in the school, which was in a purpose-built block outside the Main Gate, in the aptly named School Lane. I always suspected that the school periods taken by the generally quieter and more softly-spoken Schoolies were a blessed relief from the fiercer professional trainers. The boys were given lessons in a selection of so-called academic subjects. It was always hoped that most boys under training would learn enough English and Arithmetic in the school to pass Educational Test 1 (ET1) while at *Ganges*, but not all did! This test later became the Educational Test for Leading Rate.

Instructor Sub Lieutenants and Lieutenants on Short Service Commissions mainly did the teaching in the school. They were aided and abetted by a smattering of permanent commission or 16-year commission Instructor Lieutenant Commanders. In the early 1950s, the teaching staff still included a number of the former Warrant Schoolmasters, who were by then Instructor Lieutenant Commanders.

HMS *Ganges* – the staff in 1960

When I joined, the Senior Instructor Officer was Captain Gordon Britton and he was followed by Captain Bill Brownbill. There was also an Instructor Commander who was the SIO's deputy and ran the school on a day-to-day basis; Commander Charles Malkin was there in my time. There were also two Lieutenant Commanders who ran the school administration. One was Lieutenant Commander Harry Brierley whom I particularly remember because he had been one of the two Course Officers for the initial training of the 24 IOs of my entry in August 1956.

The teaching of classes at *Ganges* was organised with IOs working in pairs; one IO taught the non-science subjects of Naval history, English and geography while the other covered the science subjects of mathematics, general science and navigation. As the new boy, I was paired with another Short Service Officer, Lieutenant Wilmer Dykes, who was an arts graduate from Oxford.

After the initial morning parade, the training day at *Ganges* was divided into 40-minute periods for professional training, schooling and for various extramural and physical activities.

There was a lot of boat work, with both pulling and sailing taking place on the Rivers Orwell and Stour. This often provided an opportunity for IOs who liked boats to get involved, including sailing in *Sea Feather*, an ex-German Navy yacht. This was the time when adventurous training was entering the service vocabulary, and the IOs were expected to spend some weekends trekking and camping with trainees in the Suffolk countryside. Some of us, mainly the bachelors, enjoyed the opportunity, but quite a lot did not!

For active young Schoolies, *Ganges* offered plenty of sporting activities with which to get involved. All the usual team games where available and any IO who was interested could be involved either as a player with any of the establishment and Wardroom mess teams or as Officer-in-Charge with one of the boys' teams. The boys' matches were generally against local schools on either Wednesday or Saturday afternoons, though rarely against the schools' first teams because of both the boys' age and their standard. However, it was a valuable experience for the Shotley teams to get out of the establishment and meet other boys of their own age for an afternoon, even if they did not win very often!

Wednesday afternoon was when the establishment games were normally played, generally against other service sides. Our opponents were mainly the RAF stations in Suffolk and Norfolk, where there were plenty in the early 1950s, and there were various Army teams stationed at the garrison in Colchester. We rarely played another Navy side because of our isolation from other RN establishments.

Ganges had a big swimming pool where, amongst other things, the boys had to pass a swimming test as well as jump off the high board. It was also the place where young officers would sometimes go for a 'refreshing' swim after a mess dinner in the Wardroom!

A more risky activity after a mess dinner was to climb the mast. Although this only happened once during my years at *Ganges*, it was a memorable first occasion. In the summer of 1958, the Wardroom had invited a group of American Air Force Officers from their base at Bentwaters to dine at *Ganges*. The Americans were all fast jet aircrew and saw the mast as a challenge, particularly after drinking copious amounts of wine and port!

In fact, it is the iconic *Ganges* mast that is my lasting memory of Shotley. During the Ceremonial Divisions for the four Queen's Birthday Parades that I attended, I always felt a surge of pride because some mast-manners were young men from the classes I had been training.

Although *Ganges* was not everybody's cup of tea, for a young Short Service IO like me, my appointment there was my first opportunity to do a professional job that was both satisfying and worthwhile. My four-year appointment to *Ganges* combined the rewards of teaching and divisional work with many opportunities for extramural and sporting activities.

No wonder I decided to apply to transfer to a Permanent Commission.

HMS *Ganges* – the famous mast manning ceremony in 1960s
by permission of Navy News (MOD)

Postscript: Raising the school leaving age to 16 years led to the closure of both boys' training establishments: *Ganges* and *St Vincent*.

Ganges finally closed in June 1976 and training was transferred to *Raleigh* at Torpoint in Cornwall. In October 1976 the White Ensign was lowered for the last time and the *Ganges* figurehead, an Indian Prince, was given to the Royal Hospital School, Holbrook, which is a short distance away on the Shotley peninsula.

St Vincent officially closed in December 1968 and the White Ensign was lowered in April 1969.

ROYAL MARINES SCHOOL OF MUSIC, DEAL

Background: The RM School of Music moved to Deal in 1950.

The Depot occupied several separate sites and thus, was an integral part of the town. As there were no married quarters, all the married staff were scattered throughout the town.

Where: The RM School of Music was based in Deal on the east coast of Kent near Dover.

What they did there: The School provided training for the RM musicians and other ranks.

As a Lieutenant from 1960 to 1962

Ken Healey

I joined Royal Marines School of Music at Deal in January 1960 with thick snow on the ground and the temperature about zero.

I was attached to the Junior Wing. As junior bandsmen joined at the age of fourteen, they were required to attend school, as well as undergoing their musical training. Subjects included English, mathematics and science; I was responsible largely for the science subjects and had a reasonably well-equipped laboratory. There were some dozen or so Instructor Officers, about half responsible for the education of young bandsmen and half providing education for the junior marines who joined Deal at 16 years of age.

I quickly learned that music was of paramount importance; the junior band undertook a number of public events as part of their training and I was quite likely to find a depleted class, or no class at all depending on their stage of training. Not that one sat around counting the pen nibs or the test tubes; in Deal everyone played a full part in the life of the Depot and Schoolies were no exception. The Depot had a small but very good and well-equipped theatre, with a programme of events, which were always well attended by the townspeople; I found myself volunteered as the theatre stage manager, a role I kept until leaving.

During the summer term, the Depot was host for the RM Searchlight Tattoo, an annual event which rotated with Portsmouth and Lympstone. My task in the Tattoo was coordinating the arena searchlights and I was perched on a gantry at one end, with radio links to each searchlight. I had a wonderful view of the massed bands marching and counter marching, ceremonial drill, the RM motorcycle display team and an attack by RM Commandos on a fortification at the other end of the arena.

Musically there was always something happening; both the junior and the senior bands performed regularly on the parade ground and the senior wing and the instructors gave regular orchestral concerts conducted by the Principal Director of Music, Lieutenant Colonel Vivian Dunn, often with well-known soloists.

Royal Marines Drummer/Buglers
by permission of Navy News (MOD)

In early 1961, WRNS were introduced into the Depot to undertake largely administrative jobs. The first Officer-in-Charge was Elizabeth Craig-McFeely, later to become Superintendent WRNS.

During the autumn term, we had a visit by Her Majesty's School Inspectors. The one who visited me was the same person who had inspected us previously in *Collingwood*, where we had introduced the pilot scheme for apprentices leading to the award of the Ordinary National Certificate. He seemed quite content with what we were doing, although I think he was well aware of the over-riding importance of the young bandsmen's musical training and the place of education in the hierarchy.

1961 was a busy year with an inspection by the Major General Royal Marines Training and rehearsals for the Beating Retreat Ceremony in London for the Duke of Edinburgh's birthday. The summer term saw the centenary of the Royal Marines Depot in Deal with a series of events to mark the occasion in which we were all heavily involved.

Autumn term saw us return to teaching and back to the theatre for a production of 'Tea House of the August Moon'. The Colonel was determined that we should do well in the Naval Annual Drama Festival and let it be known that no effort should be spared. With a large cast, a superb set built by Lieutenant Commander Norman Kaufman, music provided by Lieutenant Colonel Dunn, we could not go wrong. Asked if there was anything I needed, I said, 'A real American jeep and a live goat would add the icing!' Both appeared in time for the first performance, although the goat was not stage nor house-trained.

Coinciding with the play, in which incidentally we came first, I was summoned to London for an interview for transfer to a full career commission; I was successful and immediately recognised that my days at Deal were numbered.

Royal Marines School of Music, Deal – the staff in summer 1961

Finally, I was ordered to oversee the arrangements for the junior band and a platoon of junior marines to go to Amsterdam and Antwerp to Beat Retreat. With two senior NCOs, we went by train to Plymouth and embarked in the destroyers *Trafalgar* and *Scorpion* for three days in Amsterdam and then to Antwerp where we spent a further three days. The junior band and the young RM recruits performed splendidly. We left Antwerp in sunshine for a very rough crossing of the North Sea to Invergordon, followed by a long train journey back to Deal. I arrived safely complete with all my young charges.

I left Deal with regret but many happy memories and a very high regard for the Royal Marines.

Postscript: The bombing by the IRA of the School of Music in 1989, when 11 bandsmen were killed and 21 seriously injured, finally caused the return that year of the School of Music to Portsmouth. A memorial was erected at Walmer and every year the Royal Marines parade there together with thousands of local people, who come to pay their respects to those who were killed and 'who only ever wanted to play music'.

HMS RALEIGH

Background: *Raleigh* was commissioned in 1940 as a training establishment for Ordinary Seamen.

In 1944, the US Navy took over the base to use as an embarkation centre prior to D-Day and it was transferred back to the Royal Navy in July 1944 to continue training seamen.

Where: *Raleigh* is based at Torpoint on the edge of the River Tamar on the eastern border of Cornwall.

What they did there: Training for new entry sailors.

As a Lieutenant from 1966 to 1968

Jeff Roberts

In September 1966, after a very happy time at Royal Marines School of Music at Deal, I went to join *Raleigh*. I travelled from South Wales and drove over the Severn Bridge that had opened earlier that day; this was not without incident, as I became the first driver to have a car breakdown on the bridge and needed to be towed off at great expense!

Torpoint was grey and wet and I approached, with increasing trepidation, the pre-Second World War huts that made up the establishment. After having served with the Royal Marines, my concern was how I would now fit into a naval training environment. This was partly because of not joining via Dartmouth, which had been the original plan for me, and the change resulting in an all too brief 4-week introduction to the Navy at *Nelson*, of which I hardly remembered anything some two years later.

My first stroke of good luck was to discover that I had been assigned to be an Assistant Divisional Officer in Frobisher Division, which was headed by a Seaman Lieutenant (SD) on his last job, following some 35 years of service. He provided all that I needed in help and support despite having a ferocious reputation, a short fuse and a pronounced stubborn streak. He ran a tight division, which was very successful.

The purpose of *Raleigh* was to take in young men and, following a short intensive training programme, turn out ratings capable of going on to complete Part 2 training at the specialist establishments.

Many youngsters who had been unruly, ill-disciplined and difficult were given a structure and a taste of discipline to which the vast majority responded positively.

The IO team at the time was made up of a group from varied backgrounds, mostly graduates, some teacher trained IOs and a couple of ex-Artificers with Higher National qualifications; they were aged from early twenties to mid-forties.

It was a lively and entertaining Wardroom with some unique characters: an eccentric who deployed a casual indifference to everything and angered the Executive Officer on one occasion by suggesting that Sir Walter Raleigh might have been gay; a deeply upset officer who had just divorced and found to his great cost that his ex-wife had employed a much more ruthless solicitor than the one he had chosen; an over-sexed bachelor who saw the arrival of the morning tea, when delivered by a Wren, as the first opportunity of the day.

The teaching for the Naval Mathematics and English Test (NAMET) was not inspiring and was not designed to stretch anyone who came into contact with it. One IO incurred the wrath of the SIO by answering the phone, after an exasperating day, with the welcome, 'University College Raleigh – Department of Fractions and Decimals'. The contrast with those over the road at *Fisgard* who were teaching apprentices and artificers was a constant topic of conversation and some envy.

Surprisingly, the system sent a Ph.D. in Molecular Biology to teach the newly-entered ratings. Possessed of a first in zoology and a Master's degree, he made a lasting impression – undoubtedly highly intelligent, but not blessed with very much common sense, he endured a culture for which he was totally unsuited and exited the Royal Navy at the three-year breakpoint.

There are two persistent recollections. The first is the contrast between the initial confusion and the dramatic improvement in performance on the parade ground: from frequent mistakes, often providing amusement to all except the GI, to a coordinated and polished marching display. There was pride and amazement shown by parents and family members as they watched the Passing Out Parade following completion of their Part 1 training, a transformation that was often described as miraculous.

The second recollection is of weekends trudging in heavy rain across Dartmoor and at Pier Cellars, the expedition training location near Cawsand, with indescribable food prepared as a pot-mess: both contributed to a philosophical consideration about what constituted effective leadership.

On reflection, there were several enjoyable aspects of my time at *Raleigh;* socially, it could not have been bettered. However, on a professional level, it was not a happy experience. I found the IO management remote and I totally failed to make a good relationship with them. After some three and a half years of basic training at Royal Marines, Deal and *Raleigh,* I received my Naval Report (the S206) which to use a cricket term, 'Did not trouble the scorers'.

At this time, the Times Education Supplement became obligatory reading and I started to plan a civilian career, and I would use the £600 gratuity for my 5 years' service as a deposit for a house purchase. Then a stroke of good fortune! I was appointed to RNAS Culdrose to be the Assistant Education Officer. There I worked with Lieutenant Commander John Lamerton, a man who was truly inspirational and exerted a profound influence on my future. The Times Ed was discarded, as I became enthused by the Fleet Air Arm and was very pleased to be selected for a 16-year commission leading to METOC training.

Some five years ago, an IO with whom I had worked, commanded *Raleigh* and invited me back to attend a Passing Out Parade. Much was the same as before, but there were some differences, including females under training. Afterwards, I overheard some parents in conversation, 'What an amazing change – truly miraculous!'

Some things do remain the same.

Postscript: Many changes have taken place including all Artificer training moving from across the road at *Fisgard* when that closed and females joining for new entry training with the closure of *Dauntless* in 1981.

Raleigh is also now the home of:

- Defence Maritime Logistics School providing training for the Royal Navy's Logistics Officers, chefs, stewards, writers, and supply ratings.
- Seaman Specialist School
- Submarine School
- the Royal Marines Band, Plymouth.

HMS SULTAN

Background: The military connections go back to the 1850s when Forts Grange and Rowner were built as part of the defensive ring around Portsmouth, known as Palmerston's folly. These two forts are within the perimeter of the establishment.

The site was originally one of the earliest airfields in the country for the Royal Flying Corps and Royal Naval Air Service.

Many RN air squadrons were formed and trained here for service in France during the First World War. It became a permanent RAF station in 1918, but was transferred to the Navy in 1945, as RNAS Gosport *(Siskin)*.

The present *Sultan* was commissioned in June 1956 as a Mechanical Training and Repair Establishment after transferring from Portsmouth.

Where: *Sultan* is based in Gosport, Hampshire.

What they did there: *Sultan* provided Marine Engineering training.

Sultan was home to the Admiralty Interview Board and the Central Air and Admiralty Medical Boards.

As a Lieutenant Commander from 1971 to 1972

Keith Hart

In April 1971, I was appointed from the Royal Naval Engineering College, Manadon to a new post as Training Design Manager under Commander Ken Harper whose Staff Officer was Lieutenant Tom Wright. The Captain was Ronnie Harcus who had been the Commander when I served at *Caledonia* ten years earlier.

Sultan was a large training establishment with about 1,000 on the staff and under training.

The methodology of Objective Training was taught at RNSETT at *Nelson.* It started with an analysis of engineering tasks in HM ships to determine what skills and education were needed to perform a range of technician jobs, to what standards and under what conditions. These were called the Operational Performance Standards.

These were brought back from the ships and then broken down into:
- What should be done in the training establishment?
- What could only be accomplished at sea?

These were called the Training Performance Standards and they were then turned into teaching notes and practical training. This is a much-simplified structure where at each stage there was feedback to make sure the requirements were being met.

My terms of reference were interesting:

- To introduce an objective training design organisation.
- To analyse training and educational career requirements of marine technician engineers.
- To design in-house courses for technician engineers.
- To be the works-liaison Officer for the establishment's rebuilding programme.

An air station in 1940s before becoming HMS *Sultan*
by permission of NMRN

My task was to sell the methodology to higher management and to those who would do the analysis and teaching. The detailed analysis was carried out by a small group of experienced technical ratings. To some it was a logical development but others opposed it for a variety of reasons.

Notwithstanding, CINCNAVHOME said it had to happen; I enjoyed the challenge and the procedures were introduced.

However, I was not to see the results, for a new opportunity arose with an unexpected appointment as the first SIO in *Intrepid,* which was with the Dartmouth Training Squadron.

I was sorry to leave after one year before the implementation of my plans could be validated.

Postscript: Many changes have taken place subsequently:

- Artificer Apprentice training was transferred from *Caledonia* at Rosyth when it closed in 1982.

- Marine electrical training was transferred from *Collingwood* in 1987.

- Air Engineering training moved to *Sultan* in 1995 when *Daedalus* closed.

- The postgraduate training of Air Engineers and Marine Engineers began in 1995 following the closure of the Royal Naval Engineering College, Manadon at Plymouth.

- The Department of Nuclear Science and Technology moved in following the closure of Royal Naval College, Greenwich in 1998.

- Some elements of submarine training were integrated when *Dolphin* closed.

- Training of Army and civilian personnel has taken place with *Sultan* taking a tri-Service role in engineering training and with Flagship capitalising upon the facilities in the establishment.

HMS DRYAD

Background: In 1940, the owners of Southwick Estate allowed the Royal Navy to use Southwick House to accommodate overnight the students of the RN School of Navigation, *Dryad* that was based in Portsmouth Naval Dockyard. In 1941, after heavy bombing of the dockyard, the house was requisitioned and became the new home of *Dryad*.

Shortly afterwards, the establishment was used as Eisenhower's Headquarters (Supreme Headquarters Allied Expeditionary Force) for planning D-Day (Operation Overlord).

Where: *Dryad* was based in the village of Southwick, near Portsmouth.

What they did there: Training for Seamen Officers in Navigation, Direction and Warfare, and Radar Plot for ratings; later *Dryad* became the School for Maritime Operations (SMOPS).

Dryad was also the home of the Maritime Tactical School.

As a Lieutenant Commander from 1973 to 1974

Roger Drury

During the Second World War and the years following, a warship was fought by the Commanding Officer receiving inputs from his specialists – TAS Officer (Underwater), Direction Officer (Air) and the Gunnery Officer (Surface). Nor should we forget the Signal Communications Officer, whose role was to ensure all communications met the operational needs of the ship and the Navigating Officer, who was responsible for the safe passage of the ship and the navigation planning for groups of ships.

By the mid-1960s, this system began to be questioned as the speed of maritime warfare increased and there was a need for a rapid coordinated response to all threats. Ships began to experiment with the concept of the Principal Warfare Officer (PWO) whose role was to coordinate inputs from all threat scenarios and to take action or advise the Command.

It was obvious a new approach to warfare training was necessary – previously the long courses (TAS, Navigation, Direction, Communications and Gunnery) had been almost a year long and the concept of three years of training to produce a PWO was clearly undesirable and impractical.

The problem faced by the Training Command (Commander-in-Chief, Naval Home Command) was twofold:

- What training was necessary to produce an operationally effective PWO?
- What was to be done with the four Seaman schools *Vernon*, *Excellent*, *Dryad* and *Mercury*?

Additionally, the size and cost of the Royal Navy was under review, and the inevitable conclusion would be a reduction in overall size with the closure of some shore bases. CINCNAVHOME decided, therefore, to set up a small group of specialists to examine the way ahead and to set out the available options. At this time, I was in *Vernon* and in my tenth year of service, having served previously in *Ganges, Albion* and *Dryad*. Somebody must have thought I was a specialist, not only in training, but also Seaman Officer training.

By this time, the design of training had become progressively more objective; at *Vernon*, I had been immersed in these training technologies and this is what I brought to the new Operations Training Cell, OPSTRAIN.

I returned to *Dryad* in the company of Commander Jonathan Findlay, a communicator, who was relieved later by Commander John Condor, a Gunnery Officer, and a number of other Seaman Officers. Both officers had considerable staff experience and it was a privilege to serve with them. During the next two years, my learning curve was vertical as I gained skills in the collection and analysis of information and in drawing conclusions. These skills were to be invaluable to me for the rest of my life.

This was incidentally, my introduction to stable living, as our offices were in the old stable block at *Dryad;* some two years later when I moved to *Mercury,* I again found myself in the Ostler's Bungalow. However, I can report that the accommodation of horses in the 19th Century was probably better than for Naval Officers in the 20th Century.

In the late 1960s and early 1970s, many millions of pounds were being spent at *Dryad* on Ops Room models for all the major classes of ship currently at sea, Type 42 destroyers, Type 21 and *Leander* class frigates, in order to train their command teams. The logical conclusion was to focus all Seaman Officers' training from Sub Lieutenant to Captain at *Dryad,* which became the headquarters of all warfare training and named the School of Maritime Operations (SMOPS). Some training continued to be provided at the other parts of SMOPS at *Mercury, Excellent* and *Vernon*. In addition, the Maritime Tactical School had moved from Woolwich to Southwick. In this School, Commanding Officers and those in the Command Task Groups were trained prior to taking up their commands. Those involved included national and NATO maritime and air staffs.

As we examined the training given to the 'Long' Course Officers, the area that came under greatest focus was the in-depth technical training that had been given on the various weapon systems. In my previous time at *Dryad*, I had taught the Long Navigation and Direction Officers' course six weeks of 'Radar Principles' and two weeks of 'Introduction to Computers'. This depth of knowledge was not compatible with the need to produce a capable PWO in a reasonable period of time. Training would have to be based on a working knowledge of the operational capabilities of weapon systems, but the main focus would have to be on their tactical application. This reduction in systems training was greeted with horror by many and much debated over the next few years. The eventual solution was the introduction of the advanced warfare courses for those going into specialist roles at a senior level where the emphasis was put on developing in-depth knowledge of specific weapon systems.

Where PWO training would be based was pre-ordained by the fact that all tactical training would be based at SMOPS. The period of moving away from the specialist Seaman Officer structure and towards the PWO concept were difficult, and the OPSTRAIN team was actively involved in smoothing the transition.

HMS *Dryad* – the Wardroom in 1970s
by permission of Navy News (MOD)

Looking back some 30 years later, it is good to know that the PWO concept has stood the test of time, and the development the OPSTRAIN team did provided a sound basis for the training of these Warfare Officers.

Postscript: All the seamen training establishments closed over the following years:

- *Excellent* – the Royal Naval Gunnery School closed in 1974.
- *Mercury* – communications and navigation training finished in 1993.
- *Vernon* – the last seaman training took place in 1995 and the establishment closed in 1996.
- *Dryad* – the majority of training moved to *Collingwood* in 2004, although the Ops Room model trainers in Cook Building continued until 2011.

In 2005, the establishment was renamed Southwick Park and became the home of Defence Policing and Guarding for Navy, Army and RAF Police.

HMS DOLPHIN

Background: The Royal Navy built the establishment in 1904 around the site of the fortifications known as Fort Blockhouse.

The name *Dolphin* was taken from an old training vessel that had been berthed alongside and used as a submarine depot ship.

Where: *Dolphin* was located at Fort Blockhouse in Gosport at the western side of the entrance to Portsmouth Harbour.

What they did there: *Dolphin* was the home of the Submarine Service and the RN Submarine School.

As a Lieutenant Commander from 1976 to 1979

Ken Langley

Joining *Dolphin* submarine base after two years on the staff at Britannia Royal Naval College, Dartmouth was a sort of culture shock. The tight professionalism of an officer training establishment presented a widely different environment to the equally professional but more relaxed submarine world.

My duties as Base Education Officer were, in the main, quite standard in that I had to cover the education and resettlement needs of the submarine base personnel. However, in addition, I was the Submarine Squadron Education Officer, which meant I covered similar needs for the operational submarines based at *Dolphin*. This meant that I had to examine the educational records of each submarine's nominated Education Officer; he had many other duties and so his education responsibilities were low on his priorities.

In order to understand the Education Officer's duties and problems, I spent four days on board *Orpheus* sailing from Dartmouth to London. This was a fully operational trip during which I experienced a dive and witnessed the true meaning of 'hot bunk' routine. I quickly appreciated the minimal free time and the limited space available to carry out any extramural activities. I understood, therefore, why on returning to base, the Education Officer usually had a pile of notes and lists regarding his education duties and the needs of the submarine's crew.

My role was to assist the Education Officer and deal with particular needs of individuals. The way that I was able to operate with the individual submarine Education Officers worked well and, from my personal point of view, my understanding and respect for the submariner increased enormously. However, for me this task was much easier in the comfort of a well-located and attractively appointed office within *Dolphin*.

The Base Education Officer's resettlement role was clearly important for those coming to the end of their service. This was particularly so for submariners, as the opportunities to utilise specific submariner skills were quite limited. Consequently the refreshing of other latent skills, as well as learning new ones, were essential considerations.

In general the Training Services Agency Opportunities Scheme was often a popular choice for officers and senior ratings. This scheme offered many facilities to enable the submariners to retrain and prepare for civilian life and a second career.

HMS *Dolphin* with submarines alongside and the escape training tower in the background
© MOD Crown Copyright by permission of RN Submarine Museum

The pre-release Vocational Training Course, for up to 28 days, was a popular opportunity, particularly amongst junior ratings. At *Dolphin* we were fortunate to have an excellent RN Vocational Training Centre located in Portsmouth. As a result, submarine personnel were within easy reach of courses covering everyday skills including domestic electrics, carpentry and bricklaying. These were all very popular.

Occasionally, some personnel would prefer to advance their academic qualifications by taking a GCE course. This could be done through commercial outlets, or by using the RN Correspondence Course Section based in *Nelson*. This was another advantage for *Dolphin* personnel, as the service was prompt and of great benefit to many users.

The whole resettlement service offered by the Royal Navy was high-class and, apart from courses, there was a steady stream of information and advice provided by a number of publications including Service Resettlement Bulletins and Resettlement Notices. Some personnel in *Dolphin* would be seen waiting in the Education Centre early in the morning on the due date of publication.

Another important facility for *Dolphin* personnel was the ship's library. Apart from a huge selection of lending books for leisure, there was an excellent Reference Library that was used a great deal. As the

Base Education Officer, I was responsible for the Library's upkeep and security. However, the base was always well served by leading WRNS (Education) who dealt with an enormous amount of administrative tasks, including the organisation of the library.

There was always another IO in *Dolphin* in the Submarine School as the Training Support Officer. During my time it was Lieutenant Commander Ralph Thomas whom I eventually relieved in that job.

Postscript: *Dolphin* closed as a submarine base in September 1998, although the last submarine had left there four years earlier.

The RN Submarine School remained there, however, until December 1999 before moving to *Raleigh* in January 2000. The Submarine Escape Training Tower still remains at Fort Blockhouse (2012).

HMS DAEDALUS

ROYAL NAVAL AIR STATION LEE-ON-SOLENT

Background: The Royal Navy established the airfield at Lee-on-Solent in 1917, then transferred it when the Royal Air Force was created in 1918. It served as the HQ Coastal Command until 1939 when it moved back to the Royal Navy as *Daedalus* and the HQ of Naval Air Command.

The Air Engineering School moved from Worthy Down (*Ariel*) and RNAS Lee-on-Solent was renamed *Ariel* from 1959 until 1965 before reverting to *Daedalus*.

Where: Lee-on-Solent, Hampshire.

What they did there: Training at the Air Engineering School.

Daedalus was home to many lodger units including 772 SAR Flight and Naval Hovercraft Trials Unit.

As a Commander from 1977 to 1979

Mike O'Reilly

Settling in as the Senior Instructor Officer at this Naval Air Station was not difficult, as I had come from *Blake* with 820 Squadron, following three years at RNAS Culdrose. A decade earlier, I had served as senior forecaster at *Daedalus,* which was then *Ariel;* I also had broad sporting interests.

The main role of *Daedalus* was the Air Engineering School where training was provided for mechanics, apprentices, mechanician apprentices and Air Engineering Officers. In the school, three commanders formed the senior management team and they worked closely together from adjoining offices near the parade ground.

Some 30 IOs served at *Daedalus* with an intake each term of newly joined IOs hot from Dartmouth and their initial training in the Royal Navy. These officers were encouraged to join in as much of the life of *Daedalus* as they could manage, in addition to their training commitments, and to assist with the running of the establishment extramural activities.

There were four key Instructor Lieutenant Commanders in the school and they were all there to support the new IOs as they settled into their respective training groups: my deputy, the Education and Resettlement Officer and two others.

Visual aids and graphics of a high quality were available as the school kept up with the latest developments in training technology. Close contact was maintained with other establishments including the new entry training establishments *(Fisgard* and *Raleigh)*, RNSETT and the Naval Air Command Instructor Officer, who were all regular visitors to *Daedalus*.

Linked with other Naval Air Command bases by 781 Squadron's Devon and Heron aircraft, it was relatively easy to move around Flag Officer Naval Air Command's air stations and other locations, either for meetings or sport. Former colleagues in the various messes invariably made Fleet Air Arm personnel most welcome; it was a club within a club.

As in all training establishments at the time, fitness, sport and adventurous training played an important part in the lives of the trainees and the staff. The Indoor Sports Centre, two former hangers, was ideal for physical training and indoor sports. Football and rugby were played on site and at Manor Way. Cricket was played at Seafield Park and tennis at the Lee-on-Solent civilian club. Competitions were held also with other Part II training establishments. *Daedalus* fielded mid-week teams in most sports and did well in the various Trophy Competitions. At weekends, many sports were available on the RN grounds in Portsmouth and adventurous training activities, including sailing and gliding at *Daedalus*, on the Gosport side.

As well as providing training and management expertise to the School, the Senior Instructor Officer served on various committees – Heads of Department, Establishment Development and Computer Steering, and was frequently called upon to make presentations on training. With responsibility also for public relations and establishment development, I was involved in hosting many visitors, addressing career and work experience groups and preparing ratings for their Admiralty Interview Board.

I remember the Captain saying to me, as he left, that he was very impressed because everywhere he went he found IOs doing extra tasks. The establishment had a lot to offer in terms of sport and social life to the new IO as he settled into his first appointment.

I look back with very happy memories of serving at *Daedalus* as the SIO.

Postscript: Routine naval flying ceased in 1993, but Air Engineering training continued at *Daedalus* until 1995 then moved to *Sultan*.

Daedalus finally closed in 1996.

HMS COLLINGWOOD

Background: *Collingwood* was commissioned in early 1940 as a new-entry training camp for hostilities-only ratings.

After the war, the Electrical Branch was formed and *Collingwood* became the School of Electrical Engineering in 1946. This was the start of electrical training.

Where: *Collingwood* is based at Fareham, Hampshire.

What they did there: *Collingwood* provided weapon engineering training for the Royal Navy, except the Fleet Air Arm.

As a Captain from 1981 to 1983

Chris Young

Arriving at *Collingwood* to take up the most senior Instructor Specialisation post in that vast establishment as Director of Training Execution, with the lace of my fourth stripe getting its first outing, was both exciting and challenging.

I had joined the Royal Navy at *Collingwood* 26 years earlier, under the excellent tutelage of Lieutenant Terry Carter, and after brief excursions to the RN Barracks, Portsmouth and the Home Fleet Training Squadron in *Theseus* had returned there for my first proper job, teaching radio and radar theory in the Radio School; those early years had a lasting influence on my view of naval life.

In those distant days, one had very little contact with the Instructor Captains, though I remember Captain Frank Westwater inviting a group of us new entry officers to help harvest sweetcorn at his house in the Meon valley; he gave us a good tea and regaled us with stories of his experiences as the Met Officer for the first British nuclear tests at the Montebello Islands, off north-west Australia. His successor was Captain Bill Watts who was always game for any sailing ideas. Their office in one of the wooden blocks near the gate still existed, but my new office was in a large new concrete block, Atlantic Building.

Many things had changed: Instructors and Weapon Engineers (WE) were more integrated at all levels, but the size and tasks of the School still made a federated structure the most effective. The working unit was a school, under a Commander, who could be of either WE or I specialisation. The schools varied from a basic training group, taking sailors from initial training at *Raleigh* and giving them the basic technical education they needed to become useful members of a ship's WE department, through to higher technical education, and training specific to the equipment, which the trainees would be required to maintain in their designated billets at sea. There was a bewildering variety of different courses, many of them for just one or two students. We had a staff of around 1,200 officers and senior ratings, and an average of about 1,600 trainees at any one time.

One reason for the very large staff was the immense effort put into making the training courses effective and up-to-date as new equipment came into service or was modified, and as lessons were learned from experience of its use. This task of training design was primarily a WE responsibility, so the basic situation was that the Director of Training Design and his staff specified what the content of the training should be, and the Director of Training Execution (me), through the various schools, ensured that it was properly carried out.

Chris Young and his training team

A simple idea you might think, except, of course, that it was far from simple. Any attempt to run the two sides of the training organisation in isolation from one another would have seriously damaged our ability to respond to change and feedback and, therefore, we worked very closely together. It helped that my opposite number, a Commander WE, was someone to whom I had given his very first sea experience by taking him, then a trainee Radio Electrical Mechanic, and his classmates for a sail in the yacht *Wal* one recreation afternoon. Ah, those were the days!

My predecessor, Captain Trevor Quarendon, departed, leaving me to ponder the question: what am I here for? I was well aware how large organisations manage to carry on as normal despite someone coming in and trying to make his name by radical changes, and equally I knew the dangers of allowing the organisation to get too comfortable and resistant to necessary evolution. The Commanding Officer, a Captain WE, set much of the agenda, so strictly my remit was just to deliver the training, but that did not mean that matters of morale and discipline did not concern me – far from it. What about the need for leadership? Well, of course that's a prime responsibility, but one must be careful – the whole reason for breaking the training organisation down into schools was to ensure that trainees and staff identify with a unit of manageable size. Whilst you want to set a high standard in all ways, you must concentrate your efforts on motivating and helping the School Commanders to make them as effective as possible, while ensuring that methods and equipment are kept up to date across the board.

In such a large organisation, there was constant coming and going; all kinds of people have a reason to visit you from time to time and there were constant staff changes. As you were the local tribal chief for the Instructor Specialisation, its members needed your special care and encouragement. The other function, perhaps the trickiest, was to plan for the future, in both short and long timescales. In general, the future of Weapons Engineering training was clearly the concern of the WE Specialisation and the Training Design staff in particular. However, there were also questions of what sort of framework, both material and human, was going to be needed. At the time I took up the post, the way equipment was maintained at sea was changing fast, and the response to a fault was more likely to be to plug in a replacement module than to poke around with a meter or monitor and a handbook, let alone a circuit diagram. Consequently, the jobs of the maintainer and operator were tending to grow together, and this presented quite a challenge in specifying how people were to be trained and where the hugely expensive equipment was to be based.

This sounds a lovely intellectual exercise, but my experience was far more mundane, as we were also beginning to experience the inexorable shrinking of resources, without any corresponding reduction in task. The whole organisation had to shrink, not just the coalface. The effects could be serious. Appointments to *Collingwood* had afforded senior ratings who had worked round the clock at sea a chance to get home to their families in the evening and to take proper leave; their time at *Collingwood* now became much more pressured. Contact hours for instructors were relentlessly increased, squeezing out all the peripheral activities that contributed to the life of the establishment.

Perhaps I exaggerate, but the fun factor, which is so important when you want to weld a group of people together for serious purposes, was being eroded and I could do nothing about it – in fact I was probably blamed for some of it, since I often had to adjudicate on where the reductions were made. Still, I reflected, 'that's why you've got four stripes'.

I've stressed some of the limitations, but that does not mean it wasn't a tremendous experience to head such a vast and dedicated team in a place that had meant so much to me in my first years in the service. And there were plenty of good things – *Collingwood* had been rebuilt and offered so many facilities, including a fabulous sports centre where we all tried to raise our fitness level with some lasting longer than others. Fond memories include a weekend for the senior officers at the activity centre in the Black Mountains, where I disgraced myself by spending about 80% of my time in a canoe in the inverted position and chickening out from an abseil; a bad morning! Maintaining morale among the School

Commanders and other senior officers was deemed such fun that the wives formed the Why Not Club, which was ready for anything.

The elephant in the room issue, rarely even mentioned, was whether it was really necessary to have an Instructor Captain. At the time, and this has since changed subtly with the proliferation of Commodores, Captains were Captains, with full command of a large body of service men and women; a spare Captain, however you loaded up the job with responsibility, was in a slightly anomalous position, especially as it was clearly understood that the incumbent was not in the succession to command. At the same time, the Instructor Specialisation had always struggled to find and keep senior officer billets, especially for Captains. *Collingwood* for many years had about a seventh of the entire specialisation – in fact with RNEC Manadon was the nearest thing to a tribal home that we had. This made a strong argument for a Captain's post, and the anomaly was just something to be lived with.

Anyway, there were compensations. At a Ladies' Night Dinner, the Wardroom was saying goodbye to a group of Chilean officers who had been on courses. Their wives attended and were uniformly gorgeous, and all of them wished to make a good impression by kissing the Captain, but there were two of us. Since there was no obvious way of telling which was which, they kissed both.

After barely two years, we were packing our bags for a NATO appointment in Norfolk, Virginia. It seemed all too soon, and I was genuinely sorry to leave a people job for a desk, even in the United States!

Postscript: *Collingwood* has grown as several establishments have closed and transferred their tasks:

- A Communications Faculty was added when *Mercury* closed in 1993 and Navigation training moved at the same time.
- Further expansion followed in 1995 when training of junior Weapon Engineer Officers transferred to the site following the closure of RNEC Manadon.
- *Collingwood* became the lead establishment for the Maritime Warfare School in 2002, following the closure and transfer of warfare training from *Dryad*.

The Maritime Warfare School is now part of the Flag Officer Sea Training organisation, delivering warfare training on five sites:

- *Temeraire, Excellent* and Horsea Island, all in Portsmouth, Hampshire.
- *Raleigh* in Cornwall and *Collingwood* in Fareham, Hampshire.

NAVAL HOME COMMAND

Background: The post of Commander-in-Chief, Naval Home Command was created in July 1969 as a result of the merger of the posts of Commander-in-Chief, Portsmouth and Commander-in-Chief, Plymouth.

The Admiral and his staff were located in Admiralty House and the Old Naval Academy, which dates from 1733 when it was set up as a school for young Naval Officers.

Where: Admiralty House and Old Naval Academy are in Portsmouth Naval Base.

What they did there: This Command was responsible for Naval Training (except for the Fleet Air Arm), and for the Naval Reserves and Naval Security.

As a Rear Admiral from 1987 to 1989

Jack Howard

In January 1987, I was told by the Naval Secretary that I had been selected for promotion to Rear Admiral and that my first appointment in April of that year was to be Chief of Staff to the Commander-in-Chief, Naval Home Command, Admiral Sir Peter Stanford, until he was relieved by Admiral Sir Sandy Woodward.

Since at the time I was the Commodore, *Nelson* this meant a mess change from Anchor Gate House to Trinity House in the Portsmouth Dockyard. Although my *Nelson* appointment was a very special one and undoubtedly the best job I had ever had, the change, the nature of the role and the range of Chief of Staff duties were, to say the least, very significant.

As the Chief of Staff, I had line supervision of twenty-three shore establishments, ranging from major establishments like *Dryad, Collingwood, Sultan, Mercury* and *Vernon* to the officer training homes at the Royal Naval College, Greenwich and Britannia Royal Naval College, Dartmouth and the Royal Naval Engineering College, Manadon. In addition, there were the ratings training establishments like *Raleigh, Fisgard, Caledonia* and *Excellent*, together with the smaller but no less vital teams at RNSETT, the Physical Training, Regulating, Diving and NBCD (Nuclear Biological and Chemical Defence) Schools. Other parts of the empire were the Royal Naval Reserve and Naval Home Security.

All of these had to suffer CINCNAVHOME's supervision, but their needs were different in nature and scope. The major establishments had both to meet CINCNAVHOME's requirements in training numbers and in standards of all-round efficiency and effectiveness. They also had responsibilities to the MOD departments in London and Bath.

The tightropes that Commanding Officers had to walk presented major challenges. They were generally at the top of their promotion lists and also had critical roles and responsibilities for their specialisation. Smaller establishments had what were, in some ways, more direct and shorter-term responsibilities to their sub-specialisations. Not the least of these were the beady eyes of their fellow sub-specialists ready with feedback and advice. Many will recognise that these were living icebergs. What outside observers saw were the tips of activities while the majority were carefully managed to deliver the goods without benefit of external fiddling.

Admiralty House, Portsmouth Naval Base
Residence and headquarters of Commander-in-Chief, Naval Home Command

A vital role that I undertook for the Commander-in-Chief was the confidential reporting on Commanding Officers. As the Chief of Staff, I had, in addition to CINCNAVHOME inspections, the responsibility for carrying out a programme of formal visits to make sure that Commanding Officers knew that CINCNAVHOME was aware of their problems and successes. My Marine corporal driver and I covered many miles, waited in lay-bys in order to arrive dead-on-time and attended, additionally, quite a few guest nights. Getting essential but informal feedback at 0030 was an invaluable source of perspective. *In vino*, perhaps, *veritas*? As a former labourer in the vineyards of training and from my subsequent appointments, I knew that we could take pride in the quality of naval training and the teams that delivered it.

To discharge these responsibilities, we had a CINCNAVHOME staff of some 300. We had to manage the personnel in the Command, both service and civilian, get the resources and budgets from MOD and act as a lightning conductor when difficulties arose in managing men, money and facilities. We also had responsibilities for the Royal Naval Reserve and for the security of the entire Naval estate.

This staff had to provide the continuity and stability needed in the face of demands of thrusting Commanding Officers and bean counters. In general our staff had the experience and memories required to keep the Command on a steady and realistic course.

Each establishment had a dedicated staff officer of varying seniority to give us a fair picture of the real needs and to err on the side of the establishment. This meant that failures on the part of CINCNAVHOME could be blamed on the Chief of Staff!

Old Naval Academy, Portsmouth Naval Base – the offices of CINCNAVHOME staff

What was most encouraging was the way in which the staff listened to us Johnny-come-latelies, gave their balanced reaction and then fell in behind when logic and reason failed to change our minds. In retrospect, I think the system moved perceptibly but steadily.

Those who have served in many shore establishments will realise that the challenges and complexities faced by their staff were only rarely raised to CINCNAVHOME level. The inherent loyalties of the Naval service were – quite properly – used to present confident and positive pictures upwards. Changes proposed from above which caused pain and anguish were, of course, more vigorously challenged. All in all, the way in which establishments managed to change, whilst maintaining the confidence and capabilities of their people, was in the best tradition of the service. When all had been lost, they fell back on the response, 'Aye, aye sir!'

To become somewhat more parochial in tone, I may remark that Instructor Officers were a significant minority in the establishments of the Command. The combination of experienced specialist officers and enthusiastic young IOs proved to produce a training system acknowledged to be world-class. Specialist officers and senior ratings combined with graduate Instructor Officers have brought to Naval training, over the years, vigour and responsiveness to change that has kept our standards as high as they have ever been.

But it's not only in respect of our training standards that IOs have played a vital role. In the social, sporting and cultural activities through the Service, Schoolies have always been a catalyst for change and improvement. Wine caterers, Navy rugby captains and ship pantomime producers are eloquent testimony to the Schoolie tradition.

Now to the finale: personal assessments of what an individual has achieved are inevitably myopic. Outside of promotions, they can only be subjective and 'rose-tinted'. My predecessor as Chief of Staff was a highly experienced submariner; my successor was an eminent Supply and Secretariat one. They brought to the job a wider range of skills and experience than mine. But I had, after all, worked as an Instructor in Naval education and training with some exposure to Polaris, H-bomb testing and command. I had also enjoyed my involvement with rugby, cricket and Field Gun training. The most valuable to me, as a person, was the rapport and awareness I developed through involvement with all levels and ranks in the Naval Service across the board. I particularly treasure the times spent teaching a three-badge able seaman to pass the 'Educational Test for Leading Rate', after his five previous failed attempts, and in teaching celestial navigation to would-be Royal Marines landing coxswains – all this in a brown Army tent on Christmas Island.

I never resented being called Schoolie. With the confidence that the Appointers gave me in many General List appointments, that name summed up the vital essence of what I and the Instructor Branch brought to the service.

Postscript: The posts of Second Sea Lord and Commander-in-Chief, Naval Home Command were amalgamated in 1994 following the rationalisation of the Royal Navy after the end of the Cold War.

The new command was based in Victory Building in Portsmouth Naval Base before moving to a new headquarters at Whale Island. There he is co-located with Commander-in-Chief, Fleet.

Chapter 4

We Saw the Sea

Many people outside the Instructor Specialisation perceive that IOs spent their whole career ashore in the UK in a training environment. This was far from the truth since most IOs served at times in other roles and all IOs on a Medium or Full Career Commission served one appointment or more at sea; many also served abroad in national, NATO or exchange appointments.

When compiling this chapter, therefore, there were many different stories to choose from but the focus here is on those related to war, operations, or conflict. However, there are some other interesting stories that have been included, because they show other, different roles in which IOs have been involved.

The first experiences recounted begin in the Second World War, continue through the Cod and Cold Wars, the Falklands War and include various other skirmishes. They involve IOs serving in a range of ships and submarines, in appointments in the UK and abroad, with the Royal Navy, the Royal Marines and in the Submarine Service.

The stories are all written for this book by the people themselves except for two – the one involving Rear Admiral Sir John Fleming, which comes from his obituary by Rear Admiral Guy Liardet, and the other about Commander Douglas Steel.

They all cover the period up to 1996 except for one, which describes another interesting, timeless job that Schoolies did.

During the Second World War

Emerald and Gold

Brin Morgan

I joined the light cruiser *Emerald* at Chatham in July 1939. The Commanding Officer was Captain AWS Agar VC DSO, who had been awarded his Victoria Cross in 1919 when, as the Commanding Officer of a three-man motor torpedo boat, he sank the Russian heavy cruiser *Oleg*. His second in command in *Emerald* was Commander Fogarty Fegen, later Captain F Fegen VC of *Jervis Bay* fame. The other officers were a mixture of serving, reserve and retired officers. The Wardroom and small Gunroom included one future Commander-in-Chief and three future Rear Admirals.

No time was lost in making me responsible for the Wardroom Officers' mess bills. The Commander, Chief Engineer and Captain Marines were all addicted to liar dice and woe betide any officer unwise enough to get involved. Finding that the Wardroom mess had no refrigerator, the First Lieutenant, whose seniority as a Lieutenant Commander was 1924, went ashore and bought one. The ship's company was composed mainly of Reservists.

From Chatham, we proceeded to Weymouth where His Majesty King George VI reviewed the Reserve Fleet from the Royal Yacht *Victoria and Albert* on 9 August 1939.

The 133 Ships of the Reserve Fleet had assembled in Weymouth Bay, including three battleships, the aircraft carrier *Courageous*, and 16 cruisers. The BBC broadcast the review from *Emerald,* but this did not attract the notoriety of the famous 'The Fleet's lit up' broadcast in 1937. I remember in particular, Sunday Morning Divisions on the Quarterdeck dressed in frock coat and sword, then compulsory church service followed by inter-ship visits for pre-lunch drinks.

After the review, the ships dispersed to their war stations and, with exercises in the North Sea en-route, *Emerald* proceeded to Scapa Flow and joined the 12th Cruiser Squadron commanded by Vice Admiral Sir Max Horton, later the renowned Commander-in-Chief, Western Approaches. War had not yet been declared, which gave us a few more days for exercises, and during that time, I was sent ashore to Kirkwall to buy a piano for the Wardroom. To everyone's surprise, not least my own, I found one. It was lucky to survive its transport from the shop to the jetty, transfer to the ship's cutter and hoisting aboard; it subsequently more than earned its keep.

We sailed from Scapa on 31 August 1939 to patrol the gap between the Faeroes and Iceland where our task was to intercept all merchant ships, irrespective of nationality, bound for Scandinavian or German ports, and enemy warships, raiders or supply ships attempting to break out into the Atlantic. Northern Patrol was generally uneventful and I remember only one interception and boarding of a trawler, though we saw a fantastic display of the Northern Lights, and I learned later from the Captain's memoirs that we had had several narrow escapes from U-boats. We returned to Scapa about once a fortnight to refuel, collect mail and for a night's sleep in harbour.

At sea, the Schoolmaster and I ran the plot on a 'watch on, watch off' basis; a boring occupation memorable only for the fact that whatever time he took over, be it midnight or 0400, he always appeared wearing a stiff wing collar.

I had the aftermost cabin in the ship over the propellers and shared a Marine Steward with the Torpedo Officer in the next cabin. At sea, the constant vibration and, in bad weather, shuddering movements of the ship's stern were very unpleasant, but it is extraordinary what one can get used to. There were two ways of getting from my cabin to the 'plot' abaft the bridge: either along the upper deck, weather permitting, or between decks, which at night meant working one's way in a stooped position under sailors sleeping in hammocks slung in the passageways.

After about a month, we were ordered to proceed to Plymouth with all dispatch. There, our anti-aircraft armament was supplemented by some 0.5-inch machine guns. We topped up with stores and ammunition and were told to get tropical uniform, which led to the not unreasonable mess-deck buzz that we were bound for warmer climes. Not a bit of it. Before sailing, a railway truck arrived alongside the ship and an Admiralty signal directed the Captain personally to unload the explosive stores. This was done in great secrecy at 0300 by six sailors who manhandled boxes each weighing 130 lbs from the truck into the small arms magazine. Only the Captain knew that the boxes contained gold bricks from the Bank of England destined for the United States and that we were to take them to Halifax, Nova Scotia. We sailed the same morning and, as we emerged from Devonport into Plymouth Sound, were waved goodbye by wives and friends who had assembled on the Hoe.

HMS *Emerald* in wartime camouflage
by permission of NMRN

A few days later, I was told that the Captain required a weather forecast; our RNVR (Special Branch) Met Officer had been put ashore because he was totally incapacitated by seasickness. I had no idea where to start, but got a copy of the Naval Weather Manual and turned to page one. After a while, I thought that I had the hang of what was required, found some charts, and got weather messages from the Wireless Office. Unfortunately, the messages didn't make sense. It turned out that this was because I was unaware that they had to be decoded. Then, when I thought I had more or less cracked it, the Communications staff switched from UK broadcasts to reading the weather messages from Canada, which required a different code book. It took me two days to produce my first weather forecast. I don't think the Captain cared very much what this and my subsequent forecasts said, as long as he had a forecast.

Our passage to Halifax took ten days and on arrival, the bullion was transferred, under cover and guarded by the Royal Canadian Mounties, into a special train waiting alongside. There used to be an Order in Council dating back to the Napoleonic Wars that the Captain of a man-of-war carrying bullion was entitled to one eighth of its value when the cargo had been safely delivered. Unfortunately, sometime between 1936 and the outbreak of the war, someone in the Treasury had this Order in Council cancelled. The value of this first shipment at 1939 prices was £2 million, which at today's prices would be about £190 million; the Bank of England Securities transferred at the same time were probably worth ten times the value of the gold.

There were 50 to 100 ships in Halifax harbour, all fully loaded with food and war materials for England, and our first convoy (HX1), consisting of 40 ships, left the following morning. *Emerald* stayed behind until they were 50 miles clear of the harbour, whereupon we left, caught up and took station for the night one mile ahead of the convoy. While steaming out of Halifax our departure was broadcast from Germany by Lord Haw Haw in his best English style, which later became so familiar, 'Germany calling….Germany calling…The British cruiser *Emerald* is now leaving Halifax harbour with a large convoy …' So much for security!

The convoy practised signalling, emergency turns and zigzagging, and the crossing to the UK took 13 days. It was not easy for the older ships with a maximum speed of 10 - 12 knots to keep station and avoid making smoke, and occasionally we spent some time whipping in stragglers. We had no alarms during this trip and the inshore destroyer escort from the UK took over about longitude 15° West, which was the furthest point west that U-boats were likely to be working. *Emerald* then left the convoy and zigzagged at high speed to Portsmouth, luckily avoiding U-boats in the SW Approaches, which later sank two ships including that of the Commodore of the Channel part of the convoy.

At Portsmouth, each watch was given two days leave, a primitive form of heating was fitted on the mess-decks, the ship was painted by dockyard mateys and, after six days, we sailed again for Halifax, stopping briefly at Plymouth to pick up another three tons of gold. After a high speed crossing, we arrived at Halifax and went to Bermuda for firing practice before returning to Halifax to be part of the escort for the first Canadian Troop Convoy (TC1). This convoy included five of our largest Atlantic liners and on this occasion it was the battleship *Resolution* which limited the speed of the convoy to 20 knots – much to the concern of the Masters of the faster liners. Halfway across, the convoy escort was reinforced by units of the Home Fleet, including *Repulse*, *Furious* and a flotilla of destroyers. We turned back then to Halifax.

As we entered Halifax, we encountered biting westerly winds with frequent snow blizzards, and how the fo'c'sle party managed to work the paravane lines in these conditions was beyond comprehension. The Royal Marines Band had as usual assembled on the Quarterdeck to play as we entered harbour, but had to pack it in when their wind instruments froze. Winter clothing supplied by the pusser was totally inadequate, but within 48 hours, thanks to the Canadian Red Cross, cases arrived on board containing warm horsehide gloves used by Canadian lumbermen, woollen scarves, sea-boot stockings, leather headgear lined with wool and fur outside for ear protection, and woollen underwear of long pants and vests, enough for every man in the ship. In spite of the cold, I enjoyed our time in Halifax. Not so enjoyable was a flight in the nose cone of a Hudson bomber, or a cold, wet and windy afternoon in the ship's whaler.

Our next convoy was a slow one that took 18 days. We sailed on 20 December with fog and gales dogging us all the way. On Christmas Day, the wind reached almost hurricane force and by daylight next morning, we had virtually lost the convoy. Between the hailstorms, there were no more than a couple of ships in sight. However, one by one they linked up again, all except a few Greeks and

Panamanians, and by the time we reached our rendezvous with the destroyer escort at 15° West, they were once again in convoy. *Emerald* suffered only minor damage during the gales, but most of our boats and life-rafts went overboard.

Emerald was not designed or suitable for service in the North Atlantic. Her low freeboard meant low gun platforms and the seamen had to keep watch as lookouts, day and night, at the guns, which were not in turrets, and in other exposed positions. They simply had to face the weather, whatever it was, and stick it out – as did the watchkeeping officers on the open bridge – sometimes for nearly three weeks on end. In fact, the weather gave us much more trouble than the enemy, as the U-boat menace had not yet hotted up and spread west to the mid-Atlantic; otherwise I fear my story would have been very different.

We arrived at Portsmouth in early January 1940 and were given nine days for rest and repairs, and to get ready for another gold run to Halifax.

The one thing that was neglected during this period was the instruction of *Emerald's* six Midshipmen in navigation. I rarely saw them, as there were always reasons why they could not be made available. How they managed to pass their Midshipman's examinations remains a mystery.

So ended my first six months in the Royal Navy; it was unforgettable, but hardly what I expected when I joined.

Only Three Survived

Commander Douglas Merson Steel

Douglas Steel was only 21 years old when the First World War ended, but he had already gained an MA at Cambridge University and seen military service: he was commissioned as an officer in the Royal Field Artillery, was wounded once and reached the rank of acting Captain.

Following the war, he resumed his academic studies and then in 1922 took a commission as an Instructor in the Royal Navy. By 1927, having served in three sea-going jobs, he had been promoted to Lieutenant Commander and subsequently served for two years on the staff of the Royal Naval Engineering College, Keyham, Plymouth *(Vivid)*.

From 1930 until 1932, he served in the cruiser *Dorsetshire,* and then in the battleship *Resolution,* followed by the Met course. On promotion to Commander in 1935, he was appointed to *Ganges,* the junior rating training establishment at Shotley, near Ipswich.

After *Ganges*, he was sent in 1939 to the Portsmouth-based battlecruiser *Hood.* When war with Germany was declared, *Hood* was operating in the area around Iceland and spent the next several months hunting between Iceland and the Norwegian Sea for German commerce raiders and blockade-runners. After a brief overhaul, she sailed for Gibraltar as the flagship of Force H and participated in the destruction of the French Fleet at Mers-el-Kebir, French Algeria.

Relieved as flagship of Force H, *Hood* was dispatched to Scapa Flow, and operated in the area as a convoy escort and later as a defence against a potential German invasion fleet.

HMS *Hood* between the wars
by permission of NMRN

In May 1941, she and the battleship *Prince of Wales* were ordered to intercept the German battleship *Bismarck* and the heavy cruiser *Prinz Eugen*, which were en route to attack convoys in the Atlantic. On 24 May 1941, several German shells struck the *Hood* early in the Battle of the Denmark Strait and the ship exploded; the loss had a profound effect on the British. The Prime Minister, Winston Churchill, ordered the Royal Navy to 'Sink the *Bismarck!*' and they fulfilled his command on 27 May.

There were 1,418 crew on board *Hood* at the time of her loss and only three men survived; they did not include Douglas Steel.

North Cape and Normandy

Rear Admiral Sir John Fleming DSC

John Fleming joined the Royal Navy as an Instructor Lieutenant in September 1925. His subsequent appointments included the cruiser *Frobisher* and the battleship *Royal Oak*, followed by Britannia Royal Naval College, Dartmouth.

In 1933, he was the Cypher Officer in the cruiser *Leander* and qualified as a German interpreter. After again serving in *Royal Oak*, he returned in 1937 to the classroom at the Royal Naval Engineering College, Keyham in Plymouth.

When war broke out, he joined the Admiralty in the Meteorological Forecast Section. A subsequent move in 1942, as the Home Fleet Meteorological and Education Officer, took him to the battleship *Duke of York*, flagship of Admiral Sir Bruce Fraser. Here he took part in the chase and sinking of the German battlecruiser *Scharnhorst*.

HMS *Duke of York* – flagship of Commander-in-Chief, Home Fleet
by permission of NMRN

On 26 December 1943, this powerful warship was at sea in appalling weather near Bear Island, between North Cape, Norway and Spitsbergen, endeavouring to intercept a large convoy bound for North Russia. The convoy's close cruiser and destroyer escort had fended off an initial attack, but they had then lost *Scharnhorst* in the murk. A sound appreciation of her probable movements and some skilful shadowing allowed the *Duke of York*, in company with the cruiser *Jamaica* and four destroyers, to close at night from a considerable distance and sink her, the only remaining operational German capital ship in that theatre.

The control exercised by Admiral Fraser over his numerous and originally widely separated forces had been masterly and this had in turn depended upon the collation and clear plotting of all relevant information. As the *Duke of York's* tactical plot officer, John Fleming was described as 'cool and skilled' and was awarded the DSC for his contribution to this strategically significant outcome.

In June 1944, Commander John Fleming was one of the meteorologists on the staff of Admiral Sir Bertram Ramsay, Commander-in-Chief of the Allied Expeditionary Force for Operation NEPTUNE, the naval component of the Normandy landings. With Group Captain Stagg RAF and Colonel Yates, US Army Air Force, he provided the weather forecasts that enabled General Dwight D Eisenhower to make his momentous decision to proceed with Operation OVERLORD, the greatest amphibious operation in history.

Early on Sunday morning, 4 June, Eisenhower postponed the invasion for 24 hours due to strong winds and low cloud. This was the limit of possible postponement. The meteorological team at the headquarters at Southwick House near Portsmouth was being asked for three-day forecasts, difficult enough even today, but then on comparatively scanty information, which naturally lacked observations from occupied Europe to the east. Weather forecasting had made great progress during the war, but was still more art than science.

At 0400 on 5 June, Eisenhower and all his senior British and American leaders were gathered around the fireplace in the large drawing room in Southwick House, with violent gusts of wind and rain cannonading against the French windows. They were contemplating Stagg's weather map for 0700 hours that day which showed a deep slow-moving depression of 978 millibars over the Shetlands and a steep pressure gradient rising towards a High in the south-west, causing strong Westerlies up the Channel. Stagg and his team predicted a slackening of this pressure gradient and a 36-hour opportunity from dawn on 6 June. Eisenhower was leaning against the mantelpiece and, after a long pause, quietly said, 'OK. Let's go'. In fact, the weather eased for nearly a week. On the next remotely possible invasion date, 17 June, it was blowing a gale.

John Fleming would later become Rear Admiral Sir John Fleming, the Director of the Naval Education Service and the head of the Instructor Branch from 1956 to 1960.

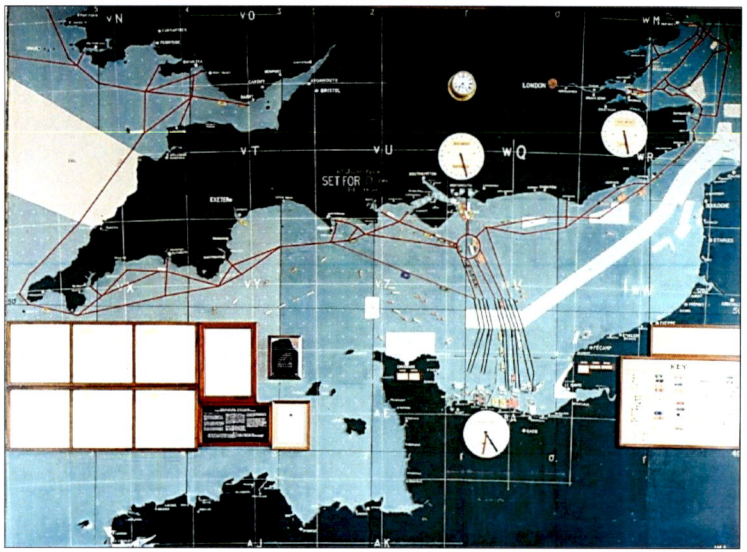

HMS *Dryad* – the Wall Map Room set up for 6 June 1944

During the 1950s

Way Up North

Derek Blacker

I joined the Royal Navy on a Short Service Commission in 1950. Following a six-month intensive course in meteorology, I was appointed in 1951 as the senior, and only, Met Officer at RNAS Gosport (*Siskin*) and continued there, after I was awarded a Permanent Commission, until 1955.

During this time, in February 1953, someone in the Ministry of Defence decided to check if I was a suitable candidate for a future life at sea and, together with one Met rating, I was given a temporary appointment to the Fishery Protection Squadron. Accordingly, in February, I arrived at Hull to join *Truelove*, a 1100-ton *Algerine* minesweeper, in which I was to take passage to join *Coquette*, another *Algerine*, at sea. A short time earlier, some trawlers had run into serious black frost off Iceland and one indeed had capsized, when the combination of freezing air temperatures and spray from rough seas produced a uniform layer of ice on all surfaces. A Fishery Protection *Algerine* minesweeper had also been damaged and so *Coquette* was sent to replace her.

Before we sailed from Hull, a neighbouring fishing trawler captain had presented the ship with a large quantity of kippers; this was to have some significance later. Leaving Hull, the ship turned left and headed north into a Force 8 gale which continued unabated, until we rendezvoused with *Coquette* a couple of days later. This passage was my introduction to very unpleasant seas and to the delights of naval catering. I had taken precautions to equip myself with a good supply of Avomine and, although I felt awful at times, I was never sick.

Eating in the Wardroom was one of the more difficult evolutions; naturally it was impossible to eat at table and officers would find a suitable bench near a stanchion, jam themselves into the seat by putting both feet on the stanchion and in that way hold the plate in a stable condition in order to eat. My recollections of menus during the voyage are hazy but those of breakfasts are locked in my mind. Every day, we were offered a choice of kippers or tinned tomatoes on toast and for ten years afterwards, I could never face a kipper or tinned tomato. However, because of the unsatisfactory living conditions on board, members of the crew were awarded sea-going hard lying allowance and I think mine was something in the region of three shillings a day.

We joined *Coquette* at night in a sheltered anchorage to the south-east of Iceland; the whaler was lowered and Lieutenant Blacker, wearing greatcoat, cap and carrying duffle bag, together with the Met rating were transferred to *Coquette*. If we thought that the weather had been inclement on the way up from Hull, we were in for a nasty shock as we set off northeast heading for Tromsø. Immediately, we left the shelter of Iceland, we ran into N to NW storm force winds with huge seas and this continued nearly all the way to Tromsø. My berth was a shared cabin with the Gunnery Officer beneath the 4-inch gun on the fo'c'sle. The scuttle would not close properly and there were one or two inches of water constantly sloshing round the deck. The ship rolled 35 degrees in the rough weather and at night we had to strap ourselves into our bunks.

HMS *Coquette* – *Algerine* class minesweeper
by permission of NMRN

As the air temperature was below freezing, the spray quickly adhered to the ship's superstructure as ice. Every morning, therefore, lower deck was cleared and everyone turned to chipping away the ice. With the ship moving around so dramatically and ice quickly forming on it, making weather observations was a very hazardous activity at night on the upper deck with an Assman psychrometer, which measured the humidity; I decided to suspend, temporarily, the taking of midnight and 0300 weather observations for which I was subsequently criticized by an uncomprehending senior Met Officer in the Admiralty Forecast Section.

Several days later, we arrived at Tromsø, a very pleasant place, but at this time of year in near twilight or darkness. After a little leisure, including skiing for some, *Coquette* set off north again, reached the pack ice near Bear Island before turning south-east to administer assistance to any trawlers needing our help in the White Sea. Since leaving Tromsø, we had been accompanied almost constantly by Soviet naval shipping and, surprise, surprise, we had the odd spy on board too, listening to them.

Leaving the White Sea, we turned west and arrived at Honningsvåg, at 70° 58' N, the most northerly habitation in Europe and the world. The inhabitants were very pleased to see us for the mayor organised a dance and made sure all the Honningsvåg girls came; no Norwegian men were allowed and a terrific time was had by all. The rest of the voyage back to the UK was very dull by comparison.

Finally, I think I can say that I acquired my sea legs and certainly earned my hard lying allowance.

Interesting Times

Anon

I joined the Royal Navy in September 1951 and within six weeks was at the Met School at Kete in Pembrokeshire on course M5. My first full Met appointment was quite a stroke of luck to be in the Fleet Weather Centre based at RNAS Hal Far in Malta and in the Mediterranean Fleet proper on the staff of the Commander-in-Chief, no less than Admiral Mountbatten. I had some trips to sea as his Met officer; he was a man of great charisma with expectations of grandeur.

In the Mediterranean, we were playing a part in the work-up of carriers and their squadrons as they proceeded to the Korean War, which the US Navy referred to as World War Three, and we witnessed the return of those same squadrons on their way back to the UK six months later, often quite decimated in aircrew, with having had to engage with modern MIG fighters in their Sea Furies and Fireflies, both Second World War types of aircraft.

My time in Malta included cruises around the Mediterranean in the submarine depot ship *Forth* and one back to UK in 1953 for the Coronation Review. On our way back from the review, we were central to the early stages of SUBSMASH when one of our submarines failed to make a surfacing report, but we found her – and towed her into Gibraltar!

Coronation Fleet Review at Spithead on 15 June 1953
by permission of NMRN

Whilst at Hal Far, there was a hair-raising 24-hour watch on Christmas Day 1953 when we had a very deep low pressure area to the south of the island, resulting in a very active Gregale wind and many hours of stress for the Met staff. Other major incidents included a Greek earthquake and searches for two Comet aircraft that had crashed in separate events within days of each other. An interesting serial that took place was the making of a feature film 'Single Handed' which was shot on location around Malta; this was the story of the commerce raider *Essen* in the Second World War, with the fast minelayer *Manxman* taking the place of the German ship.

Like others, I had the opportunity to fly – and on one occasion was in the back seat of an aircraft on a dive-bombing sortie, where the pilot was a good friend. All went well and with all the obvious features leading up to the pullout not much above sea level and well below the cliffs of Malta. But the end of the story is that my friends had to call me to say that our undercarriage was not showing locked down and after several over-flights of the Control Tower, we put down hoping for the best and observing other friends pulling out in the Blood and Fire Wagons as we passed them at the near end of the runway – but the undercarriage did hold up!

Back in the UK, I served in *Vidal* on survey duties in the Barents Sea and then we annexed Rockall and made front page news in the main newspapers. Later in another Met appointment, I was serving in *Tyne*, the flagship at Suez in 1956. The big question that I had to answer was, 'But can I drop Paratroops?' when all the soldiers minds, including that of the General in command, were full of the disaster at Arnhem.

I served ashore at many Royal Naval Air Stations including Lossiemouth (Morayshire, Scotland), St Merryn (Padstow, Cornwall), Abbotsinch (Paisley, Scotland), Mackrihanish (Campbeltown, Argyll, Scotland) to mention some that have been closed for many years.

My Met life also included the light fleet carrier *Vengeance* in which I made my first forecast at sea, got it spot on and after which the Commander mistakenly made out that I was always right; much later I served in *Ocean*. This all shows how much I enjoyed Met!

Long Way Round

Chris Young

Towards the end of the one-term Permanent Commission course at Greenwich, learning about serious navigation and other useful nautical arts, we learned what our next appointments would be. Our first proper sea job! Since studying a 1937 edition of Jane's Fighting Ships throughout the Second World War, I had absorbed the details of every RN ship and now I was actually going to belong to one of them.

It was a bit of a let-down to find I wasn't appointed in 1958 to a ship, but rather as the 6th Frigate Squadron Instructor Officer, which was made up of anti-submarine frigates, mainly Type 15s, which were conversions from the War Emergency destroyer class. With a new aluminium superstructure and the latest in sonar and anti-submarine weapons, they were pretty state-of-the-art for their time.

We were to be on a General Service commission, meaning about a year in the Mediterranean and a year in Home and north European waters. However, even squadron staff officers needed a base and mine was to be in a private ship, *Ulysses,* and not in the squadron leader, which was already topped up with officers.

I joined *Ulysses* as she lay in dry dock in Devonport Dockyard. My day job was to see to the educational needs of young sailors who needed to pass the Educational Tests for advancement. Since *Ulysses* was the only ship of the squadron within reach, I got on with it or at least tried to. It seemed that the junior rating training establishments, *Ganges* and *St Vincent,* had accumulated a residue of trainees who persistently failed to pass educationally, and a smart drafting officer had decided to send them off to a ship which had a Schoolie.

After two years teaching some very bright apprentices at *Collingwood*, I now had a more challenging teaching job. These young sailors were well motivated, as they could only rise from the lowly Ordinary Seaman level if they passed the educational test, but their failure to pass the test at the training establishments left them in need of encouragement as well as a brisk classroom discipline.

The ship was soon out of dock and I was gaining a little more confidence as Officer of the Day. After we set off for the Mediterranean, I asked the Captain if I could keep bridge watches at sea. He agreed, but pointed out that as I used contact lenses he would not be able to give me a full ticket, however good I was. I still wanted to have a go, nevertheless, and the prospect of an extra watchkeeper was welcome to those in the Officer of the Watch union.

HMS *Ulysses* – Type 15 anti-submarine frigate

We joined Captain F6 with the other three ships in Naples – he had been Naval Attaché in Rome, and had huge delight in leading his small flock at high speed round the Bay of Naples. This turned out to be the only part of the commission when all the ships were together. We returned to Malta for a minor refit in the dockyard; the tricky bit was working out whether the dockyard workers were on strike or not. I had a chance to take my class of sailors, now boosted by lads from other ships, for several weeks of preparation for the exams, after which a surprising number of them passed. A hot Maltese summer was spent living at RNAS Hal Far (*Falcon*) and travelling into the dockyard early each morning. There was still plenty of time for exploring the island, swimming, sailing and enjoying the social life associated with the Mediterranean Fleet.

Having with some difficulty extricated the ship from the dockyard, we were sent on Cyprus patrol, trying to inhibit the flow of arms and agitators from Greece into the island. The weather was glorious, but the patrol routine was very boring for the ship's company. One of my treasured memories is of doing the morning swim around the ship to check for limpet mines when we were anchored off north Cyprus. The water was so clear in the early morning sun that you could see the whole ship's hull and the complete catenary of the anchor chain stretched out ahead.

HMS *Ulysses* ship's company

We went back to Malta and exercises in the Central Mediterranean as the weather broke, and I learned just how vicious that sea can be. Asian flu was rampant and we picked it up on a visit to the Mediterranean base for the French fleet at Toulon. Though we left early, by the time we got back to Malta there were just enough in the Engine Room department to get us back, and they had to stay on watch until we were safely in Sliema Creek.

We were back in Devonport for Christmas 1957. I half-expected a move to another ship of the squadron, but there was a major change of plan which meant that *Ulysses* was to go off on her own to support the H-bomb tests in the Pacific, codenamed Operation Grapple. To my great satisfaction, it was decided that a supernumerary officer such as myself could make himself useful on such a mission. As it was a very long trip for what should be just a few weeks in mid-Pacific as naval guardship round the testing area at Christmas Island, it was planned that we would go on to Singapore after the tests and take part in a major exercise in the Bay of Bengal before returning to Devonport, so it would be a round-the-world trip.

It is difficult to avoid making the ensuing twelve months sound like a tourist itinerary. To put it as concisely as possible, we went Devonport, Jamaica, Panama, Christmas Island, then diverted to New Zealand via Fiji because the Grapple H-bomb test was delayed. After the test, which was an unforgettable experience, we went via Tarawa and the Gilbert and Ellice Islands to Singapore for a maintenance period in the dockyard, thence to the exercise, Trincomalee, Mombasa, where instead of accompanying *Bulwark* back to the UK via South Africa as planned, we were diverted to deal with a Jordanian oil crisis at Aqaba. Finally, we headed home via Suez, Malta, Gibraltar to Devonport.

What did the squadron Instructor Officer do? Apart from basic education, and I had a very competent Leading Coder (Education) to help with that, and marking the Midshipman's and Captain's astro-navigation sights, there was no lack of useful jobs. The Navigator and I, who got on very well, decided to put the rapid-reduction method of astro-sights to the test on the 4,000-mile voyage from Panama to Christmas Island; we could warn the Captain when the first sight could be expected of the island, a flat atoll with a maximum elevation of a 40 feet flagpole in the middle of an empty ocean.

In port, there were public relations and trips for the crew to be organised. Around Christmas Island, we were using our radar to track Met balloons to measure wind strength at various altitudes and I was roped in by Lieutenant Commander John Taylor, an IO, to work watch-and-watch with him. By this time, I was trusted with a straightforward bridge watch on my own and persuaded the Captain to give me a certificate to say so; this proved useful in later appointments, and I also deputised for the navigator when he was struck down with a virus. Thus I made myself as useful as possible and in the process learned a great deal. This was just as well, as it was twelve years until my next sea appointment!

My experience, like that of others, of being appointed to a squadron of ships was almost meaningless since the ships of the squadron had quite separate programmes. It would have been better if the job spec had included something more crucial to the ship's role. Being known as the Laundry and Morale Officer (anybody remember the film 'Captain Roberts'?) or the Tourist Divisional Officer, as listed in the book of the commission (OK, I edited it), even affectionately, gives the wrong vibrations somehow.

However, the privilege I enjoyed of my two years in a frigate gave me a grounding that stood me in good stead for almost 30 years.

Christmas in the Pacific

Don Cripps

My task as the Met man was to head a team of five senior ratings to provide regular weather reports upwind of Christmas Island, which is about 1,200 miles south of Hawaii; these reports would be used to decide when to drop the hydrogen bombs, without the ensuing debris risking the health of people living on islands in the Pacific

In January 1957, we joined the light fleet carrier *Warrior* for passage out to the test area via Jamaica, the Panama Canal and Honolulu. During the passage, however, the Captain decided to keep the crew occupied by painting the flight deck. As we left the Gulf of Panama, the bright blue sky was dotted with little bunches of white cloud which sometimes scattered light rain. The Captain called me to the bridge and said, 'Now Cripps, we have just painted the flight deck and I do not wish it to be rained upon yet. As a Met Officer you are to take command of the ship's steering and ensure that we pass between these rain clouds and the deck remains dry.' I am pleased to report that I did manage to complete my watch without a speck of water getting on the flight deck.

At Christmas Island, my team transferred to the Loch class frigate HMNZS *Pukaki* and the other team, run by Lieutenant Andrew Chadwick, went to HMNZS *Rotoiti,* another of the same class. Both ships, out of sight of each other, were positioned about 150 miles upwind of the small, uninhabited island which was to become the focus of the H-bomb tests.

Loch class frigate
by permission of NMRN

Our task was to send regular weather reports back to Christmas Island including measurements of the wind speed and direction at regular heights up to 30,000 feet. To do this, the team launched a balloon from the ship's stern and the ship's radar operator would track this, then pass on the readings at set time intervals to me. I could calculate from these the wind speed and direction at set heights and they would be passed to the Commander-in-Chief who would decide when to drop the hydrogen bombs without the danger of debris being blown towards the Pacific Islands within range.

Between each trial, we would steam off to relax in the lagoon of a nearby island. One of these was particularly beautiful, with the only inhabitants being a lovely Polynesian lady with a Scots husband who would walk round the shore of the atoll gently playing his bagpipes every evening.

Pukaki carried out her diplomatic task thoroughly; we visited the Cook Islands and were made most welcome wherever we went and treated to fine entertainment of music and Polynesian dancing. Conditions in those days were pretty basic in these islands with no forms of transport or trade, and most food was grown or caught by each family. However, the people were delightful.

One thing I shall never forget was the time when we visited a large island with about 30 inhabitants. They had all originated in another of the Cook Islands about 40 miles away, but very few had ever had the opportunity to go back to visit their families. The Captain decided to put this sad omission right; he offered to take anyone over to the other island and return them next day. Everyone went and we had a delightful journey with our deck full of very happy passengers.

At Rarotonga, the largest island of the group, we received a signal from *Warrior*, 'We shall visit Rarotonga before leaving for the UK and need a liaison officer to plan our stay. Put Cripps ashore and we'll pick him up in four weeks' time.'

I was accordingly put ashore to stay as the only guest in the New Zealand Government hotel, where I spent a magical time getting to know the local people and joining in their frequent festivities. In return, I was asked to give several talks on the conduct of the H-bomb tests and what we had done to protect the Cook Islands; they were obviously concerned.

After *Warrior's* successful visit to Rarotonga, we managed to collect all the crew and set off for Peru calling at Pitcairn Island on the way. We were circumnavigating South America on our way back to the UK, paying diplomatic visits on the way round, but on arrival at Peru, I was ordered to be flown home to take some leave since I would be required for a second set of H-bomb tests which were to be held in the autumn.

Afterwards, *Warrior* was sold to Argentina (and renamed ARA *Independencia*) and operated until being replaced in 1970. The replacement, ARA *Veinticinco de Mayo*, became well known in the Falklands war.

Send a Gunboat

Peter Rogers

From April 1959 until September 1960, I was the 3rd Frigate Squadron Instructor Officer based on the Far East Station. At my first meeting with Captain F3 on board *Cardigan Bay*, he greeted me with the words, 'Ah Schoolie, now you're the most important man in my ship'. It transpired that he had started his naval life as a junior rating at *Ganges*, and never forgot the efforts of one of our predecessors. He was keen that, in all the ships of his squadron, I had total involvement in all activities.

During my time in *St Brides Bay*, the Commanding Officer, who was an RN aviator, insisted that I was his Met Officer, although it was to be another four years before I attended the Met course. Life at sea was very varied with taking educational classes, current affairs, supervising astro-navigation for the young officers under training, including checking morning and evening stars, as well as undertaking bridge watchkeeping and other ship duties.

HMS *St Brides Bay* – *Bay* class anti-aircraft frigate
by permission of NMRN

At the end of August 1959, we had returned to Singapore, following a spell as guardship at Hong Kong, when a buzz went round the ship that we were immediately to prepare for sea. The next day, we sailed and learned that we were to relieve *Cavalier* as guardship at Addu Atoll in the Indian Ocean.

It transpired that there were local difficulties between the Maldivians living within the atoll, and the Pakistani workers who were extending the runway at the RAF airfield on the island of Gan. On passage, a number of us requested to discontinue shaving and I have had my beard ever since. Apart from diverting to land a casualty in Ceylon and the Crossing the Line ceremony, which was great fun, the rest of our passage was pretty uneventful.

After a brief turnover, we parted company with *Cavalier*, which turned away from us and came steaming past in a huge sweep at 30 knots, quite a sight. We anchored near the centre of the lagoon for what was to be the best part of six weeks. We sailed twice to show the flag, but mostly worked Tropical Routine from 0600 to 1400 to make the best use of 12 hours of daylight. Fortunately, we had access to all the islands of the atoll, whereas the RAF contingent ashore was confined to Gan and their communications facility on Hittadu. The next island to Gan was uninhabited, only about a quarter of a mile long, and we used it as our own banyan island, irking our light blue friends.

Sporting activities included sailing, snorkelling, swimming and, of course, football. We played against the RAF but we also played matches against local teams from all the major islands on their home pitches, which were mainly sandy surfaces with scant grass. The locals played with bare feet and boundless enthusiasm. The object of the exercise for them was to keep the football after the match, whatever the result. When we ran out of footballs these games fell into abeyance, but were resurrected when we replenished the stock at a scheduled Replenishment at Sea, one of the two occasions when we left the lagoon. The ship was open to visitors for the locals and, being a Muslim community, the ladies wore their Sunday best. The men rowed their families round and round the ship, but eventually only the men and younger children ventured on board.

We had many opportunities to see how they lived. Fishing was a main source of food and so the fishing boats and nets were kept in good order; areas on the islands were laid aside for drying coconuts. Our contact with the RAF at Gan was limited; we had a couple of standard lunchtime invitations to drinks on board followed by low-key return matches. It was after one of these that our Navigating Officer and the Engineer decided to paint a message on the new runway. The upshot was that a Wardroom team painted 'F600 – Under Royal Navy Protection' on the Gan main runway, F600 being the pennant number of our ship. Security patrols had failed to spot us and the following day was interesting to say the least. Apparently, lots of scrubbing failed to remove the slogan.

Officers from *St Brides Bay* showing the locals how to pull

Soon after this it was our turn to be relieved. Far from being a dangerous or arduous mission, it proved to be an interesting and challenging period during which we gained the hearts and minds of the locals. The reward was an unforgettable six weeks.

There is a postscript to this story. In June 1965, I was returning from Singapore to the UK in the carrier *Victorious* and recounted the runway-painting incident to some of our aircrew as we crossed the Indian Ocean. A couple of days later, I gave the Met brief to our Gannet aircrew who flew into Gan for the mail run and to pick up some essential items. They reported back that they could still discern the lettering after more than five years, although by then it was very faint.

Great Variety

John Franklin

The 5th Frigate Squadron went about its business in the early 1950s in the Mediterranean and comprised four W class anti-submarine frigates: *Wrangler, Whirlwind, Wakeful* and *Roebuck*. As squadron IO my main task was the education of Upper Yardmen ratings for advancement and Midshipmen for navigation. Bearing in mind that I had had no previous experience in teaching and had just emerged from the navigation course at Greenwich, learning on-the-job was the order of the day.

I was required to meet my responsibilities in the four ships by frequently going from one to another either by boat or by jackstay transfer. The latter was quicker and much more exciting.

HMS *Wrangler* – W class anti-submarine frigate
by permission of NMRN

When we had a spell in Malta, I was involved in cultural activities such as on board entertainment and, being able to play the 'organ portable small', I got together a small band of singers and 'musicians', who played the Jew's harp and a comb and paper. With this motley crew we managed to win the Maltese radio's prize for amateur entertainment, using the names of Maltese villages strung together as the libretto for a popular song.

A number of interesting incidents took place during our cruises in the Mediterranean. One was the journey to north-east Italy to take off the last of the British Element Trieste Forces. As we sailed up the Adriatic, we had on board a full pack of journalists and when I quizzed them on how they were spending their time en route they said they were writing their reports on 'How the British troops left Trieste'. Having remonstrated that this was a bit premature, I was told that on landing they all had to race to the nearest phone to get their story to their editors as soon as possible, since there was no instant communication in the 1950s. Their reports were greatly elaborated to make a good story with gory tales of how the troops had embarked accompanied by jeers and stone-throwing. In fact there was hardly anyone on the quayside other than the troops and not a single untoward incident occurred. I learned then not to rely on the papers if you are researching history.

Another trip up the Adriatic landed us in Split, where we indulged in harmonious social intercourse with the Yugoslavs. Part of this included yacht racing, water polo in the sea and various dinners. On one of these occasions, it fell to my lot to give the response to the host's opening speech. As my knowledge of Croatian history was non-existent, I fell back on the politician's standard patter and spoke of our great bonds of friendship and our admiration for what they had achieved not knowing at all what this was. The great thing was that I had an interpreter who must have embellished at length what I said and the evening was a great success.

Other memories of this time included my appointment as the local 'Provost Marshal' in Gibraltar when, arrayed in gaiters and with a baton and accompanied by two CPOs, I roamed about the town looking for malefactors and drunks.

My second tour at sea was as a Commander from 1968 to 1970 in *Bulwark* whose motto 'In which we trust' was inevitably popularised as 'The rusty B'. There was a great crowd of IOs on board and, with such an efficient staff, I was without a real IO's job. However, having an engineering background, the Captain (Templeton-Cotill) appointed me Refit Coordination Officer, which entailed liaising between the ME and WE Departments in planning the ship's refits and maintenance to ensure no conflicting overlaps of time and space.

Another enjoyable task was making the arrangements for the ship to participate in the Kataklysmos Fair in Larnaca, Cyprus. As *Bulwark* was nearby, we agreed to send one of the helicopters to lift Aphrodite, a member of the Women's Royal Army Corps, from the sea to mark the start of the festivities. Other Mediterranean highlights included a helicopter visit to an otherwise virtually inaccessible monastery on Mount Athos and our visit to Venice where we were then the largest ship ever to moor off St Mark's Square.

After returning to the UK, we set off for the Far East. Keeping fit on board was not easy and repetitive runs around the ship and volleyball in the aircraft lift-well had to suffice, although swimming was greatly welcomed when it became possible. Memorable events included Crossing the Line, where I got the full treatment, and Cape Town which provided a welcome trip ashore. After visits to Brunei, which was fascinating to see by helicopter, we reached Singapore and immediately went into dry dock for refit.

I finished my time in *Bulwark* towards the end of the refit and travelled home by a most uncomfortable propeller aircraft, stopping off en route at Gan in the Maldives and Cyprus.

During the 1960s

Up North

Dick Abram

With no leave between appointments and no hirings or married quarters available, my wife and I with two boys under four years old moved on the Friday from Lossiemouth to an unseen renting in Aberdour, prior to my joining *Malcolm* in Rosyth Dockyard on the Monday. I had previously received a letter from the Captain stating that *Malcolm* was not expected to sail until the Friday; she would then visit Aberdeen before sailing for an Icelandic patrol.

I arrived about 0730 to find that, on the Sunday, one of the trawlers had had an argument with one of the Icelandic gunboats, so by 1000, my turnover from Lieutenant Scott Farquharson had taken place, he had departed and we were making best speed for the fishing grounds.

Fortunately, the only good thing about the rented accommodation was that it had a telephone, so I was able to warn my wife that I would not be home that night and did not know when I would next see her. As it turned out, it was about five weeks before we returned to Rosyth and, as we were not allowed into ports in Iceland, an RFA had to provide fuel. When things settled down again, we refuelled in Reykjavik the capital, or in Seydisfjord next to a very smelly fish factory. There in the winter, the ship often had to provide heating for the pipes from the storage tanks to the jetty so that the furnace fuel oil would become sufficiently viscous to flow downhill.

HMS *Malcolm* – *Blackwood* class anti-submarine frigate
by permission of Navy News (MOD)

The Captain Fishery Protection Squadron was the CO *Duncan* in which I managed to do only one patrol but, apart from leave periods, I was normally at sea in one of the other Type 14s and was able to spend patrols in *Palliser*, *Russell* and *Keppel*. In addition to the Met advice for the ship, duties involved broadcasting twice-daily forecasts for the British trawlers with additional gale warnings as necessary. The Fishery Protection Squadron frigates were there to provide as much assistance as they could to the trawlers and this turned out to be mainly medical, electrical, mechanical or removing wires wrapped round the propeller. The ship's company lived very healthily as the reward was usually cod, halibut or prawns; the prawns would otherwise have been thrown back by the trawlers as there was then no demand in the UK for them.

Met advice was critical to the comfort of the ships company when travelling from one side of Iceland to the other; the choice was 'clockwise or anti-clockwise' but the comfort much depended on whether the wind was on the bow or up the stern. However, it was not always possible to avoid a few days with the Wardroom table lashed upside down and everyone sitting on the deck eating hash, which was all that the galley could produce.

It is interesting to note now that, in the early 1960s, there were times when areas of ice and bergi-bits extended from Greenland to close to the Icelandic coast and they were sufficiently dangerous to prevent the thin-hulled Type 14s breaking through, forcing the ship to go the long way round.

The new volcanic island of Surtsey, the southernmost point of Iceland, erupted in early 1963 and during a patrol shortly afterwards, when the eruptions were still significant, *Malcolm* went as close as safety allowed and did briefly land some sailors by sea-boat, but it was deemed not politic to raise the Union flag or the White Ensign.

Between January and Easter, Fishery Protection Squadron frigates also supported UK trawlers fishing outside Norwegian territorial waters and this meant that we could visit several ports in the north of Norway. On one occasion in the Barents Sea, we were sufficiently far to the east for a claim to be made for East of Suez Allowance. Unsurprisingly, that got a biblical 'not granted' from the Admiralty.

In the summer of 1965, shortly after my two years in the squadron, I did return to Icelandic waters. I was lent for a few weeks to the diving ship *Reclaim* to provide Met support for that ship and a group of minesweepers, which were being sent to Iceland to sweep the fjord to Akureyri and Seydisfjord of moored mines, thought still to be in position from the Second World War. These mines were designed to be detonated from the shore as necessary, but when hostilities ended and the shore controls were removed, some of the mines remained. I recall that three mines were cleared from Akureyri fjord and detonated by gunfire, but despite much sweeping, none was found in Seydisfjord. The locals later told us that Seydisfjord had been swept a year earlier by a large whale, which killed itself in the process.

Versatility

Roger Drury

A characteristic of a career in the Instructor Branch was that one was continually learning new skills to equip you for the next appointment.

In mid-1966 when I was appointed to the commando carrier *Albion*, I was despatched to the 14-week Photographic Interpretation (PI) course at RAF Bassingbourne, north of Cambridge. At that time, the principal Photographic Reconnaissance aircraft, the Canberra, was based there and so the training was co-located with the equipment to obtain the necessary photographs. All the RN aircraft carriers had a PI capability. On the fixed wing carriers, *Ark Royal, Eagle, Hermes* and *Victorious*, an Observer from one of the squadrons fulfilled the role, with the primary objective of assisting not only with target identification, but also to direct strikes to maximise damage. On the commando carriers, it was often the role of the Instructor Officer (Education) to carry out the PI task, advising the Commando Unit on board on the topography for a shore landing, as well as what enemy threats there could be facing a landing.

The art of PI is to take a series of aerial photographs all of which overlap by 60% and then study pairs under a binocular instrument that forces each eye to focus separately on the image. The brain interprets these two received images as a 3D image from which the object can be more readily identified and, more importantly, be accurately measured.

The course members were an interesting group – RAF pilots, many with Second World War experience, who had reached the ends of their flying careers, Army Majors and Captains going to a range of staff appointments mainly with the British Army of the Rhine facing the might of the Russian Bear and, with me from the Royal Navy, were Observers from *Ark Royal* and *Eagle*.

The course was absolutely fascinating. We studied industrial complexes, transport systems, aircraft recognition, weapons systems and a great deal more – I could distinguish between a Russian 105mm and 115mm gun from 35,000 feet without difficulty. We spent much time analysing target potential, where measurement was often the key to identification. Additionally, we examined many Second World War photographs and were faced with the same problems that arose then – what exactly were we seeing?

One of the most horrifying parts of the course was the section on camp identification across Europe, primarily aimed at knowing where the POW camps were. However, slipped into this section were photographs of the concentration camps taken quite early in the war – they had a very different layout but, at the time, their function was not known.

In the 1960s, the Vietnam War was raging and we were given access to early satellite photographs, which graphically showed what was happening on the ground. You could see the sophistication of the United States pitted against the peasant culture of Vietnam and I clearly remember to this day scenes of Hanoi. Some 40 years later, I visited Vietnam and many of the images I had studied were still there on the ground.

HMS *Albion* – *Centaur* class light fleet carrier
by permission of Navy News (MOD)

The opportunity for me to use these newly won skills in Europe quickly disappeared as a number of RM landing exercises were cancelled as *Albion* was despatched to the South Atlantic to watch over a little local dispute. In mid-1966, Nigeria was on the brink of civil war and *Albion* was sent under great secrecy with a Commando Unit to occupy the airport at Port Harcourt to evacuate British civilians. In the end, we were ordered to retire 200 miles out to sea and avoid all contact – there then followed six weeks of incredible boredom.

This was very sensitive at the time, as the Six Day War was taking place in the Middle East and there was media speculation that *Albion* could be involved.

Later, *Albion* was involved in the Aden withdrawal in November 1967 and there was little opportunity to undertake any photographic reconnaissance; not until the following year did my chance come. We were going to Perth, Australia, and the Royal Marines were planning a series of exercise landings on the Western Australia coast and had obtained photographs from the Australian Navy. My analysis of the sites selected for landings was that they were totally unsuitable, as deep ravines inland would have made movement off the landing sites impossible. I then had an anxious wait until my observations proved totally correct and the Royal Marines began to think PI might be useful after all.

However, my learning curve was not over. I was sent for by the Captain, Godfrey Place VC who had been awarded the Victoria Cross for his part in the midget submarine attack on *Tirpitz*. He informed me that the ship's NBC organisation was not up to scratch and I was to deal with the problem before an Admiral's Inspection, scheduled two months away.

My immediate ploy was to request a return to the UK to attend the appropriate course at *Phoenix*. When that fell on stony ground, it was a question of getting the books out and learning what was required. I was greatly helped by the arrival in Hong Kong of two Canadian frigates, which had been designed to be semi-submersible thereby washing their decks clear of any radioactive materials – they were the real NBC experts.

Over the next two months, my team of a petty officer, two leading seamen and ten hands set about creating an organisation following the training manual page by page. The Inspection came and went and much to our delight, and to my Captain's shock, we got a Bravo Zulu – the fact that they found a defective light bulb in one of the cleansing stations still annoys me to this day!

Shortly afterwards, I was summoned to the Offices of Commander-in-Chief, Far East Fleet to be told by the Fleet TAS Officer that, as I was the only NBC expert in the Far East, I was to be seconded to the Admiral's staff for a month to work-up the Royal Fleet Auxiliaries at the Supply depot.

This was the perfect job; I would arrive about 1000 in a staff Land Rover and then examine equipment and offer advice until 1200 before retiring for a long, leisurely and, dare I say, alcoholic lunch.

The prime benefit to the Royal Navy of the Instructor Branch was that it provided a pool of extremely intelligent and motivated young men, who were highly adaptable. It was said that give a Schoolie 24 hours and a set of training manuals and he could become an over-night expert! I often reflected that the training I had received in the Royal Navy equipped me for a whole range of situations in later life.

Out East then Back for Good

Alan York

After joining *Victorious* in 1965 as the ship's Education and Resettlement Officer, followed by two shakedown cruises in North Sea and North Atlantic, we were ready for a 13-month deployment in the Far East. We were based in Singapore, leading a Task Force to support Malaysia in its confrontation with Indonesia and to provide air support for Royal Marines troops ashore in Borneo. After Sukharno gave up his ambitions, we had four visits to Hong Kong, patrolled the South China Sea, extracted our troops as necessary and took part in major exercises with Australian, New Zealand and US Navies in the Pacific, including two visits to the massive US base at Subic Bay in the Philippines.

Following our main exercises with the Allies, we visited first Sydney and then Perth, Australia. After a successful application to organise an expedition to cross Australia by ship's Land Rover in conjunction with an Army Ground Liaison team, we travelled 3,500 miles from Sydney to Perth via the Nullabor Desert where there was no tarmac road or reliable water for 1,000 miles.

I also ran the shore side of a coastal survey, planned by Lieutenant Jock Slater, the Second Navigator and future First Sea Lord, to update Admiralty charts of Direction Island in the Cocos Keeling Group. This resulted in a superb week ashore on a deserted coral island, once used as the Repeater Station for the Cable and Wireless Indian Ocean telegraph cable.

As Education Officer, I produced VICNEWS, the ship's newspaper published every morning that we were at sea during the commission; this was recognised as a great morale booster and a source of considerable talent and humour. Excellent cartooning skills included many by the very successful Tugg Wilson. Our Captain passed a copy to the Captain of the USS *Enterprise,* who admitted he had nothing similar to compare.

HMS *Victorious* – *Illustrious* class aircraft carrier built during the Second World War
by permission of Navy News (MOD)

Finally, after the aviators helped our troops out in the Aden area, *Victorious* and her escorts were the last RN Task Group through Suez Canal before the Seven Days Arab-Israeli War started. The Strike Planning and Operations teams were joined by MOD Intelligence personnel who came on board to collect information on Soviet and other weapons and electronic equipment used by the Egyptians as they advanced east over Suez. *Victorious* was then held over in Malta for the duration of that war and its aftermath in order to convince the Soviets and the world that we were not involved. This delayed our return to the UK after over a year away and hit the headlines at home.

The commission was an unforgettable and unrepeatable experience, but tragically it turned out to be *Victorious'* last – she caught fire whilst in Portsmouth Dockyard and it was decided that she would be scrapped.

Part of a Large Operation

Richard Yeomans

On completion of the Seaman Direction Officers' long course in September 1967, I was appointed to *Eagle*, then in Singapore. After an eventful flight in a trooping aircraft with several aborted take-offs and stops in Istanbul and Bombay, I arrived after 26 hours airborne; *Eagle* was the largest ship in the fleet and at 54,000 tons full load displacement, she looked huge.

After two weeks alongside, we sailed for Aden where we were the flagship of a flotilla of 20 ships, tasked to provide the air cover for the evacuation of the colony.

HMS *Eagle* – the largest aircraft carrier built for the Royal Navy
by permission of Navy News (MOD)

The Aden evacuation was in the UK news, mostly as the result of the exploits of Lieutenant Colonel 'Mad Mitch' Mitchell, as he was affectionately known, who had recently led his Argyll and Sutherland Highlanders to retake the terrorist-dominated Crater district of the city.

It was a period of intense activity with everyone in *Eagle* working at full capacity. Our 899 Squadron Sea Vixens were on constant combat air patrol, 800 Squadron Buccaneers carried out frequent strikes on rebel positions and 820 Squadron Wessex helicopters provided anti-submarine protection and extensive transport around the fleet and ashore. In the latter role, they were fitted with additional machine guns for self-defence. Lastly, 849 Squadron airborne early warning Gannets provided long-range surveillance.

I was fully occupied as the Picture Compilation Officer running the team providing the air picture for our ADA computer system, as first Officer of the Watch and as an aircraft controller. The atmosphere and teamwork on board were excellent and the disciplinary problems, with 2,700 people confined in a relatively small space, were remarkably few. There were not many opportunities to land and none for strictly social purposes. On the rare occasions that we did step ashore, it was sad to see so much equipment being abandoned, but it would have cost more to bring it back to the UK than it was worth. Cars were used until they ran out of fuel and then abandoned; quarters and offices were simply left full of domestic equipment, but this did provide an opportunity for improvements and quite a lot was retrieved, including a fridge for every mess-deck in the ship. Beer was a lot more drinkable thereafter!

In December, with the evacuation almost completed, we were relieved by *Hermes,* which came from Mombasa and we were sent to Singapore for Christmas. This was unexpected and many on board changed their plans to bring their wives out for a few weeks. I sent my wife a cable with three questions: 'Do you want to come to Singapore? Shall I book a flight? Shall I find a hotel?' I received a prompt reply: 'Yes, Yes, Yes.'

When we arrived at Singapore, we had spent an eventful 88 days at sea and had taken part in the historic change-over from the British colony of Aden to the beginning of a new country, the People's Republic of South Yemen, which continues to be in the news.

During the 1970s

I Saw the Sea and Liked It

Bert McDowell

My first day at sea in the early 1970s in *Grenville* was spent on passage from Portsmouth to Tangier in convoy with other ships of the 2nd Frigate Squadron, a motley collection of some of the RN's oldest ships, sadly long since razor blades. Some of these lovely old frigates had seen service in the Second World War; the exhilaration of working on an open bridge more than made up for their lack of modern facilities. At times, one felt just like Jack Hawkins in one of his many roles as a sea Captain, minus the duffle coat of course. Keeping a chart dry and free from smut was always a challenge.

An hour into the passage, the Captain of the Squadron summoned me on board *Undaunted* for a first meeting. Minutes later, I was jackstay transferred from ship to ship over a lumpy swell to spend an hour being briefed on the duties of the squadron Schoolie. At this particular moment, I must confess to being more interested in gaining some experience of watchkeeping on the bridge rather than teaching NAMET. Anyway, by the time we were passing Plymouth, I was back in *Grenville* keeping duty as Second Officer of the Watch, encouraged to develop my seamanship skills by my Captain.

I had joined the Royal Navy at Dartmouth some ten months before this as the oldest trainee there since the war. There may well have been many older students since but, at that time, I was the first and only over 30-year-old in the College. After Dartmouth, I had a nomadic existence, first a few months with the Royal Marines at Lympstone starting a Green Beret course only to get a pier-head jump to an Education Centre, followed by another pier-head jump to sea. Oh, and in between, I found enough time to get married on a 24-hour pass to South Armagh, well known bandit country in Northern Ireland. So within a year of joining, I was enjoying the summer in the Mediterranean with other ships of the squadron, a far cry indeed from my life as a master in a grammar school and, to my mind, much more exciting.

HMS *Grenville* – with Bert McDowell on the bridge wing

Two years later, I was back at sea in *Fearless* and training Midshipmen in the arts of astro-navigation, taking expeditions in tropical climes and spending as much time on the bridge as possible. Whilst at Dartmouth, my Divisional Officer, also an Ulsterman, had very gently suggested to me that I might benefit from elocution lessons, which I equally politely declined. My Ulster accent had not appeared a problem at my interview and, as it turned out, became something of an advantage. Some months into my time in *Fearless,* I was invited by the Captain to look after the Flag Officer when he visited the ship. He explained that this could be a challenging job as the Admiral had a fearsome reputation, but he had every confidence that as the Admiral and his Chief of Staff were Irish I could cope. His final words struck fear, 'If the Admiral demands his porridge at 58 degrees then that's what it will be, not 57 not 59, but 58!'

On the day of his arrival, I was at the tail end of the reception party, neat and tidy and prepared for a rough ride. The Admiral looked as fierce as I had expected, but his cheerful Chief of Staff examined my name tag and in a broad Belfast accent asked where my grandfather had been born. 'Ballymena', I replied. 'My wife's a McDowell and her grandfather was also born in Ballymena so you must be related', he replied. I observed the faintest smile cross the Admiral's stern face, the Captain suddenly seemed to relax and I had just acquired the permanent job of looking after the Admiral on all his future visits.

Here I should confess to a grave mistake. When I next saw my Dartmouth Divisional Officer, he was a Rear Admiral with a cut glass accent who had obviously benefited from elocution lessons. Alas, I will never know how elocution might have changed my prospects in the Royal Navy.

The End of an Era

Patrick Binks

My appointment to the aircraft carrier *Eagle* in 1971 was for the final five months of her last commission, and I joined the ship in Singapore. She had already spent many months in the Far East, in Australia and New Zealand. The Captain of *Eagle*, I G W Robertson was something of a legend; he began as a pilot in the Fleet Air Arm in the Second World War, and had been my Captain at Culdrose when completing the long Met course five years before.

My time in *Eagle* was to gain experience in the Ops Room of a computer-fitted ship prior to my next job as an analyst/programmer at ASWE Portsdown; my time was spent on board in the Ops Room during exercises, with periods in the Met Office improving my forecasting but, in the main, I carried out the usual IO tasks of teaching O levels, NAMET, resettlement and helping with the ship's library. The facilities on board included a really smart and spacious classroom although, being near the bows of the ship, the noise from the steam catapults when launching aircraft and the ship's movement in rough weather made teaching challenging at times.

The team of Instructor Officers on board was headed by Commander David Dacam as the SIO/SMetO; the others were Lieutenant Commander Iain Sidford, Lieutenant Graham Sullivan (Met and Oceanography) and Lieutenant Berny Harrison (Education, Resettlement, editor and production manager of the Eagle Express).

After a week alongside in Singapore, we headed for Hong Kong and immediately encountered two tropical storms; even though the ship displaced over 50,000 tons, huge seas broke over the flight deck and all aircraft were stowed below for safety. During an interesting visit to Hong Kong, I arranged to spend some weeks in *Glamorgan* in order to work with their computer systems at sea, again as part of pre-joining training for my next job. By good fortune, *Glamorgan* was short of accommodation and, when we sailed from Hong Kong, they had to allocate me the Captain's cabin, which was available as he occupied the Admiral's suite.

After a couple of weeks at sea in *Glamorgan*, taking part in exercises, our Task Group arrived off Singapore at the end of October; the Group was gathered to hold a ceremonial steam-past to officially mark the end of 150 years of the UK's Far East Naval Command, and the handing over of Singapore Naval Base to the Island's Government.

Glamorgan was the flagship of Rear Admiral David Williams, Flag Officer, Second-in-Command, Far East Fleet, and for the rehearsal the Commander detailed me, as the spare officer, to replace the Admiral. It was a memorable experience standing on the bridge roof with *Glamorgan* leading a dozen RN and RAN ships and RFAs in a steam-past in line astern, with many aircraft flying overhead in formation.

On the following day, the official party sailed from Singapore in RFA *Stromness* and Rear Admiral John Troup, Commander Far East Fleet, took the salute, before all the ships sailed to an anchorage off Langkawi, an archipelago of beautiful islands off the north-west of Malaysia, where we spent a few days. At the end of my time in *Glamorgan*, my passage back to *Eagle* was by helicopter; we first returned to Singapore to pick up the mail from *Triumph*, the support ship alongside, and then made deliveries to all the assembled ships before being dropped off in *Eagle*.

Commander David Dacam surrounded by his team
Front row Iain Sidford and Graham Sullivan; back row includes Patrick Binks and Berny Harrison

For the next two weeks, we took part in more exercises in the Indian Ocean on our way via Gan to Mombasa. However, there was suddenly a serious international incident when the Iranians invaded a strategically important group of small islands in the Straits of Hormuz at the entrance to the Gulf. *Eagle* was required to remain on patrol in the area near Masirah, Oman outside the Gulf awaiting developments. After two weeks, the ship was allowed to resume its programme, but had unfortunately to miss the port visit to Kenya, and proceed to Durban where we arrived after 60 days at sea.

We probably did not reflect at the time on the long-term significance of events, as we sailed into Durban for Christmas and the New Year. However, our few months in the Far East and Indian Ocean marked the reduction in RN forces in Hong Kong, and the withdrawal of permanent RN forces from Singapore and Bahrain. This was the end of an era for the Royal Navy.

White Funnel Line

Tom Wingate

My appointer said, 'You're going to *Hecla* as Scientific Officer, so get your tropical kit sorted – all they do is wander the South Seas'. The reality was rather different.

The complement in the *Hecla* class ships included an IO as the Scientific Officer whose main purpose was to operate some of the new and fairly complex survey equipment, some of which was associated with the development of the Polaris programme. The domain of the IO was the dry laboratory and his duties included Met and Flight Deck Officer.

My pre-joining training courses began with a few weeks of loan to the Hydrographic Office. This was followed by a course at the Met School at RNAS Culdrose to qualify as the ship's Met Officer for normal operations, helicopter flying and for when the survey boats were operating remote from the ship; later, there was a spell at *Osprey* to qualify as a Flight Deck Officer. All this took several months while I commuted from my normal day job in the development of a Programmed Learning course, which I was doing in *Collingwood*.

I joined *Hecla* in Harwich towards the end of the first commission when all the interesting things like tropical trials and ice trials had been done. The joining interview with the four-stripe Captain let me know that I was the Scientific Officer; there would be no Education Officer role, as there is no time for this, and I would do bridge watchkeeping duties.

HMS *Hecla* – lead ship of four ocean-going survey ships

The IO Scientific Officer was in charge of two sets of major equipment in the ship:

- The magnetometer: this was easy. You streamed it when well out at sea and the actual readings came up on the counter continuously. All the Survey Recorder rating had to do was to note in the log the reading every time the ten minute buzzer went.

- The gravity meter: this was another matter. Although it was large, it was a very delicate heavy lump on gimbals, driven by a gyro system and mounted in the ship's main compass compartment. The meter was looking for small variations in the gravitational field although it did not measure actual values of gravity, only the changes from when you last calibrated it alongside. Measuring gravity changes or actual values on a moving platform, particularly one that moved like *Hecla,* was a complete contradiction as the movement of the ship varied the gravitational field; similarly changes of course also varied the reading.

In congested waters, the equipment could not be used because of limitations on streaming, so I would not see it in operation until we reached the North Atlantic where, for two years, I became very familiar with the Faeroes-Iceland Gap. The standard trip was about three weeks away at sea followed by a weekend alongside, mostly in Londonderry or Stornoway.

Ocean surveying is rather like ploughing a large field; you go for several hours in one direction, then turn and go in the opposite direction a short distance away, in parallel with the original track. You do this for many days, gradually covering your survey chart with a series of parallel or nearly parallel tracks, showing the ship's position every ten minutes.

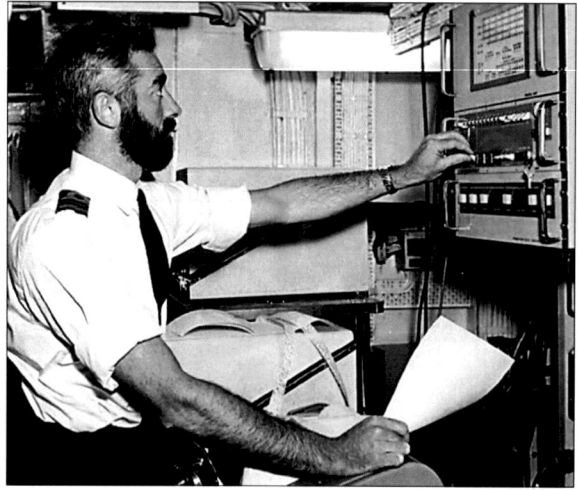

Tom Wingate operating survey equipment

If the weather during a trip was bad and the ship rolled more than 20 degrees each side then the meter fouled the mounting and the shocks with each wave were not good for the expensive piece of kit. This meant that if you could not get the Captain to vary course or speed, the meter had to be locked, thus making a mess of your calculations of start and finish value on a trip and the drift of each measurement during the day.

After a few months, we returned to Devonport as *Hecla* was to be the first recipient of an Automatic Data Logger, a commercial computer system that was made sturdier to go to sea. The aim of this equipment was to record automatically some 16 devices which previously required ratings to sit with pens and logs.

I had to go to the manufacturer for courses in machine programming and system maintenance and to stand by the system being built at Bracknell. It progressed as far as it could there, before needing to be fitted in the ship at Devonport. As the survey programme could not be delayed, we departed with a lot of problems left for me to sort out.

Our LORAN C navigation system was used in ocean surveying when a long way from shore; setting the system up at the start of a survey trip gave us a fixed start point, from which we could hopefully know our position. Nevertheless frequently, sometimes four or five times a night, the call went out 'LORAN has lost lock'. This meant that we did not have a true reading, so I had to sprint to the bridge to set up the system in the dry lab again before we lost track.

We had an Admiral's inspection and this included a visit by an Instructor Captain. I sat with him in the Captain's cabin and he stated the need for IOs to do lots of educational work in the ship, and my Captain giving him a much stronger statement describing my actual duties. Not for the last time, I was piggy in the middle. We also went for our sea trials to Flag Officer Sea Training at Portland where the staff didn't know what to do with us and we departed after four days to return to what counts as normality on a survey ship, deep sea surveying. On that trip, we had a foreign visit to Stavanger, which was a welcome change and still allowed us to do surveys on passage.

In the North Atlantic on our traverses, we normally saw Rockall with waves breaking clear over the top of the rock. This small rock, protruding from the sea about 160 miles west of Scotland is disputed by the UK, Ireland, Iceland and Denmark. On one occasion, the very rare sea state allowed us to land, raise the flag and leave a plaque. I was part of the landing party which involved jumping from the ship's Gemini dinghy as it passed the cliffs on the crest of the wave and hanging on before climbing the rock. Six of us landed and made the climb. We landed from the sea and made a double page spread in a national newspaper, the Daily Mail.

The area that we covered over the two years was nearly always between Rockall, Iceland and Greenland, although there was little excitement of going 'foreign' in the way that the Appointer has suggested. At least as a designated Land Rover driver, I was able to do some training in Northern Ireland, and I managed to drive in Southern Ireland in uniform.

Rockall – the 20-metre high rock, 160 miles west of Scotland

We had one very rare moment of general duty work when we were assigned to shadow a Russian flotilla transiting the Atlantic in a westerly direction. As we could only manage 13 knots 'downhill with the wind behind us' and all three engines operating at their maximum, we had some difficulty in the chase. We fell rapidly behind and, after a day or two, had to give up.

All in all this was an extremely challenging and technically interesting appointment, but a fair to middling non-event in adventure.

Not Just Met

John Hartley

I joined *Antrim,* a guided missile destroyer, in my first sea appointment as a Lieutenant Commander in early 1973. Fresh from Met course and with little forecasting experience, a six-month Far East deployment was a challenging and exhilarating undertaking. However, the port visits were exceptional: Mombasa, Port Sudan, Massawa (for Haile Selassie's last birthday), Jeddah, Gan, Singapore, Thailand, South Korea, Japan and Hong Kong; then home via Mauritius, Beira patrol and the Cape.

The weather in the South China Sea was appalling, with three typhoons in July and two of these, close together, meant our having to sail from Hong Kong. As a department of one officer and one leading hand, such incidents made for hard work and long hours on the bridge, as we had no ships in company. The sight of ocean-going Japanese tugs poised as the *Glomar Challenger* drilling rig dragged her anchors in the Taiwan Strait will stay with me forever.

In a ship the size of a guided missile destroyer, many extraneous lurks come your way: Confidential Books Officer, Flight Deck Officer, prisoner interrogation team leader, and oh, of course, education and resettlement. Balmy nights on the flight deck in the Indian Ocean at flying stations contrast with recovering the helicopter at anchor in Mauritius with the aircraft facing aft, with me in the flight deck netting and the tail rotor inches from the hanger bulkhead; hours spent page-by-page mustering books of dubious value were followed by dashes ashore with bags of classified paper to burn conscientiously in the nearest large incinerator; time spent with the Master-at-Arms practising interrogation techniques and trying to get information from captured enemies in exercises, alternated with watches in the Ops Room writing the diary. All these combined to make a varied and edifying experience.

HMS *Antrim* passing Haile Selassi's Flagship, *Ethiopia* at Navy Day at Massawa 1973
by permission of Navy News (MOD)

My next sea appointment, also as a Lieutenant Commander, was to *Ark Royal* in early 1977 for her last commission. This was a much more challenging deployment for a METOC, with five types of aircraft embarked and many aspects of meteorology and oceanography to explore and exploit. Again, there were extraneous tasks to carry out and the post of Confidential Books Officer went with the appointment. I had thought that managing confidential books in a guided missile destroyer was hard. Looking after a carrier's books, and often the ships-in-company as well, followed by the return of them all to the depots and issuing authorities when *Ark Royal* paid off was a step increase in intensity, not least because the Captain was anxious to get the ship's clearance certificate before moving on. I was very lucky to inherit a comprehensive and detailed system set up by my predecessors, and no pension traps crept from the woodwork.

On the meteorological front, another brush with a tropical disturbance, the tail end of Hurricane Flossy in the Norwegian Sea, Mistral winds off Toulon and strong Etesian winds off Piraeus, made forecasting for carrier operations in this busy deployment a challenge for us all.

Another job, as a Commander stands out. I was appointed to Portugal to IBERLANT, a small NATO command based near Lisbon, with a British contingent of about 18 officers and a few more other ranks, and manned by a representative selection of the older NATO nations. As Staff METOC to Commander-in-Chief, IBERLANT, my peripheral involvements dominated and included local school liaison as a governor, supervision of the Ibershop where British families could buy their much needed sausages, legs of lamb, brown sauce and firelighters, and the duty free drink store, convincing host nation personnel that a limit of five bottles of whisky did not mean five one-gallon flagons.

Unusual Piece of Kit

Derek Thomas

'I am sorry, sir, the underwriter is not prepared to insure it in such circumstances.'

So ran the conversation that I thought would put paid to taking my harp on board my first sea appointment to the County class guided missile destroyer *Devonshire* after the Met course in 1974; up to that time the harp had gone into every Wardroom with me starting at Dartmouth, where it was described as 'one of the more unusual pieces of officer's kit'. After mess dinners, its capacity to still the most boisterous heart was remarkable.

As a METOC trainee whose first six weeks at Culdrose were spent growing an extra layer of skin, I had become impervious to many ribald comments.

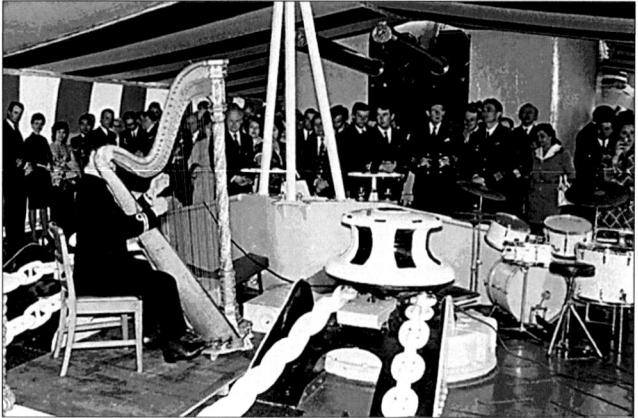

Derek Thomas performing on the fo'c'sle of HMS *Devonshire*

I was more or less resigned to being harp-less during my time in *Devonshire*. However, a tiny part of my job was as the Band Officer and, when I went to see the Royal Marines bandmaster to get acquainted with the ship's volunteer band, he mentioned that the RM School of Music at Eastney had amongst its instruments, one concert harp gathering dust in their store. Hot-footing it to Eastney, I managed to negotiate for use on board the loan of the harp, which they agreed also to re-string. The ship's Land Rover soon brought the harp to South Railway Jetty and an ingenious stowage was found in number six trap of the Officers' heads.

What music in general did I play? Sailors being sailors requested music that ran through a rather catholic repertoire, from *Greensleeves*, through *Penny Lane* and *A Nightingale Sang in Berkley Square* to Welsh Airs.

Memorable amongst the musical interludes with the harp was taking part in the ship's concert held on the flight deck whilst we steamed slowly over the glassy surface of the Aegean. All manner of talent sprang forth from every deck: stand-up comedy, humorous sketches and instrument solos from members of the volunteer band appeared as the ship's company was entertained in splendid fashion.

As part of the cruise around the Mediterranean, we called at Odessa, where *Devonshire* was the first RN warship to visit for a generation. A reception was held under awnings rigged on the fo'c'sle and harp music wafted through the somewhat bemused audience of Russian Officers and their wives, standing in the shadow of the 4.5-inch guns.

Finally, at the end of my appointment, the harp was returned, undamaged, to Eastney and I am deeply indebted to the Royal Marines for their generous loan.

In the Squadron

Mike Pengelly

In June 1974, I completed what was then called the Instructor Officers Long Course; this was mainly for those IOs who had not taken up the METOC option. The course consisted of a mixture of training such as two weeks at RNSETT, two weeks at the Fire Fighting School *Phoenix* and nearly five months on a navigation course at *Dryad*.

On completion, I was appointed to the 4th Frigate Squadron and to *Sirius*, where I spent 12 months before she commenced long refit. I enjoyed my time in *Sirius,* where they had an excellent Captain and the other officers accepted me as one of their own. I qualified as a Second Officer of the Watch and soon became an operationally qualified Flight Deck Officer; all this was on top of my duties as Education and Resettlement Officer, of course.

As *Sirius* was going into long refit, I had to jump ship, so to speak, and so in September 1975, I joined *Mohawk,* a Tribal class frigate based in Plymouth. I joined the ship in Liverpool and I soon discovered that life was a little different in *Mohawk*; when I asked the Navigator if I could keep a watch on the bridge, he stated in no uncertain terms that he would not allow a Schoolie on his bridge.

Luck then took a hand as *Mohawk* commenced a six-month refit, and many of the officers changed. I also took the opportunity to visit the other ships in the squadron, especially if they were visiting places with good runs ashore.

My Captain asked if I would take on the responsibility of Refit Liaison Officer. I was uniquely qualified for this position, as I had been a Devonport Apprentice, worked in the drawing office there and my brother was an Inspector of Joiners, all of which was very useful. Near the end of the refit, the new First Lieutenant asked if I would take on the duties of the NBCD Training Officer; he said that, as he was Fleet Air Arm, he knew little if anything about NBCD.

HMS *Mohawk* – one of seven Tribal class frigates, under floodlight
by permission of Navy News (MOD)

On completion of refit, we were sent for work up at Portland and this was a very interesting period. We passed that and, after a brief but interesting visit to Amsterdam, joined the NATO Standing Naval Force in the Mediterranean. We stayed there for six months and this became the pattern for the year, changing between Plymouth and the Mediterranean.

Upon reflection, I thoroughly enjoyed my time in *Mohawk*, made many friends that I still see today, and I am sure the experiences made me a better Instructor Officer.

Unseen Up North

Guy Warner

I had already served at sea as a seaman officer in two diesel submarines and then had been in the first 'S' class SSN for over 18 months, when we started on special operations. I had been on operational patrol in *Swiftsure* before – in the Mediterranean – but this time it was different. We were to gather intelligence on the Soviet Fleet at close quarters in their own backyard. Any mistakes could mean spending the rest of our lives in Siberia, as the Captain was fond of saying.

First there was a special work-up which was overseen by Captain Sandy Woodward and Commander Mike Boyce – both severe taskmasters. During this phase, the Executive Officer and Navigating Officer were both replaced as being not up to the job. I survived – mainly I suspect because I was the officer who 'understood' DCA, our new computer driven Action Information system, and the Captain had boldly done away with all the manual tools.

We duly sailed from Faslane for the Barents Sea with special intercept equipment on board and Russian speakers to operate it. Also we had an extra Command Qualified officer whose job it was to take charge of one watch with the Executive Officer taking charge of the other, leaving the Captain free. We kept six-hour watches – six hours on, six hours off – with both watches able to conduct all evolutions, so we were permanently at Action Stations. This was necessary as, once in the patrol area, we were always in contact with Soviet forces. The downside of this was that when you came off your six-hour watch you had to reconstruct what had happened during the watch by drawing up and analysing manual plots on the Wardroom table. This sometimes took the full six hours before you were due back on again! Years later, this motivated me into including post event analysis in the replacement computer system even though it wasn't in the specification.

Our mission was to gather as much information as possible on new Soviet ships, submarines and weapon systems but, above all, remain undetected. While trailing Soviet submarines, we used to keep in their stern arcs to avoid detection, but every so often they would reverse course and come at full speed down their previous track to ensure there was nobody behind them; this manoeuvre was known as 'Crazy Ivan'. You had to sidestep smartly to avoid counter-detection or collision. However, this was not as hairy as 'underwater looks' when you sailed under a hostile ship with your partly-raised periscope a few feet from her hull, taking photographs. We also did this on their submarines! The trim had to be perfect with neutral buoyancy and I happened to be the Trimming Officer. It reminded me of the Byron quotation, 'My hair is grey though not with years'.

HMS *Swiftsure* – the lead in a class of seven nuclear powered attack submarines
by permission of Navy News (MOD)

This task was particularly appropriate when we had a rare reactor system leak in the primary coolant. This had to be repaired and immediately meant a reactor compartment entry – not an evolution to be conducted at sea and certainly not in hostile waters, as the reactor had to be shut down resulting in zero propulsion except for a minute electric motor rightly called the 'eggbeater'. The Captain asked the MEO, who was to do the entry alone with all the protective kit on, how long he would need. 'Fifteen minutes,' he replied. So that was the period in which we had to keep a 'stop trim', that is one not assisted by forward motion. I just about kept the trim in equilibrium for 15 minutes and then we started to oscillate. As we started to come up, I would flood water in and then pump it out as we started to sink – *in extremis*, a choice between inadvertently surfacing surrounded by Soviet warships or exceeding our crushing depth. After 30 minutes, things were looking grim with the Captain breathing fire at me, but the repair was just completed in time. The MEO subsequently got the MBE!

I had my share of operational pressure also as Communications Officer. After observing especially important missile firing tests or other significant events, a signal had to be sent back to HQ with details so that other assets could be tasked immediately. During this particular operational patrol, we sent over 40 Flash signals, each of which necessitated special encryption action by the Communications Officer alone and as speedily as humanly possible without any mistakes. Also, if our communications mast played up or communications could not be established, guess who got it in the neck.

Moreover, when we got back to Faslane, the Captain said, 'Warner, you haven't done much this trip. You can take charge of preparing all the material of Top Secret and above for my presentation in the Ministry of Defence to First Sea Lord and others next week and it had better be good'. He was awarded the OBE following this patrol, so I suppose the presentation was all right.

I ended up serving nearly three years in the submarine *Swiftsure*, under three different captains, much of it on operations, during which we never failed to sail on time. I certainly 'Saw the Sea' even though most of it was from below the surface. I wouldn't have missed any of it!

A Lucky Squadron

David Bittles

Following various courses including the Lieutenants' Greenwich course and the Frigate Met course, I joined *Salisbury* as the 1st Frigate Squadron Instructor Officer. She did not have a flight deck and was to operate primarily in UK waters, so from a Met point of view the regular forecast from CINCFLEET sufficed. The Captain agreed that I would contribute to the ship by working towards a Bridge Watchkeeping Certificate, standing watches on the bridge as a Second Officer of the Watch (OOW) in addition to my IO duties.

About a year later, I was told by my Captain F to join *Alacrity* at short notice and that she would be away for several months. He said the ship was short of a bridge watchkeeper and it was an ideal opportunity to progress towards my Bridge Watchkeeping and Ocean Navigation certificates. Although my main job was as a watchkeeping officer, I maintained the usual responsibilities of an IO and additionally, the role of Entertainment Officer and Censor Officer. Censoring mail required having to hand copies of the Bible and the Oxford Dictionary of Quotations, because it is amazing how inventive sailors can be in trying to 'beat the system' in their messages home.

Following a short break, I re-joined *Salisbury* for a Joint Maritime Cooperation Exercise, but luck was with me as the Captain sent for me and asked, 'Do you believe you can drive the Gibraltar guard boat which needs an officer for a 24-on 24-off watchkeeping system?'

What a choice! Two weeks in the North Atlantic or two weeks in Gibraltar! *Salisbury* was the next guard ship and the condition on my being released was that I had to organise a cocktail party to welcome *Salisbury* when she arrived.

With a crew of off-watch Polaris submariners, it was a very interesting couple of weeks in the guard boat and it was almost disappointing when *Salisbury* arrived in Gibraltar and I had to hand over my command. Re-joining *Salisbury*, I completed the passage planning and navigating part of the Ocean Navigation Certificate.

On returning from the Mediterranean, my next change was being told that, as she had lost some quarter of the ship's company because of salmonella poisoning, I was to join the squadron leader, *Galatea* the next day and go through Basic Operational Sea Training as a bridge watchkeeping officer. I joined and found that in addition to normal watchkeeping, I was to be also the Special Sea Dutyman OOW.

HMS *Salisbury* – one of four air-direction frigates named after cathedral cities
by permission of NMRN

The next two months were probably the most hectic and tiring of my life, where I spent most of the day on the bridge, either as the OOW, or as Second OOW, helping out during busy exercise periods. At this stage, I was still not a fully qualified OOW, but I was learning quickly! Despite all the trials and tribulations, Basic Operational Sea Training was successfully completed and the Captain awarded me my Bridge Watchkeeping Certificate with the threat that if I bent any of his ships, he would haunt me for the rest of my life.

Thus, as a qualified bridge watchkeeper, I returned to *Salisbury* as part of the steaming and training crew to take the ship to Egypt after she had been sold to their Navy. We embarked some 200 Egyptian officers and ratings, all their kit and what seemed like half of Curry's electrical shop and set sail for Gibraltar to paint ship. It was disappointing when, after a spell in Gibraltar painting ship and preparing her for the final passage to Alexandria, the decision was taken to cancel the sale. After returning to Plymouth to disembark the Egyptians and all their kit, *Salisbury* was directed to Chatham Dockyard to end her active career, giving me the opportunity to take a ship through the Dover Straits as the OOW and this was exciting to say the least!

From the graveyard of Chatham, I next found myself on an RAF flight to Malta to re-join *Alacrity* in an OOW role. I did not know at the time that it would be nearly two months before I spent any time on her bridge, as she had limped into Malta with a seriously damaged gearbox. When it was finally repaired and tested, *Alacrity* joined *Galatea* for passage to Malaga; this was the first RN ship visit to a Spanish port for many years, because of the dispute over Gibraltar. It was a good visit with many Spanish dignitaries coming on board. I particularly enjoyed the visit, as it was my last in the squadron because, on our return to Plymouth, I left the ship and the squadron before taking up my next appointment.

Those two years passed very quickly and turned out to be not at all as I expected when I was preparing for what I thought would be a conventional sea job for an IO. I was extremely lucky to have been appointed to a squadron where all the Commanding Officers were very positive in providing the opportunity and encouragement for me to work towards doing something slightly different for an IO at that time.

In His Footsteps

Clive Holtham

In 1845, on his last expedition trying to find the North West Passage, Captain John Franklin, RN sailed in *Erebus* and *Terror* from Disko Island on the west coast of Greenland. His route took him through Baffin Bay into Lancaster Sound and to Beechey Island off the southwest coast of Devon Island, where he camped through the winter. In 1846, he left and sailed down to a spot just north of King William Island where he became trapped in ice for 18 months. He eventually abandoned the ships in April 1848 and was not seen again.

In 1975, when working as an Assistant Divisional Officer at Britannia Royal Naval College, Dartmouth, through a contact in the Canadian Navy, I was invited to take a party of ten Midshipmen to join a group of Canadian militia trekking in the same islands to the north of mainland Canada that Captain John Franklin visited; this was an annual exercise for the Canadians designed to prove their sovereignty of these islands.

After a short and interesting stop in 'the wooden-house' sprawl of Churchill on Hudson Bay, we flew on in an RAF Hercules to Resolute on the south coast of Cornwallis Island at approximately 75° N, 95° W. Here we camped in Tent City where, over the following four days, we were taught how to survive in the

Arctic. Summer in the Arctic means 24 hours of daylight, but even so, the temperature varied from cold to very cold and even icy-cold on higher ground. The terrain changed from stony rocky scree on the higher ground to wet clingy mud and large tufted grasses in the low-lying areas. Occasionally, we encountered snow flurries or freezing fog, which added to our navigational problems.

We lived on dehydrated meals, chocolate bars and occasional fresh-cooked arctic hare, provided by our two Inuit hunter-guides. We made two-man tents using four ponchos, with everything tied together using two rifles as tent poles. With the magnetic north well to the southwest, we navigated using an astro compass and simple line-of-sight dead reckoning when in freezing fog. We saw many arctic hare and arctic foxes and quickly learned to give a wide berth to the several small herds of musk oxen, which grouped in rather threatening defensive semi-circles on seeing us.

At the end of the four days of training, we each shouldered our 50 lb rucksacks containing provisions, two ponchos and a rifle, and trekked to Assistance Bay, which was steeped in RN history. We camped a short distance from the sea at Barrow Strait, between Nelson and Hardy Lakes in the Trafalgar complex. On the foreshore, we found large piles of opened bully beef tins, metal casks, ships nails and many pieces of assorted timbers. Between the lakes, we saw four unidentified cairns. Although this site was not recorded as having been used by Franklin, it was undoubtedly a base used in 1850 by some of the 15 vessels searching for signs of Franklin's expedition.

After the one-week survival course and despite two members of the team hobbling badly with tendonitis, we flew further north to a small Met station at Eureka on Ellesmere Island at 80°N, 86° W. Here we applied our new skills in survival for the next ten days, trekking widely around Eureka.

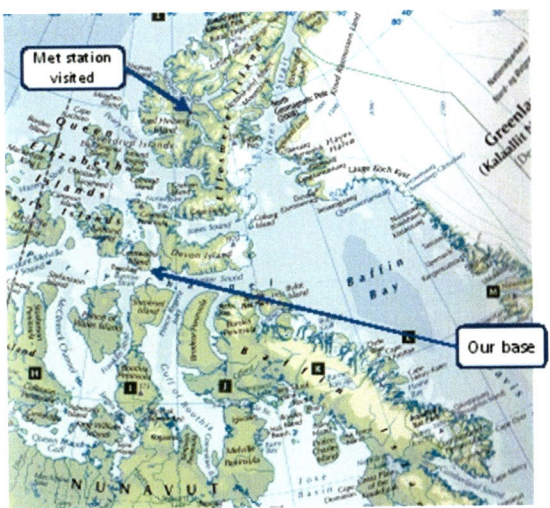

Area of Canada visited by the BRNC party

This time in Northern Canada was an exciting, once-in-a-lifetime experience and a great privilege to trek in such a remote area. The scenery was bleak but spectacular with large glittering ice flows littering the seas. Yet as time progressed and the weather deteriorated into freezing rain and fog, it became more monotonous and rather dreary. The need for warmth, cleanliness and dry clothing became both increasingly important and problematic. Breaking ice in the gullies to get to water to clean one's teeth, and coping with the most basic sanitary facilities became more and more troublesome. We were delighted and relieved when we finally flew back and could enjoy warm showers, a change of clothing and an excellent three-course meal at the only hotel in Resolute, which was a very large, simple wooden shack.

Later, it was particularly gratifying to receive a warm 'thank you' letter from the Canadian expedition leader for a job well done in helping maintain the sovereignty of the Canadian north and keeping the Russians at bay – or was the threat really from the Americans?

Another Cod War

Des Malone

Just after Christmas 1975, at the start of three months Foreign Service leave following an appointment to the Royal Observatory Hong Kong, my leave suddenly disappeared when I was told on three consecutive days, to join three different ships in three different bases. The end result was that I joined *Mermaid* in Rosyth.

She was a ship that had originally been built for President Nkrumah of Ghana, but had been commissioned into the Royal Navy after he was deposed. Smaller than a frigate and totally unsuitable for operating in the North Atlantic, *Mermaid* had Captain Ted Anson in command, who was to become Commander Task Group of the RN ships in the 1975-1976 Cod War on his arrival off Iceland.

My arrival was not a particularly happy event, as the First Lieutenant was clearly under a lot of pressure and there were no cabins available. I would have to make do with the presidential suite, which turned out to be a rather large, totally bare compartment with absolutely no fixtures, except for one camp bed placed in one corner. I settled in by securing one end of the camp bed by line to the nearest door handle and the other end to a bracket halfway down the compartment. My suitcase was then strapped to one leg of my camp bed. As was to be expected, every time the ship rolled, I was tossed out of my camp bed into what was a totally unheated compartment. The Fishing Fleet Liaison Officer, a huge, friendly ex-Grimsby trawler skipper with lots of fishy stories, was also allocated a similar unsuitable compartment and we both agreed we would sleep in the Wardroom at night; this was much to the annoyance of the First Lieutenant.

Arriving off Iceland, I found that weather forecasts were provided twice a day at 0600Z and 1800Z to the trawlers by the UK Met Office forecasters, on board a Ministry of Fishing vessel. There was also an RFA present with a full RN Met team on board. I sent them both a signal to say that I would be issuing weather forecasts to the RN ships and trawlers at 1000Z and 2200Z based on the 0600Z and 1800Z data. Neither replied to my signal, which I found rather surprising! I plotted my own charts with very limited local area data and then, based upon these charts and the fax charts from Northwood and the Met Office, I produced my twice-daily forecasts. At no time did the RN team on the RFA send me a copy of their forecasts, or attempt to discuss the weather with me – again a big surprise, as I had attempted to talk to them on several occasions.

HMS *Mermaid* – a frigate built for Ghana and taken into service in the Royal Navy
by permission of Navy News (MOD)

The Icelandic gunboats including *Tyr*, *Aegir* and *Thor* soon appeared and each in turn, over several days, tested *Mermaid's* manoeuvrability. She surprised most of us by her ability to out-turn the Icelanders and to 'stop on a penny' when they cut across her bows. But after several days of intense manoeuvring, one of the gunboats rammed *Mermaid* and caused major damage just ahead of her main bulkhead. Water was pouring in at a serious rate and all pumps had to be put into action just to stay afloat.

The Icelandic gunboats would generally approach from the port quarter, with their Captain leaning out of the bridge window and giving hand signals to his helmsman on the bridge. We, however, had to relay our bridge orders to our helmsman several decks below by phone hence they had the advantage of a speedier response. Why we were never allowed to use high-pressure water hoses to wash away their Captains I will never know, nor why we were not allowed to trail steel cables from our stern to stop them approaching so close – but those were the rules imposed upon us by the MOD.

About a week after our major ramming, and with several other more minor collisions, we still had to pump huge amounts of water from the forward compartments in order to stay afloat. One evening, the Met Office forecaster issued his weather forecast for the next 24 hours with SW Force 4 - 6 winds.

I thought this was a very conservative estimate of the likely wind, as a depression was approaching from the SW and was liable to deepen rapidly. However, I decided to await the next 24-hour Met Office prognosis chart, which confirmed my worst fears. Before issuing my 2200Z forecast to the RN ships, I briefed Captain Anson that Force 10 winds were highly likely within six hours, with gusts to Force 11. I was very impressed, and a little surprised, that Captain Anson never questioned my forecast and within minutes of my briefing issued the order that all RN ships and trawlers were to disperse immediately, then heave-to. Needless to say, there were many comments from the trawler fleet, as to why my forecast was so very different to that issued a few hours earlier by the Met Office team, embarked in a Ministry of Agriculture and Fisheries Support Vessel. Captain Anson made the very brief comment that it was based on the very latest information received – diplomatic but true! I still do not understand why the Met Office team did not delay the issue of their forecasts by a few hours in order to make use of the latest UK Met Office prognosis charts.

HMS *Bacchante* with gunboat *Aegir* and British trawler in close quarters
by permission of NMRN

The winds steadily increased, reached Force 10 within five hours and did not moderate for some 22 hours afterwards. In the meantime, the water inflow dramatically increased, and this was a great concern – so much so, that we were told that the problem was not to be openly discussed. Needless to say, I did not sleep very well, constantly monitoring the wind strength and the prognosis charts. The waves were huge and awe-inspiring with the tops ripped off by the force of the wind. The ship took a great pounding when ploughing down into a trough, with screws making a considerable noise as they neared the surface. Very few on board were sick, but mostly suffered from headaches due to the constant thumping of hull against sea. Fortunately, the wind dropped, as predicted, and no ships or trawlers were lost, but several vessels reported major damage.

Within a week, I transferred with the Task Group team to *Juno* where the accommodation was a little more spacious. The remainder of my time was extremely interesting, but fortunately, there was no more bad weather and only a few minor collisions. However, there was one occasion when an Icelandic gunboat suddenly decided to cut across our bows. The OOW was perhaps a little late in ordering full astern and the result was that our bows took off a good slice of the gunboat's starboard side and funnel. This slice was duly cut up into many pieces and presented to all the officers and senior rates on board; my bit is still in my garage.

The ship handling displayed by the Captains of all the RN ships was just superb and I felt very privileged to have served with them in this Cod War.

Reporting back to MOD a few days later was an eye opener and a bit of a let-down, as nobody asked how I had got on, nor what they could do to assist the RN Met man on the Task Group team. Needless to say, I attempted to tell them, but I am not sure they listened!

A Focus on Technology

John Franklin

An unusual appointment in the Royal Navy occurred in 1970 when I was sent to the United States to the Massachusetts Institute of Technology (MIT) in Cambridge, Massachusetts; this is a relatively old university having been founded in 1861. My appointment to MIT came about when I was at Manadon as Head of the Thermodynamics Section.

To keep up with developments in the subject, and to be at least one step ahead of the students, I had attended as many engineering conferences as I could get away with. At these, I got to know a number of American professors and one in particular, Professor Joe Keenan from MIT, who wrote to me suggesting I might like to spend a year with him at the Institute. I duly passed this letter to higher authority and to my surprise and delight, was given leave to take up the offer.

In preparation, I spent time at both the University of Reading and University College London as a Research Associate. It was whilst I was at the latter that I responded to an advertisement by an American professor, who was due to spend a year at University College London at the same time I was to be at MIT. In exchange for seeking out suitable accommodation for him in London, he agreed for me to rent his house near Boston and take over his car whilst he took over mine.

I flew over to the United States ahead of my family and arranged to meet the professor at his house. We duly met as he and his family were heading for the airport. I asked about an inventory and was told that as I was an RN officer, this was unnecessary. He handed over the keys and with that I took over the house – complete with a magnificent library, record collection and all mod cons; coming from the UK at that time this was a cornucopia of luxuries.

I was admitted to MIT as 'Guest of the Institute', which allowed me to use all the resources available, both academic and social. I was given the honorary title of Assistant Professor and helped to mark students' test papers and to assist in tutorials. I engaged in research and in association with others, published two papers whilst I was there. My favourite task was acting as guinea pig for distinguished academics who were drafting their books. I bombarded them with questions and was encouraged to challenge them on the principles on which their thesis rested. I managed to get away with being ignorant, pompous and pedantic without too much rancour and made many friends of long-standing! It was a most wonderful year, and in the summer vacation with my family I spent five weeks criss-crossing America and Canada. As senior UK service officer in Massachusetts, I was given the onerous task of researching and advising on the elements that made up the overseas cost-of-living allowance!

Another different appointment was in Intelligence. After leaving Manadon in 1979, I was appointed to the Defence Intelligence Staff for nine months of experience with Technical Intelligence (Navy). This provided a wonderful insight into how intelligence was gathered and analysed and drew me into many areas that I had only heard of from afar. At that time, the various Intelligence organisations such as MI5, MI6 and GCHQ were not only hidden away, but indeed, were not even officially recognised to exist. My visits to these organisations had to be kept under wraps – even from my wife!

After a year at Royal College of Defence Studies as a student, I was appointed Captain Technical Intelligence (Navy), and was based in London, near Whitehall. Here I found myself responsible for advising all and sundry on the technical abilities of foreign navies. I was fortunate in having an experienced staff with much specialist knowledge and expertise, which made my task much less demanding that it might have been. This was particularly important during my second year of office when the Argentine forces invaded the Falkland Islands and the pace of our activities increased dramatically. Daily signals went out to the fleet giving the latest intelligence on the capability of the Argentine Navy and Air Force, which gave us the feeling that we were really part of the action – albeit from afar.

Whilst the job provided much of great interest and satisfaction, there were many drawbacks. It was essential that I had accommodation in town as I had to be on call 24 hours a day – particularly during the Falklands War. With the 'need to know' paramount, I had to quickly decide whether the subject under discussion was public knowledge, or classified in my social and professional conversations at that time. If one ended up saying nothing that did not enhance one's social attributes.

This was my final job in the Service and although tinged with inevitable sadness, there was relief that normal conversation could be resumed!

Two Invasions

Bob Young

Apart from brief attachments to the Submarine Service and the occasional Fleet Air Arm squadron, I was perhaps fortunate to experience two real operations. The first was when I was serving in the guided missile destroyer *Devonshire* and was associated with the 1974 Turkish invasion of Cyprus, and the second was whilst I was in the carrier *Invincible* in the 1982 Falklands War.

The Cyprus conflict involved the assembled RN ships carrying out a major airlift of British residents and tourists off the island. As one of the IO's duties in a guided missile destroyer was that of Flight

Deck Officer, I recall spending seemingly endless around-the-clock hours guiding vast numbers of helicopter landings and launches as wave upon wave of evacuees were airlifted to safety. Certainly, when the operation was over, to go back to the IO's routine tasks of NAMET teaching, weather forecasting, entertainments and Confidential Books Officer was somewhat of an anti-climax and gave one the yen to get back to more exciting times!

Be careful what you wish for, as in my case the exciting times re-started with a vengeance eight years later. As SMetO/SIO in *Invincible*, I was on Easter leave when I received, along with many others, a telephone call at 0400 instructing me to return immediately to the ship which was under short notice to sail to the South Atlantic. I remember at the time thinking that this was like something out of a movie!

Bob Young and his team on winter exercise off Norway

Although the IO complement in an *Invincible* class carrier listed two METOC Officers for the ship, one METOC Officer for the embarked helicopter squadron, plus two Education Officers, everyone was tasked with a myriad of secondary duties from bridge watchkeeping, entertainments officer and public relations.

As *Invincible* sailed from Portsmouth, one of the hot topics of discussion was what would happen if either *Invincible* or *Hermes* was disabled or destroyed. Indeed Admiral Woodward was reported as saying, 'Lose *Invincible* and the operation will be severely jeopardized; lose *Hermes* and the operation is over'. Thoughts such as these certainly began to focus the METOC team on the importance of the forecasting tasks ahead, particularly after having researched the expected South Atlantic winter weather conditions. As it happened, the team of forecasters and meteorological ratings performed tremendously under some extreme conditions, often with very little information available.

As events evolved and the ship went into an Action Stations status, it was discovered that I had been a naval architect before joining the Royal Navy and as such had the wherewithal to help correct any trim or stability problems resulting from enemy damage. Hence my action station became HQ2 (Damage Control Headquarters) which was a back-up station to the main HQ1, and the METOC forecasting team was immediately reduced in numbers. Thankfully, such damage control services were never needed, despite the Argentine claim that they had crippled the ship, but the long hours spent in a small space deep in the bowels of the ship with six other members of the ship's company provided an experience far from the normal routine for an IO.

HMS *Invincible* – lead of three light carriers
by permission of Navy News (MOD)

For a large number of the ship's company, Action Stations meant long hours of inactivity punctuated with the odd incident. For the most part, in HQ2 we fell into that category. Memories include the sinking of the Argentine light cruiser *General Belgrano* on 2 May and the muted sadness that prevailed among the HQ2 team who felt empathy for the enemy sailors who died doing their duty. These emotions progressively changed over the period of the next three weeks when news of the sinkings of *Sheffield, Coventry, Ardent* and *Antelope* reached our ears; certainly the sinking of the *Atlantic Conveyor* on 25 May was a little too close for comfort.

Enjoyable distractions during Action Stations included the action messing meal breaks. Even though getting to the mess meant negotiating a multitude of Zulu Alpha hatches and doors, these excursions provided welcome breaks from the confined surrounds of HQ2. Added to this, there were a few occasions when an hour or so after sunset, the Wardroom bar would open for a short period for two beers max, and I can report that even in a Wardroom stripped to its bare essentials, a pint of Courage Special Bitter never tasted so good!

Meanwhile, back at flight deck level, the METOC team, often devoid of the usual plethora of information, was quickly learning the art of single observer forecasting and how to draw and extrapolate weather charts with only half a dozen observations on which to base their analyses. On reflection, during the 45 days of war, the ship spent 15% of the time in fog, which was often very welcome, and over 30% of the time in Sea State 5, that is wave heights of two metres or higher. So heavy were the South Atlantic seas that on one occasion an 'on alert' Harrier jet was lost when it slipped off the flight deck into the ocean; fortunately, the quick thinking pilot ejected safely.

Returning to the mundane theme of secondary duties, another of mine was that of ship's Public Relations Officer. Just prior to sailing to the South Atlantic, I was delighted that an intense period of press interest associated with the 1981 Defence Review's intended sale of *Invincible* to Australia was over and the sale had just been rescinded. However, on the morning of 5 April 1982 when *Invincible* left Portsmouth for the South Atlantic, press interest was to escalate way beyond our expectations when five major newspaper journalists embarked for the duration of the conflict.

I very soon realised that being the Public Relations Officer was not going to be a 'walk in the park', particularly as we had on board Prince Andrew who was serving as a Sea King helicopter pilot with 820 Squadron. Throughout their time with us, the journalists had to produce continuous copy to feed the demands of their editors for 24/7 news.

Bob Young keeping his distance from the press pack encircling Prince Andrew

What had hitherto been a secondary duty assumed much greater proportions and was to do so during the Falkland operations and through until 17 September when Her Majesty, the Queen, and a host of journalists boarded *Invincible* off the Solent on our return to Portsmouth.

We had been at sea continuously for carrier operations for 166 days and during that time had steamed 51,660 miles in support of the recapture of the Falkland Islands.

Around the World

Terry Le Manquais

Early in my career, I was fortunate to get an appointment as a squadron Schoolie, where I was responsible for education and resettlement in a squadron of frigates as well as additional duties such as Met Officer and Flight Deck Officer. I found that I adapted well to life at sea in a warship; the teamwork, close-knit community and the matelots were all terrific. Furthermore, I was awarded my Bridge Watchkeeping Certificate during this first sea job. Subsequently, I was lucky to enjoy several sea appointments.

My time as the squadron Schoolie in *Berwick* included a nine-month world deployment and a three-month deployment from Rosyth Naval Base to the Arctic during the Third Cod War in 1975 – 1976. During the Cod War operations, frigates acted as fishery protection vessels and attempted to protect British trawlers when Icelandic gunboats conducted trawl-cutting operations. Few shots were fired, although several ships were rammed. In total, 22 frigates were deployed, including *Falmouth*, *Brighton*, *Mermaid*, *Bacchante* and *Galatea*, although only six to nine ships were together at any one time. Some ships had their hulls reinforced with railway sleepers. Moreover, *Berwick* was plastered with Killfrost, a thick greasy substance that prevents upper deck icing. *Berwick* was the last Royal Navy distant-water fishery patrol ship.

Undoubtedly, the most demanding sea time for me was during the Falklands War in 1982. I was the senior bridge watchkeeper in *Penelope*, a *Leander* class frigate fitted with Exocet missiles. As well as providing escort and close-in support to the main units of the Task Force, we spent a lot of time defending the amphibious assault force in San Carlos water, which became known affectionately as Bomb Alley.

Terry Le Manquais – in the Falklands

Initially, *Penelope* was tasked as an escort to the Main Battle Group in the Total Exclusion Zone and with collecting stores from RAF Hercules airdrops. During this time, the Battle Group came under attack from Argentine Super Étendard aircraft, armed with Exocet missiles and accompanied by Skyhawk attack aircraft.

At night, we escorted convoys into the inshore waters of the Falklands. When we detached from the Battle Group to enter Bomb Alley then our routine changed. The days were spent at full Action Stations from sunrise to dusk; there were frequent Red Alerts as Argentine aircraft made a determined effort to blitz San Carlos and the supply chain of merchant ships.

The nights were spent at Defence Stations, usually escorting fast convoys of troop and supply ships to and from their landing zones. These ships included the troopship *Sir Galahad* taking the Welsh and Scots Guards to Bluff Cove where, sadly, many of the soldiers perished when the ship was attacked by Argentine aircraft. Night-time operations, with steaming lights turned off and in radar silence, in gales and blizzards, proved to be particularly challenging for watchkeepers.

It is claimed that *Penelope* was the last intended victim of a missile assault when we were escorting a merchantman east of Fitzroy on the day before the surrender. Despite coming under attack, *Penelope* escaped without damage or injury to the ship's company. We were one of the first warships to go into Port Stanley after the liberation of the town from the Argentine forces.

HMS *Penelope* returning to Plymouth after the Falklands conflict

In a later appointment to Royal Marines Poole, I was in command of the training vessel HMFT *Aberdovey* and responsible for navigation training for the Landing Craft Company and the Special Boat Service (SBS).

I was very lucky with my sea time: in the Cod War in the Arctic, the Falklands War in the Antarctic, the Dartmouth Training Squadron and in command of *Aberdovey*.

During the 1980s

A Terrible Ending

Jeff Buckley

I joined *Sheffield* as Squadron Instructor Officer in November 1981 and after a half-day turnover, sailed for Gulf patrol the next day. Gaining my sea legs en route to Gibraltar across the Bay of Biscay, I clocked up quite a few hours as Flight Deck Officer; by the time that I returned to Portsmouth, I should have completed over 160 day and more than 30 night landings of the ship's Lynx helicopter. I must say that I enjoyed this aspect of my sea time as it gave me the opportunity to become involved operationally.

HMS *Sheffield* – carrying out an NBCD exercise
by permission of Navy News (MOD)

As we made our way to the Gulf of Oman via the Mediterranean and Red Sea, it became increasingly apparent to me how much emphasis the ship's company placed on the prevailing weather conditions. They wanted to know how cyclones were formed and whether waterspouts were dangerous, presumably after seeing three of them following each other in the Gulf. The differing winds and climates that we encountered were all a bit much for a short-course Met man, which became my lame response to many questions, before I hurriedly read up on whatever it was we were encountering. SIO's corner in daily orders explained it all the next day. Suffice to say that I became known as 'Dai the Weather' and the flight crew emblazoned this dubious name across my FDO's jacket.

A Sod's Opera organised by yours truly was well received on New Year's Eve. The next day was, inevitably, very quiet! We then went to Mombasa, experienced many cyclones off Mauritius, encountered sharks near Diego Garcia before handing over to *Cardiff* in the Red Sea. Along the way, education and resettlement had remained a priority, and I was pleased to have helped some of the ship's company gain qualifications that made them eligible for promotion.

Our final destination was to have been Gibraltar and, after Exercise Springtrain, we would return home after a four and a half month deployment. To our surprise, we turned south at Gibraltar instead of north because of the Argentine invasion of the Falkland Islands on 2 April 1982.

Our passage down to the area around the Falkland Islands over the next few weeks was interesting; we were in company initially with the Task Force and then sent ahead by Admiral Woodward to establish a presence with the destroyers *Coventry* and *Glasgow*, and the frigates *Brilliant* and *Arrow*. The Falkland Islands were not really that cold when we got there – grey skies and some fog were generally the norm.

On 2 May, the whole operational situation changed dramatically when the Argentine light cruiser *General Belgrano* was sunk by the RN nuclear submarine *Conqueror*.

Two days later, I can remember going to the bridge at about 1400 to make a routine weather check, having just left the Communications Office a few decks below. The visibility was quite good on that particular day and I remember seeing a puff of smoke on the starboard horizon. 'Hello', I thought to myself, 'what's that smoke trail heading towards us?' The OOW and Flight Commander had also observed this and, after a few seconds, the Flight Commander uttered an expletive that made it obvious to all that this was an incoming Exocet. Feeling extremely vulnerable and subconsciously knowing that this was a low-level missile, I felt as though I needed some cover above my head just in case it wasn't an Exocet, so I made for the hatch leading to the deck below. I was too late though, as the missile struck and hurled me through the air, ripping off my spectacles in the process. As I am very short sighted, my first thought was to regain my vision, so gathering my wits I dashed down to my cabin to pick up a spare pair.

Seeing Captain Sam Salt on the way, I informed him what had happened and then made for my action station as Flight Deck Officer, which was not made any easier because of the flames leaping out from either side of the ship. After I eventually got to the flight deck, I remained at action stations for about four hours before we were given the order to abandon ship. By this time, *Yarmouth* had appeared alongside and while some of the ship's company were trying to jump across to her, others were jumping into the sea. Observing this perilous scene from the flight deck, one of the PWOs and I decided to hail our passing Gemini dingy, we dropped down to the quarterdeck through the flight deck hatch and then lowered ourselves into the dingy.

What a sorry sight 'Shiny Sheff' looked just then, but we could not dwell on this, as safety was uppermost and there was no telling what hostile threats there were around or what might happen next. *Yarmouth* and *Arrow* picked up all those who abandoned ship and then we were all re-united in RFA

Fort Austin. However, a support ship laden with – who knows what – was not my idea of a safe haven. We transferred yet again to a small oil tanker and this took the remaining ship's company on a two-week passage to Ascension Island from where we flew home.

In the relatively short time that I had been at sea in what was to be my first and last sea-going appointment, I had witnessed history in the making and an equal dose of tragedy as 20 of my shipmates died on that fateful day.

In the Very Centre

Alan York

Whilst serving in *Victorious* as the ship's Education and Resettlement Officer and with the ship still in dockyard hands, I attended the Photographic Interpretation course at RAF Bassingbourne; this may have led to me being appointed years later as one of the secretaries responsible for the work of the Joint Intelligence Committee (JIC) Secretariat.

I am delighted to have had the opportunity for such a unique experience, as Secretary to a Cabinet Committee in Whitehall. My job involved interdepartmental work, liaising with the MOD, Departments of State, Intelligence Agencies and NATO Allies, where we produced staff work to highly classified levels of security involving policy advice for senior members of government and the Civil Service. This period of time was particularly interesting being able to observe and take part in the events leading up to, during and after the Falklands War, and also the Cold War in the early 1980s.

This was a unique 'pool' appointment for any specialisation and I was lucky to get it. My RAF predecessor had done a Joint Staff course and two years in MOD RAF Intelligence in preparation for the post, but the Royal Navy did not have anyone available with that sort of pedigree. Advice from Vice-Admiral Sir Louis Le Bailly, who had retired as Director-General Intelligence in the MOD, told me something about Intelligence Officers: 'You are going into the most thankless of staff jobs, telling people who do not want to listen the things they do not want to hear'.

This was a most exciting and challenging job, giving a unique insight into the workings of the governmental machine and the upper echelons of the Civil Service. I am still not sure about disclosure, given all the security restrictions and remembering that in 1980, it was not even acknowledged that the Joint Intelligence Committee was part of the Cabinet Office and the government refused to talk at all about intelligence matters until much later.

The Joint Intelligence Organisation is based in the Cabinet Office and is responsible for providing assessments on a wide range of external situations and developments for the Prime Minister, the Cabinet, other Ministers and Officials. Its assessments were made on the latest information available from diplomatic reports, Government Departments and secret intelligence reports. Assessments were usually considered before circulation by the Joint Intelligence Committee, which included representatives of the security and intelligence agencies, Foreign and Commonwealth Office, Ministry of Defence (Intelligence) and the Treasury.

I was thrown in at the deep end, having had no previous experience in the Directorate of Naval Intelligence, although my time in photographic interpretation in *Victorious* had given me experience of work in the field and contact with Joint Intelligence outstations in the Mediterranean and Far East. I had to visit the UK Intelligence organisations to lecture on the Cabinet Office and JIC structure and explain how they were all coordinated. Among my many tasks was to oversee the arrangements for the weekly JIC meetings; produce draft minutes; see to their production and distribution; liaise with the Foreign and Commonwealth Office and other Departments and Agencies, including the Intelligence Allies. I would also take part in regular exercises (WINTEX and others involving the government's crisis response organisation COBRA), where I would stand in for the Cabinet Secretariat. At a social level, I managed to attend embassy receptions, the best being held on the roof garden of New Zealand House with its unparalleled panoramic views across London.

Writing minutes to the Cabinet Secretary, who was also Head of the Civil Service, passing information for him or the Prime Minister's Office, was always a mind clearing exercise, for which our MOD standard (JSP 101) was absolutely no help! We had to use a special minute sheet, not much more than 6x4 inches! The senior officials in the Cabinet Office preferred short, succinct, well-phrased papers in elegant English, preferably with some memorable phrase and a minimum of technical jargon.

There was not really an RN course to prepare for such a job. My years at Manadon as a history graduate covering Strategic and Defence Studies and Nuclear Disarmament at least enabled me to comment intelligently in the rarefied atmosphere of the Cabinet Office.

Little did I realise that my Photographic Interpretation course might have led to such an interesting job in the Royal Navy several years later.

Never a Submariner

Des Malone

I was appointed in the early 1980s as Acoustic Training Officer on the staff of Flag Officer Submarines to work at the Joint Acoustic Analysis Centre (JAAC) based in the Admiralty Research Laboratory at Teddington. This proved to be a most unusual job, especially for someone with my background as a METOC and never having served in submarines.

The JAAC had effectively three Heads; an Officer-Commanding RAF (Squadron Leader), a Commanding Officer RN (Commander) and a Senior Principal Scientific Officer. I was to work for both RAF and the RN heads. The only other RN officer on the staff was a Lieutenant Commander submariner, who was the Acoustic Analysis Officer. Initially I shared an office with two submarine sonar chiefs, which was extremely fortunate as my learning curve was to be almost vertical and it was thanks to these two that I learned my new trade.

JAAC issued monthly training schemes. These were made up of audio tapes of all underwater noises of ships, aircraft (yes aircraft) and submarines, whales and dolphins, and also paper acoustic sonar grams showing noise levels, pitch and frequencies of all underwater noises from the various sonars used by the RAF and RN. One needed to know what a whale sounded like, or looked like on a printed sonar gram in order to tell the difference between a soviet submarine and a whale!

These training schemes were undertaken by all submarine sonar rates and all RAF acoustic operators flying with the RAF Maritime Patrol Aircraft (MPA) squadrons based at St Mawgan, Kinloss and Finningley. Monthly training schemes were also produced for the RN Towed Array ships, which included Type 23 Duke class and four *Leander* class, the Fleet Air Arm sonar rates flying in anti-submarine Sea Kings and Merlins, and the Royal Netherlands Navy MPA. These Dutch customers entailed some very enjoyable, but hard working visits to the Naval Air Station Valkenberg in the Netherlands.

The training schemes became very well known, as JAAC supplied limited editions of the UK schemes to the Canadian, Australian and the New Zealand MPA squadrons. In addition, JAAC ran Advanced Acoustic Courses, which were attended by senior rates and a few officers from the RN and RAF MPA communities and some Commonwealth countries. The standards that were set for these courses were extremely high and the failure rate was around 30% and only one further attempt at passing was allowed. Even so, the course was popular and competition to attend was fierce.

One day I received a phone call from the US Military Attaché in London asking if a visit could be arranged for 24 US officers to visit Teddington to see how we produced our schemes. I could only cater for a smaller number of visitors, but the visit was a great success in that the US Navy and Air Force set up the equivalent of around 15 JAACs across the United States, almost identical in every respect to ours.

Whilst at the JAAC, I had, as the senior Lieutenant Commander, to prepare for inspection by teams from Air Officer Commanding 18 Group and FOSM and learned that, for the first time ever, there was to be a parade in uniform. This was most unusual, as normal rig at the JAAC was plain clothes and, added to that, the RN and RAF work to different rules on the parade ground. Normal commands were amended and, although in rehearsal, all was chaos, everything went according to plan on Inspection Day.

JAAC had a great feeling about it, as everybody was so professional but, at the same time, a very friendly place in which to work. A summer garden party for all the staff at the ARE who supported us started as a low key event with wives, partners and children also invited. However, RN/RAF rivalry led to the Chief of Staff to CINCFLEET attending with a RM Band in support. The following year Air Officer Commanding 18 Group decided not to be out done and we ended up with both Royal Marines and RAF bands.

These Cold War years at the JAAC were very exciting and fulfilling, with the Soviets regularly launching many new classes of submarines and warships, which all had to be assessed acoustically, and documented in great detail in a number of JAAC publications for which I was responsible. Finally, the data had to be incorporated into our training schemes in various ways so as to highlight the differences between the many classes of submarines and warships – not an easy task!

In the mid-1980s, I was again appointed to the staff of FOSM as the Assistant Submarine Training Officer; this title amused me, as I had never served in a submarine. However, neither did it please FOSM himself, so I was sent to sea in *Superb* to gain some submarine experience. I enjoyed the experience and each day ordered a half pint of bitter at lunch and dinner just to prove that I really was a surface man. Luckily, my old CPO sonar colleague from JACC was in charge of the Sound Room and the time passed quickly, as we both tried to be the first to identify each vessel that was showing up on the sonar.

After just over a year as the Assistant Submarine Training Officer, I was appointed as an oceanographer with the Polaris team (CTG 345); this was a job that I thoroughly enjoyed. Then in the early 1980s, I was appointed, again on FOSMs staff, as the Officer-in-Charge of the Anti-Submarine Warfare Analysis Centre at Royal Aircraft Establishment, Farnborough. This involved reconstructing encounters between Soviet vessels and RN ships and submarines; the aim was to see what lessons could be learned from such encounters. In the vast majority of cases, our RN ships and submarines performed extremely well and it was only on a very few occasions that some harsh criticisms were made. My team was made up of officers from submarines, the Fleet Air Arm and the Towed Array frigates together with a great bunch of very bright and attractive Wren Weapon Analysts. When this centre was absorbed into the JAAC, I was made the Senior Analysis Officer for both Acoustics and ASW tactics.

On reflecting upon my career of 28 years, it was interesting to note that I had spent half of it with FOSM although I never professed to be a submariner!

During the 1990s

A Brand-New Boat

Bryan Newton

I was lucky to have some months of sea familiarisation in the 'O' class submarine *Olympus* during her last commission, as she paid her farewell visit to many ports. After that, I completed the Submarine Basic Warfare course at *Dolphin* followed by the nuclear course at Greenwich. I do not know how my plum appointment to the latest 'T' class SSN came about, but I was selected to join *Talent* in January 1990 whilst she was in her final three months of finishing off at Barrow-in-Furness. I was very aware that the pace of life speeded up, as we raced to completion and the technology uplift from the 'O' Class submarine world was a huge culture shock.

There was nothing for it but to get stuck in, progress through training task books, learn nuclear submarine systems and wonder what I was doing there when I could be doing some good old safe chalk and talk appointment in *Collingwood* or *Sultan*, returning every day to the warm and welcoming arms of my wife and very young family. I am not sure that I made many friends during this phase of my submarine life, but I certainly had some good laughs, plenty of opportunity to stretch the brain cells, much blood spilt from my 6 foot 2 inch frame crashing into exposed pipe work and a few tears along the way.

When *Talent* finally put to sea, she was worked from the moment she first poked her nose into a bleak, grey and windy Irish Sea, because of the nuclear reactor 'trouser leg' problem that had laid up virtually the whole nuclear submarine fleet. As she was brand new, *Talent* was about the only operational hunter killer able to go to sea. It was a great opportunity for me to press on with the tasks of being a Part Three trainee: Captain Submarine Sea Training staff work up, Head of Department examination walk-throughs, control room and bridge watchkeeping all went in a blur.

Finally, in September, I had ticked all the boxes in the training task book, passed all the Department Heads' grilling on systems, passed the ship control simulator board and was now deemed ready for my final Part Three oral board. This took place inboard on a Friday whilst we were alongside at Faslane. The grilling and testing of all aspects of submarine operations from the CO, First Lieutenant, WEO and MEO lasted for over six hours and I felt like a completely wrung out dishcloth by the end of it.

The wait seemed interminable until the CO and all the other officers entered the Wardroom, grins all round. I was handed what has probably been one of the sweetest drinks in my life, a very large glass of rum with my Dolphin submarine badge at the bottom. Swallowed with a large gulp, the Dolphin caught between my teeth, I had finally been admitted to one of the most exclusive clubs in the world.

The next piece of good news was to be told that I was flying home to Portsmouth that evening to attend the four-week ships' diving course, as I was now also to be the submarine's Diving Officer. Whilst I was fairly well up by now on submarine systems for standard watchkeeping, the dark control room arts were skills that I was desperately trying to master. Still, I thought, that time would be on my side, but unfortunately, it wasn't.

At the very beginning of January 1991, we put to sea from Devonport, destination unknown but, for the first time in RN submarine warfare, a 'T' class hunter-killer submarine was going on patrol with a full weapon load of Tigerfish torpedoes and Sub Harpoon surface-to-surface missiles. The rumour was that we had taken to sea with us the UK's full stock of submarine weapons; slim budgets were in force even in the early 1990s.

Our prompt deployment meant that we were on our patrol station well in advance of the outbreak of the first Gulf War. These were interesting times with amazing communication intercept equipment, swims in the dead of night to recover air dropped intelligence and two small discreetly placed peg-boards, one aft in manoeuvring and one forward in the control room, that advised the on-watch crew the whereabouts of the CO at all times.

Fairly soon, the conflict was over. We were greeted with the news on stopping off in Gibraltar on our way home, that our contribution to the war effort was not going to be recognised formally, as it was deemed too sensitive to admit that a Royal Navy 'T' class submarine had been deployed in the conflict.

HMS *Talent* arriving in Faslane
© MOD Crown Copyright by permission of RN Submarine Museum

As a consequence, there would be no campaign medals for the crew. We did, however, have the immense satisfaction of a visit from the US Navy Admiral in charge of all naval assets during the war, who informed us what a splendid job we had done. This was made all the more enjoyable when his Flag Lieutenant, in the process of coming aboard from the Admiral's barge, refused to hand over his two briefcases, which were handcuffed to each wrist, and promptly fell into the sea between the barge and the side of the submarine. He was promptly rescued unharmed by the swimmer of the watch and the casing party transfer team with no harm done apart from a massive dent to his ego.

I flew home from Gibraltar and spent my last few weeks on *Talent* alongside in Devonport, buried in warfare books before leaving to start the Submarine Advanced Warfare course – the submarine equivalent of the PWO course. I was pleased to be the first Schoolie to complete this intensive six-month course.

To War with the Army

Nigel Huxtable

At the beginning of 1991, I was 'invited' to join the Force Information cell that had been set up at the behest of General Sir Peter de la Billiere, the Commander-in-Chief of British Forces in the Gulf, to provide all British troops in theatre in the first Gulf War with updates on what was taking place. British Forces Broadcasting Services provided the radio; video was shot and edited in theatre by another IO Campbell Christie and good use was made of American 'Combat camera' footage.

Keeping the troops on the ground and on board ships up-to-date eventually evolved as the 'Sandy Times', a news magazine printed in Riyadh and distributed to all service units. An Army officer and an RAF officer edited the material from the British broadsheets and collated articles; the aim was to keep morale buoyant during the long months of preparation, training and international politicking with Iraq, whilst quashing rumours and answering letters from servicemen and servicewomen in theatre.

Photographs were a rarity, so having brought my own R5 Leica camera kit with me, I offered support to 'The Sandy Times' team and was given the freedom to move about the deployed British army and RAF bases on the ground and to process my work in Riyadh before having it published weekly in support of articles and in a series of centre spreads reflecting the life and times of the ordinary serviceman in theatre.

Nigel Huxtable with soldiers from the Kings Own Scottish Borderers searching Iraqi POWs on day two of the Iraq ground offensive before moving them to holding areas behind the front line

The editor's honest and sometimes pithy responses in answering reader's letters built up a reputation with the troops for honesty and lack of obvious 'message', so I was made very welcome wherever I went. As the days passed, the editor and I decided that when the coalition troops invaded Iraq, we should be there to record the event. So Squadron Leader Pat McKinley joined Brigadier Patrick Cordingley's 7 Brigade (The Desert Rats) and I joined Major General Rupert Smith's 1Div HQ team. Having settled into our new locations, been issued with our morphine ampoules and attended the briefings, international negotiations resulted in a halt to the countdown and our return to Riyadh.

When the call did come, I was able to talk my way into accompanying a Royal Signals team setting up 'Ptarmigan' radio nodes in advance of the ground troops and so was in one of the first vehicles into Iraq.

Then followed 100 hours of rapidly moving tank warfare, where I had access to the field HQ and to the front line. Typical of the support received was to be told that there was an RN Sea King due in and did I need a lift? So I left the forward POW collection team and next day returned to the front line in a Puma doing medical evacuation work. The RN pilot needed little persuasion to exceed his safe fly zone to go forward to 7 Brigade HQ area to collect blue on blue casualties. Coalition forces had advanced so quickly that safe fly zones were not keeping up with the front line. Foolhardy perhaps, but speed was of the essence in supporting the wounded.

Nigel Huxtable in the back of a United Nations Huey helicopter in Iraq in 1993

Having eventually run out of film, I returned to Riyadh only to hear at the airport that a ceasefire had been called and I was to cover the ceasefire negotiations at Safwan, over the border in Iraq.

This was not possible, as I had all my film to print up, as well as to restock for whatever came next. Charlie Lowndes the British Force Broadcasting Service journalist recorded my impressions of what I had witnessed and as the ceasefire came into effect at 0800, my words were being transmitted, unchecked and uncensored, only by our own Force Information team. Even more challenging was getting all the images from the war processed and back to our HQ, although standing watching everything being processed and printed was a small period of calm amidst extremely busy and stressful times.

Eventually, Pat McKinley returned from Kuwait City and our two eyewitness articles were written up. Together, we put together a Sandy Times edition and I had the privilege of flying copies to Kuwait City only days after the fighting stopped. Only when I returned to Kuwait did I fully realize what had been done to the city and could watch and once again record the return of the desert battlefields to their previous state by clearing away wrecked tanks and others vehicles and removing live munitions.

The images I had taken were the highlight of this period and, with those I took in the liberated Kuwait City, formed the basis of an exhibition in the MOD. They were later used in the Central Office of Information's history of the war, 'The Shield and the Sabre'.

During the 2000s

Caught on Camera

Harvie Montgomery

Having returned from Easter Leave during my stint as the Unit Education Officer at 45 Commando, I received a cryptic message from a member of my civilian staff at RM Condor, 'You need to phone Commodore Christie about your career.' However, with the unit taking leave in conjunction with the Scottish schools, I was left with a week in which I was unable to reach Commodore Christie – a week of sweating over what I now believed would be a considerably shortened career in the Royal Navy. I finally got in touch with him to find that he merely wanted to wish me well. He had heard that I had been appointed to the role of Officer Commanding the Royal Marines Video Production Unit, which meant that I was following his early career path from Commando Training Centre to 45 Commando to the Video Production Unit. Panic over!

I was absolutely delighted with this move, despite barely knowing one end of a camera from the other. I knew that I was following a long line of Commando Instructor Officers, all of whom had maintained the strong reputation of the Video Production Unit, ensuring its survival where the other RN Video Production Units had been closed.

Memorial near Fort William in Scotland dedicated to British Commando Forces
raised during the Second World War – this area of Scotland was their training ground

My first project was to update the Mountain and Cold Weather Warfare series of films, last produced in 1986 and voiced over by Lieutenant Commander Tony Miklinski. This took me to the military hostel in Kinlochleven in the Scottish Highlands to work with the Mountain Leaders course, a visit that emphasised the need to have passed the Commando course in order to do the job. Within a matter of hours, I was yomping up the first of many Munros, hills in Scotland over 3000 feet, carrying all the necessary safety gear as well as my camera equipment and doing my damnedest to get the shots I needed.

Never for a second on the Commando course did I think that one day, a crucial part of my field kit would be lens cloths and sprays, spare tapes and batteries, with my tripod 'top-flapped' on my Bergen – not ideal for balance when traversing a fairly tricky route a few hundred feet up! However, the best was still to come. Having struck a deal with the *Gannet* Search and Rescue team, I spent an afternoon being flown in a Sea King helicopter around the valley of Glencoe to get some aerial footage.

The next project was deploying at the request of Major General Andy Salmon, who was Commander UK Amphibious Forces and the last UK General Officer Commanding, South East Iraq. This was to be my second operational tour, having deployed with 45 Commando to Afghanistan. We followed wherever General Salmon went, including the Governor of Basra's compound, a bridge ground-breaking ceremony in Basra and a patrol in the back of a Toyota Hilux along the border with Iran.

Our footage was edited into a half-hour film, detailing the activity leading to the drawdown of British forces in the region. During our time there, the security situation had developed to a point that British Forces rarely had to deploy on combat patrols, thanks mainly to the capability of the indigenous Iraqi Security Forces.

Returning to UK, I faced a difficult decision. We had just taken on a large project for Captain Mike Farrage, the Director of Naval Physical Development, to make a film promoting adventurous training activities. However, we had a commitment at the same time to deploy with 40 Commando on a multi-national amphibious exercise in South East Asia.

'Monty' Montgomery with his gear in Iraq

I had to choose between three weeks in the US, Belize and Egypt filming freefall jumps, sailing and diving, or three weeks in the jungle in Brunei and Malaysia with the Royal Marines. In the end, I chose the latter and sent my Second-in-Command on the adventurous training project. However, by deploying with the Royal Marines, I was able to complete my set of having operated in temperate, desert, jungle and arctic conditions.

So, I flew out to Bandar Seri Begawan in Brunei and met the Video Production Unit on board the RN's amphibious assault ship *Ocean,* where we remained for a couple of days, before deploying upriver and into the jungle on various landing craft. In the end, my footage was used in regional news and internal communications, and the film enabled us to update our archive of amphibious operations.

My final highlight was arguably the best when I was invited to accompany seven members of 42 Commando's original HQ element from Operation Corporate on their first joint return to the Falkland Islands. The members included Major General Nick Vaux, who had been the Commanding Officer 42 Commando and Major Mike Norman, Officer Commanding J Company during the operation; he had earlier, on the orders of the British Governor of the Falkland Islands, surrendered Naval Party 8901 to Argentine Forces on 2 April 1982, following a stirring defence against overwhelming numbers. My job on the visit was primarily to capture the official presentations by the team as they re-traced their route from Mount Challenger onto the assault on Mount Harriet.

Though the technology and terminology have changed over the years, the job itself hasn't altered that much. It still involves managing a small team of specialists and liaising with customers to achieve the desired end product, be that a training, promotional or briefing film, or rushes for the media as a combat camera team. I see it as by far the best job for a Commando Schoolie working with the Corps.

Chapter 5

'... and Women may Apply.'

No story about the Instructors would be complete without recalling the significant contribution made by the WRNS.

Most that has been covered in the previous chapters applies to the WRNS – working in education and training, appointments in various specialist areas including METOC and Information Systems, jobs in training establishments and the RN Colleges at Dartmouth, Manadon and Greenwich, employment in the UK, NATO and overseas; latterly their appointments have included those at sea.

Although the stories of the Wren ratings are not covered in this book, Instructor Officers have been extremely fortunate to have Wrens working with them in the Education Centres, Training Support organisations and many Met Offices.

The first two stories have been written by WRNS Officers who went on to become the head of their Service.

WRNS through the decades
©Crown Copyright MOD 2010 from 90th Commemorative Brochure for Association of Wrens

Education – Mary Talbot

In the WRNS from 1943 to 1976

I was in at the birth of the WRNS Education Branch, which came about because the war was coming to a close, and demobilisation was likely to take time, as the Government wanted to prevent service personnel clogging up the employment market.

There were many servicemen and women with little to do. Thomas Dugdale in Winston Churchill's coalition wartime government decreed that every officer and rating should have two hours education a week; the form that it took was left to Commanders-in-Chief and varied enormously.

I had finished my Officer Training course at Framewood Manor, on the outskirts of London, after the WRNS training unit at Royal Naval College, Greenwich was bombed and, together with a Second Officer, was given a short course in London organised by the Senior Psychologist, who was part of the Instructor and Education organisation. We were told that there were two appointments available in Liverpool and Plymouth and if we could agree, then we could choose. My colleague wanted Liverpool because of Malcolm Sargent and the Liverpool Philharmonic and I was content with Plymouth. When the two appointments came out, I went to Liverpool and she went to Plymouth!

In Liverpool, I was an assistant to a Naval Headmaster on the staff of Commander-in-Chief, Western Approaches, Lieutenant Arthur Miles, who was excellent and agreed that I should arrange two-day courses. We did this, as most of the Wrens were watchkeepers and it was not possible to organise discussion groups and visits to places of interest without interfering with their watches. Arthur Miles gave me a free hand in arranging courses; these included lectures, discussion groups with the help of leaflets on current affairs and a number of visits. We went to the Courts, for example, where Judge Hemmerde, known as 'the hanging judge', was sitting and he organised special seating for the Wrens. He even stopped a case to address us and explain that it was most unusual to have a woman accused of murder.

Other visits included those to local government, where Lord Sefton was Lord Mayor of Liverpool and he arranged for us to attend Council meetings. One meeting involved a discussion with Bessie Braddock, a well-known left-wing councillor, on gas and electricity for the new council houses.

Admiral Sir Max Horton, Commander-in-Chief, Western Approaches gave strong backing throughout to our education efforts. He persuaded Lady Listowel, a friend and author, to lecture on her native Hungary and he ordered the port closed when her talk took place. Another discussion that I arranged with Tavistock Square was for Dr Gillian Kerr to give sex lectures, which were possibly the very first ones in the UK. She was factual and answered every question quite naturally. I was also able to get her to come to Chatham to the headquarters of Commander-in-Chief, Nore, when I was serving there some years later.

We were well provided with lecturers – the officers in the Naval Education Department were always helpful and sent speakers to Liverpool, and Doctor McPhee, the local Director for the national adult learning organisation (Workers Educational Association), was always ready to provide people to talk. Liverpool had the first women police officers and their senior officer came to lecture.

I tried to provide a variety of courses and was able to acquire material for crafts such as rug making, which were not available generally, and this made them popular. I also had a green goddess fitted out with cooking equipment so that the Wrens could learn to cook. We had special rations and a Petty Officer Wren to instruct us.

In 1946, I was appointed to *St Angelo* in Malta as the assistant to the Command Instructor Officer, Captain Charles Sobey. However, demobilisation meant that I had to close the Education Centre in Sliema. Another task that I was given meant rewriting the Mediterranean Station Guide book; this proved to be an impossible job in keeping it up to date, as there were frequent changes to the town mayors in the Mediterranean ports and to the medical regulations, and each meant alterations to the Guide.

I returned to the Nore, carried on my two-day education courses and held classes for the Higher Education Test. These were needed for commissions for both male and female ratings who had not been able to take School Certificate during wartime.

After a fairly short appointment as Command Education Officer on Commander-in-Chief's staff, I went to the Naval Education Department and my main tasks were organising the Command Drama competition with the help of the British Drama League and overseeing the RN side of the correspondence courses. The scheme was run by the Army at Eltham Palace, where I had two male Cadets (Education) who dealt with the requests for courses from throughout the Royal Navy. The work was relatively straightforward, so that I only needed to go to Eltham Palace once a week.

I thoroughly enjoyed my Education appointments and I travelled extensively in the UK in the three commands of the Nore, Portsmouth and Liverpool, which included the Isle of Man.

METOC, Information Systems – Julia Simpson

In the WRNS from 1963 to 1996

I wanted to go to sea, but when I applied to do a Radio Officer's course in 1960 at the Merchant Navy Training Centre at Conwy, North Wales I was strongly advised by the Officer-in-Charge not to do this, as there was not a navy in the world that would accept a woman at sea! Instead, I went to university, gained a Physics degree and in 1963, followed my other interest, meteorology.

I joined the WRNS on a Special Entry scheme for Met Officers and this gave me four weeks at *Dauntless* to learn how to salute and march, followed by the Officers' Training course at Greenwich. My first real experience of the Royal Navy was at RNAS Culdrose (*Seahawk*) on the six-month Met course run then by Lieutenant Commander Ken Cropper and Commander Jock Evans. My fellow students were Brian Beel, Dai Morgan, David Brooks and an Australian officer.

After qualifying as a forecaster, I served at Lee-on-Solent (*Daedalus*), Brawdy (*Goldcrest*), NAVSOUTH when it was in Malta and finally, at Portland (*Osprey*), where I was the only female apart from Commander Air's civilian assistant! During my time at Portland, I did manage some sea time in RFA *Engadine,* embarking with 737 Squadron for their deck landing training.

Towards the end of my Short Service Commission, the Instructor Branch was looking for candidates to work in the Information Technology field and in particular, with the development of the command systems going into ships (ADAWS and CAAIS) and their trainers; this sounded interesting and I was accepted for a Full Career Commission and invited to join Commander 'Boy' Downer and his team in the ADP (Automatic Data Processing) section at *Dryad*.

It was a steep learning curve, but in time, I became familiar with the Ferranti FIXPAC programming language and then took up systems analysis. I worked first on upgrading the Tactical Trainer for the Maritime Warfare School in *Dryad,* from where I was appointed to the Admiralty Surface Weapons Establishment, Portsmouth as the Project Officer for the Cook Building Trainer in development also at *Dryad*. These projects will be covered later in the chapter on Information Systems.

The work in Cook Building required a close understanding and knowledge of the new ADAWS and CAAIS systems in the Type 42 destroyers, and the Type 21 and *Leander* class frigates, as well as their radar systems and weapons. To achieve this, I had to do some sea time – not easy as a woman and I was off-loaded at midnight in several ports, as I was not allowed to remain on board overnight – a real green rub as the Ferranti female programmers were able to stay! I did achieve one night at sea, however, when a parachute was ingested up an engine intake and the ship could not make it to Gibraltar! Working close to the front end of technology was a challenge; we had 17 computers running the Cook building trainer, which probably could be done by my iPhone now!

In the mid-1970s, the Instructor Branch now took over my appointing from the WRNS and in 1977 after doing the RN Staff course at Greenwich, I was sent to the United States to SACLANT in Norfolk, Virginia as a systems analyst, working with the then innovative World Wide Military Communications System (WWMCS) used by the US Navy. I well remember an early occasion when Admiral Ike Kidd, then SACLANT, was able to dispute the conduct of an exercise because he had a view of the ships' plot through using the system.

On promotion to Chief Officer WRNS in 1982, I went to the Defence ADP Training Centre at Blandford, as Deputy Chief Instructor and later Chief Instructor. There I earned the right to be called a Schoolie, instructing on the Project Management and Advanced courses. It was a challenging time too: that was during the advent of PCs and it was difficult keeping ahead of the serious Basic programmers, who knew their machines inside out. Amongst other Schoolies who were there at that time were Captain Don Watson and Lieutenant Commanders Peter Marshall and John Gardiner.

Whilst at Blandford, I did a stint as Mess President – unusual for a WRNS Officer and in a tri-service mess it was fraught with differences of etiquette. One that I remember was at my first mess dinner as President, when I proposed the loyal toast and nothing happened – the band was waiting for Mister Vice to propose the toast to 'The Queen' and Mister Vice (RN) was waiting for the band to play!

After Blandford, I went back to Naval Procurement, but based in Northwood as the OPCON Project Manager involving many projects, including Naval Staff Requirement 7126, the modernisation of the RN shore communications network. This number is etched on the minds of all RN Communicators, because this project automated all shore message handling in the Royal Navy. Again there are details of this in the section on Information Systems dealing with OPCON. The new system was a revolution in communications and its success led, I think, to my promotion to Superintendent in 1988.

This was followed by six wonderful months in Rome, at the NATO Defence College in preparation for my appointment to NATO Headquarters in Brussels as Deputy Secretary of the Military Committee. There I witnessed the collapse of the Warsaw Pact; it was my job to coordinate the first meeting of the NATO Military Committee with the Russian Chief of Defence, Admiral Gorshkov.

Back home, I was appointed back to Naval Procurement as the Assistant Director Communications, where I was closely involved with the development of communication requirements for the Future Frigate. This was initially a joint development with the French and was soon followed by the Tri-Service Frigate with the French and Italians. It helped considerably when I was rebranded into gold stripes and my rank became Captain.

My final job, as Director Naval Environment and Safety, came about as a discussion on what I would do if I took redundancy. I suggested that I would like to get involved with green issues and help save the world. Within a month, I was appointed to look after the Royal Navy's environmental issues and help introduce the requirements of the Health and Safety Act into the Service. Both were testing subjects to integrate into a fighting service and I found myself embroiled in discussions about storage of waste on ships, the safety certification of ships and decontamination of armament depots.

By this time, I had become the senior woman officer in the Royal Navy and held the rather unprepossessing title of Chief Naval Officer for Women (CNOW). Apparently the Queen herself rejected the title proposed by the Royal Navy of Chief Naval Woman Officer (CNWO).

Altogether, I served for over 30 years and am delighted to be an Honorary Instructor, having begun as WRNS (Met) then becoming WRNS (IO) and finally RN (any).

Training, Information Systems – Anne Bailey (née Minard)
In the WRNS from 1969 to 1986

I graduated in 1969 with a Physics degree from Bristol University. Not knowing what to do afterwards and not fancying industrial research jobs or school teaching, I luckily met a family friend who was a senior WRNS Officer (Elizabeth Bell). She explained that the WRNS employed science graduates as Met forecasters and, as my parents' wartime naval experiences had been happy, this sounded a good option and I made the necessary applications.

I went through the selection process for Direct Entry WRNS Officers and this involved an interview panel and medical. They explained to me that, although they were not currently recruiting forecasters, they wanted to introduce women to the Instructor Branch as teachers. Despite my reservations about school teaching, by this time I was very enthusiastic about the prospect of Service life and decided that this was a good way ahead. The WRNS seemed equally keen to have me as they waived the eyesight requirement that I had failed at the medical.

As a result I joined *Dauntless* in September 1969 for a month of basic new entry training along with about 20 other young women, three of whom were also Direct Entry; the rest were joining as WRNS ratings. This period of initial training was followed by two months of port experience at RNAS Culdrose, living on the lower deck and experiencing the work of the Navy's different specialisations and branches. The time at Culdrose was an eye-opener for me but I thoroughly enjoyed it.

Instructor Officers' Short Course 1970 at Royal Naval College, Greenwich
with Course Officer, Lieutenant Commander Frank Feest

I joined Royal Naval College, Greenwich in January 1970 for the three-month WRNS Officer Training course, which was good fun, but it was not until the April that I had my first experience of teaching. I went back to Greenwich for the Short IOs course, which comprised a month of theory and practical exercise, followed by another month of teaching practice out in the field. I did this at *Daedalus*, teaching air engineering apprentices some subjects where I was only one lesson ahead of them in knowledge. After that, I was deemed fit for my first proper appointment.

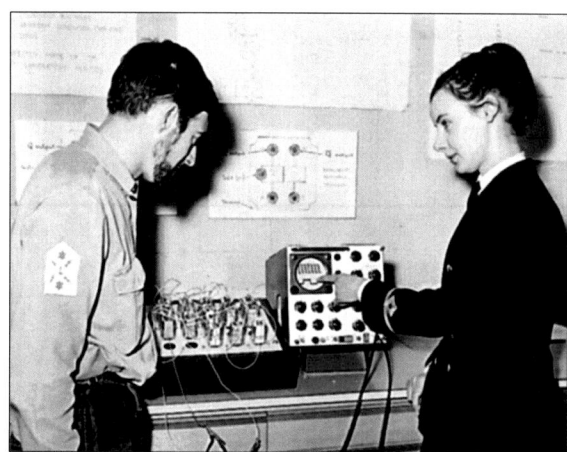

Anne Bailey carrying out training at HMS *Collingwood*

I joined the Maths Group in *Collingwood* and found myself the only woman in a group of about eight young Schoolies, several also in their first appointment. They had joined the Royal Navy only three months earlier and were already Lieutenants, whereas I had been in the WRNS almost a year, but was only a Third Officer; we were all doing exactly the same job and this seemed grossly unfair at the time. Nevertheless, I enjoyed *Collingwood*; I was teaching maths, mechanics and basic digital theory to artificer and mechanician apprentices, and courses in electrical mechanics for petty officers and leading rates. They were all quite surprised to find themselves taught by a woman and were much kinder to me than they might have been. Some years after this, I would often meet an elderly Chief, who would say, 'I remember you – you taught me maths in *Collingwood*'.

After almost three years of this, I began to feel that the powers that be might have forgotten about me, although they did select me for promotion to Second Officer. There had certainly been no talk of a new appointment. Eventually, a new position was found in Faslane at the Polaris School which was entitled Training Evaluation, but after I arrived, I found there was hardly a job there to be done. The Officer-in-Charge was not keen to have a woman on his staff. After a couple of months of doing nothing much, I went to work in the WRNS Admin Office until a new appointment could be found. This period could not be called a success and I felt that no long-term plan for this experimental WRNS Schoolie had really been made.

Six months later, I went to *Fisgard* to teach maths and mechanics to artificer apprentices again. This was much more up my street and another enjoyable appointment. By this time, the WRNS and Instructor appointers seemed to have got their acts together and my next job was at the Royal Naval Engineering College, Manadon, teaching the computer language FORTRAN to engineering undergraduates. This expanded my knowledge of programming and computer techniques, which was to stand me in good stead for the future. After a couple of years of this, I moved back to the Portsmouth area and to my next appointment in *Centurion*, as a Systems Analyst in the Drafting Section of Computer Division. However, by this time I felt that my best skills lay in teaching, so I asked for a move back to artificer training and went to *Caledonia* in 1978 and started maths and mechanics teaching again.

At the end of this appointment – 11 years since I joined up – it was deemed that I should have a general WRNS job for the good of my career. Incidentally, *Caledonia* was the first job where I was relieved by another WRNS Schoolie, Gill Ingram. I went to *Dryad* as WRNS Radar Training Officer and the WRNS Unit Officer, where I was one of the last to hold this appointment before that role was abandoned. I was selected for promotion to First Officer during this appointment, which was relatively late in the zone for WRNS Officers, and certainly late in comparison with male Schoolies who had this promotion automatically. After this, I did the RN Staff course at Greenwich in 1982; on completion, I remained at the Staff College to assist with the installation and management of a small office computer system, and teaching Staff College staff and students about word processing.

At about this time, the prospect of sea jobs came along. I decided at this point in my career, this was not something I wanted to volunteer for, especially as there would not have been any further Instructor jobs available for me afterwards. So I spent the rest of my 16 years at Greenwich and left the Service in 1986, still wearing blue stripes.

METOC Lesley Suddes (née Moore)

In the WRNS from 1984 to 2010

I joined the WRNS as a Direct Entry Instructor Officer and was, according to the Instructor Appointer at the time, the first Direct Entry female Schoolie.

This came in response to an advertisement in the 'New Scientist' for Instructor Officers in the Royal Navy, which offered opportunities to teach maths and science subjects to trainee engineers, with opportunities to expand into meteorology and oceanography or Information Technology.

I had completed a Natural Sciences degree at Cambridge, specialising in geology and physics and spent two years in various jobs – teaching sailing, running a chalet in a ski resort, and marketing food products – all of which proved fun, but were not really long term options for me. I was looking for a proper job and this advert sparked my interest.

After an interview with the Appointer, Lieutenant Commander David Bittles, I was informed that I would need to apply as a Direct Entry Wren, go through the Admiralty Interview Board, do my basic training at *Raleigh*, have three months of port experience, go for officer training at Dartmouth, Divisional Officer training at *Excellent*, and afterwards the Schoolies would pick up my training and employment.

I did all of this, joining *Raleigh* in September 1984 as Direct Entry Wren Moore to be a Schoolie on the usual eight-year Short Service Commission with a break point at five years. I was the only Schoolie on my course, although there were five other Direct Entries and one, Liz Spencer (née Alford), transferred Schoolie after her first WRNS job. We became great friends at that time and by retirement had both served 26 years, leaving within three months of each other.

I thoroughly enjoyed the Direct Entry Wren time, but was a little bothered by the fact that the system seemed slightly confused about my career route. It was clear that the WRNS system and my DOs and trainers at this time were unfamiliar with Direct Entry female Schoolies.

It was only towards the end of Dartmouth, reinforced a bit later when I arrived at RNSETT for my Instructional Techniques course that I began to realise there was a significant inequality between my pay, terms and conditions and the other dozen male recruits in my entry. As was normal for the WRNS then, I passed out as a Probationary Third Officer and was to remain so for a year before becoming a fully-fledged Third Officer. My male colleagues were all wearing two stripes already, so there was clearly a disparity, but David Bittles assured me that it would change in due course.

In 1985, I went to my first 'I' job at *Collingwood*, teaching mathematics to artificers and mechanicians. Also in the same training Group were Second Officer Jackie Norman, who had transferred to Schoolie, and Lieutenant Julia Eagles US Navy, on exchange, both teaching mathematics and computing. Later that year, I received a letter informing me that I was to be promoted to Second Officer and this would bring my conditions of service into line with my male counterparts. This was great for me, but understandably there was a deal of consternation from the other Second and Third Officers at *Collingwood*.

I leapt at the chance of doing the Met course in February 1986. I was now hoping to become an I(METOC), following in the footsteps of Nicki Hamp (née Smith), Karen Peach (née Shepherd) and others. At that time, the course lasted over nine months and included on-the-job training at a Royal Naval Air Station. I spent my eight weeks at Portland and was lucky to go to RFA *Engadine* with 702 Squadron where we went down to Lisbon and back. After the course, I was appointed to the Met Office at Culdrose and spent a most enjoyable two years there in my first job. While I was at Culdrose, Liz Spencer, Susie Swarbrick (née Elcombe), Cate Pope and Anne Sullivan (née Stanley) all transferred Schoolies, came through the Met course and went to various air station forecasting jobs.

From Culdrose, I was not very keen to start a tour of air stations, as only shore jobs were available to us then, and I asked for a broadening job. This came in the form of a six-month stint in the MOD in

London working on the EH101 Merlin helicopter project. From there, I was appointed to Dartmouth as the Training Staff Officer's Assistant, a role which nicely combined administrative tasks with responsibility for leadership training, on the river and on Dartmoor.

In 1990, as I was considering my next move from Dartmouth, the Government announced that women would be allowed to serve at sea. As a METOC, with Dartmouth experience, I was ideally placed to go to *Bristol* in the Dartmouth Training Squadron in January 1991. Before joining, I completed the Flight Deck Officers' course, so that my responsibilities on board included the Flight Deck, METOC and being a Divisional Officer to some Officers under Training. It was a great learning experience in a ship that had training at its heart, so was perhaps the ideal introduction to life at sea, especially since the only sea training I had received before joining *Bristol* was two days in the Damage Control and Fire Fighting Unit at *Raleigh*!

Around this time, we lost our WRNS status so instead of Second Officer Moore with blue stripes, I became Lieutenant Moore with gold stripes. During my six months in *Bristol*, we spent one term in the Mediterranean and one in the Baltic, so there were plenty of interesting runs ashore, as well as some different weather to forecast! One highlight was visiting Helsinki and St Petersburg, in the days of President Yeltsin leading up to Perestroika.

Bristol was decommissioned in July 1991 and I was immediately appointed as METOC to the 8th Frigate Squadron, comprising *Cornwall*, *Cumberland*, *Chatham* and *Campbeltown*. During leave, I married and so arrived in the job as Lieutenant Suddes. I served most of my two years in *Cornwall* where I eventually became the Squadron METOC and Flight Deck Officer. Again we had a great programme and visited the West Indies, the Gulf, the Baltic and the Mediterranean, in addition to carrying out many exercises around the UK, especially off the north and west coasts of Scotland in January and February. The Battle of the Atlantic Commemorations off Liverpool in 1992 were especially memorable.

By mid-1993, I was due a shore job. During my time in *Cornwall*, I had transferred to the General List and was promoted to Lieutenant Commander. My next job was as the Senior Met Officer at Culdrose and after that I went directly to be the Training Officer at the Met School, still at Culdrose. It was during the latter part of this time that significant changes took place in the Instructor Officer world. The specialisation was disbanded and we METOCs became part of the Seaman Specialisation and merged with the Hydrographers to be (HM). Thereafter, my appointments were as a Seaman, which are outside the scope of this book. This was all a far cry from the original advertisement that I saw for Instructor Officers in the Royal Navy, which had at the bottom, in brackets:

...(and women may apply!)

PART THREE - COLLECTIVE STORIES

Chapter 6

Up the Ramparts

The edict to provide 'Scientific Advice to the Command' meant that Instructors began to be employed increasingly in roles outside education and training. This began in 1935 in meteorology and then in the late 1950s in many other areas.

It is these other areas where Instructors worked, either for their whole career or for a single appointment, that are covered in this chapter.

The expression 'the Ramparts' to cover these specialist areas of employment for Instructor Officers was first used at an Instructor Officers' Conference held in the mid-1970s. The Director of the Naval Education Service showed the side of a fort with its walls and the ramparts extending upwards. He compared the work of Instructor Officers to this picture – the walls represented the main activities of education and training, and the ramparts showed the specialist areas of employment, which involved over 150 Instructor Officers at that time.

Whereas the previous contributions in this book were written by individual Instructor Officers, recounting, for example, how they joined the Royal Navy and relating their experiences in education and training, here one person has coordinated the work and been assisted by many unnamed others.

These coordinators have done a fantastic job in covering a vast area in relatively few pages; each has expressed concern about getting the information right, aware that some facts may have been missed, inaccuracies introduced or significant people not mentioned.

The sequence of the following sections follows the chronological order in which Instructor Officers became involved in the subject.

In the beginning, therefore, there was meteorology!

METEOROLOGY AND OCEANOGRAPHY

Alex Morrice and Geoff Fosberry

Officers of the Royal Navy have, from the very earliest days, played an important part in the development of the science of meteorology, with names such as Fitzroy and Beaufort, who need no introduction. Their successors as naval meteorologists may not be as well-known but, alone of the three services, the Royal Navy trains its own personnel in meteorology – a factor that has an even greater influence on naval operations today than it did at the zenith of sail in the 18th and early 19th Centuries.

The Early Days

When the Meteorological Department of the Board of Trade was established in 1854, there was no specialised service for the Royal Navy. During the First World War, a new fighting arm emerged, the Royal Naval Air Service. This spawned a requirement for specialist support, and the Admiralty set up a separate organization in 1916 to meet the requirements of the Royal Navy, called the Meteorological Section of the Naval Air Department.

Shortly afterwards, this section transferred within the Admiralty to the Hydrographic Department where it remained until 1920; then its responsibilities were taken over by a newly created Naval Division of the Meteorological Office, headed by a Naval Officer as Superintendent. Under him meteorological services were developed to meet the increasing needs of the fleet and naval air stations at home and abroad.

RNAS Hal Far, Malta in 1930s
by permission of the Fleet Air Arm Museum

Met training was also arranged to enable Naval Officers to forecast at sea. During the 1930s it became apparent that a fully equipped and adequately staffed forecasting service was required to support the RN fleet and aviation operations around the world. Therefore, in 1937, AFO 2033/37 announced the establishment of the Naval Meteorological Branch.

Prior to 1937, the Meteorological Office had trained naval officers to be forecasters but, after the Naval Meteorological Branch gained sufficient experience, forecaster training was moved to the Royal Naval College, Greenwich.

An unusual Met facility – a mobile Met Office used in North Africa
in the Second World War
by permission of FOST HM School

The number of officers trained in meteorology steadily increased to meet the requirement at sea and ashore; in 1945, there were 39 Royal Naval Air Stations (RNAS) in the UK and 20 overseas. The 1945 Navy List shows that 391 officers were Met qualified, having passed a 12-week course at Royal Naval College, Greenwich. Of these 51 were Seamen, 115 were Instructors, 180 were RNVR and 45 were WRNS.

The training for the Met ratings was mainly being carried out 'on the job' at various naval air stations. Gradually, however, during the 1940s, the Met staff serving in the Tower at RNAS Lee-on-Solent *(Daedalus)* took on more and more of this training because this was the headquarters of the Fleet Air Arm, although *Daedalus* was never officially a Met School.

After the Second World War

In 1946, Met forecaster training was moved from Greenwich, and the first RN Met School was opened at the Royal Naval Aircraft Direction Centre Kete *(Harrier)* near Dale in south-west Pembrokeshire. In the following year, the training of Met ratings was formalised and moved to *Harrier* from *Daedalus*.

After the war, the Admiralty Board considered the future organisation for providing Naval meteorological services and, in 1950, decided to set up an independent organisation, the Department of Naval Weather Service (DNWS).

During the ten-year period after the end of the Second World War, the number of naval air stations was reduced in the UK from 49 to 6 and abroad from 21 to only 2. As a consequence of this reduction in numbers of naval air stations, the number of officers qualified Met was reduced, with all the RNVR and WRNS Officers being lost. Those officers remaining totalled 190 and included 14 Seamen, (1 Rear Admiral, 8 Captains, 3 Commanders, 2 Lieutenant Commanders) and 2 Electrical (1 Captain and 1 Commander). The other 174 were all Instructors, whose number had increased from 60 in 1945.

Royal Naval Aircraft Direction Centre Kete – RN Met School for officers and ratings

In 1959, ratings training moved from Kete to RNAS Culdrose and a year later, the Met School at Culdrose was fully established with the Officers' Met courses also moving there under the guidance of the new Officer-in-Charge, Commander Norman Jenkins.

Forecaster courses lasted for six months, with students spending an intermediate week at a naval air station. On successful completion of the course, they generally did two weeks of probationary work, usually at the place where they would be appointed. Once their probationary period was successfully completed, their entry in the Navy List included the Met qualification.

In addition, several other officers' courses were run at the Met School. These included acquaint courses for Commanding Officers designate, week-long courses for navigators of small ships, self-briefing courses for helicopter pilots and shortened two-week forecasting courses for Instructor Officers appointed to frigates or as squadron Instructor Officers.

The last year in which 'Officers Qualified in Meteorology' were listed separately in the Navy List was 1960, and this showed a total of 207 with 8 Seamen (1 Rear Admiral, 5 Captains and 2 Commanders), together with 190 Instructors and 9 WRNS.

Introduction of ASW Oceanography

During the 1950s and early 1960s, the increasing importance of submarines and anti-submarine warfare (ASW) had a far-reaching effect on the Naval Weather Service. Sonar had been developed between the wars and was extensively employed during the Second World War, but knowledge of the parameters affecting its performance was extremely limited. Oceanographic studies into ASW were generally terminated after the war, and in the mid- to late-1950s, the environmental information available to ASW planners and operating forces was limited to small-scale charts and atlases, which showed mean conditions and indicated the average performance to be expected from hull-mounted sonars. Although the bathythermograph gave the thermal structure at a given position, the fleet had no method of projecting this information in time and space. With the advent of more complex ASW systems and true submersibles, detailed forecasts of operating conditions became essential.

To meet this need, the US Naval Oceanographic Office (NAVOCEANO) commenced investigations into factors affecting sound in the sea and, following research by Dr Dick James and others, set up an Anti-Submarine Warfare Environmental Prediction System (ASWEPS) in 1958. This shore-based unit was given the task of providing the operational fleet with synoptic and forecast charts, similar to weather maps, of oceanographic conditions in the western Atlantic.

In the early 1960s, the Royal Navy became involved in these developments at NAVOCEANO; furthermore, it was decided that the Naval Weather Service should address the operational impact of oceanography on sonar performance and ASW because of the relationship between the sea and the air in contact with it.

RNAS Lossiemouth in 1966
by permission of the Fleet Air Arm Museum

In December 1962, Lieutenant Commander Dennis Roe was sent to the US for five weeks of training and Lieutenant Commander David Carter was sent for two weeks to the Hydrographic Office then at Cricklewood. This was the start of a very useful cooperation between the Royal Navy and these organisations.

In 1963, at the request of SACLANT, a Pilot ASWEPS Unit was formed in the UK to provide a similar service to the US ASWEPS, but for the eastern Atlantic. This unit was situated alongside the then Fleet Weather Centre under the Admiralty Building with Dennis Roe as Officer-in-Charge and David Carter as his deputy. The US ASWEPS technique was basically to map sea surface temperatures to use as an indicator of water masses and to delineate sonar conditions from the historical and scarce bathythermograph data within these water masses. Hence the task of the UK Pilot ASWEPS was to provide strategic and tactical information for both surface and submarine sonar operations and, in particular, to enable reliable forecasts of sonar conditions to be made.

After a period of investigation, the prefix 'Pilot' was dropped. The UK ASWEPS team produced charts of sea surface temperature in the north-east Atlantic to try to identify those areas where temperature variations with depth would limit sonar ranges and reduce the detection opportunities of ships and submarines.

RNAS Culdrose – Met WRNS under training
by permission of Navy News (MOD)

Data was scarce and bathythermograph readings from the ocean weather ships and warships were all that were available. Much historical data, such as mixed layer depth, were extracted by staff at the Hydrographic Office and passed to ASWEPS for analysis. Royal Navy Met ratings were lent, sometimes under protest, to some of the ocean weather ships for periods of a month in order to produce detailed profiles. The Admiralty also put pressure on Royal Navy ships to take more bathythermograph readings. The original bathythermograph used to measure the temperature profile was a heavy piece of kit that could only be lowered and raised by cable when ships were almost still in the water. This situation eventually led to the development of the expendable bathythermograph, which could produce a sea temperature profile down to 500 metres in not much more than a minute, without the launch vessel having to slow down. The development took place at the same time of an airborne version of the expendable bathythermograph, which could be used by maritime aircraft.

In 1963, there was a convoy exercise from Plymouth, which went out due west and then back across the Atlantic for a total of nearly three weeks. A vessel in the simulated convoy was the flagship of the Royal Netherlands Navy with their Admiral embarked. He was interested in ASWEPS and Lieutenant Commander Geoff Fosberry, who had become Officer-in-Charge ASWEPS, along with a petty officer, was embarked for the exercise to demonstrate the tactical use of the analyses, using the data received by fax from UK ASWEPS. The Admiral, his Ops Officer and the ship's Captain were briefed twice daily and routed the 'convoy,' trying to escape detection by submarines that were lying in a screen across the convoy route on both the outbound and return legs. At the Post Exercise Discussion in Plymouth, the submarine Commanding Officers complained that they had been wasting their time, finding no convoy contacts at all. The Admiral, on the contrary, was delighted and sent three Dutch Met Officers for extended training at the UK ASWEPS Unit.

Following the success of this convoy exercise, UK ASWEPS personnel regularly took part in NATO exercises in the North Atlantic. David Carter took part in an exercise in the north-east Atlantic and Norwegian Sea in the USS *Wasp* together with a Met rating and a scientist from NAVOCEANO.

Around this time, SACLANT formed a Military Oceanographic (MILOC) group in which each of the NATO countries was represented. The MILOC Chairman was the US Navy Captain who was SACLANT's Chief Oceanographic Officer; the Vice-Chairman was the Fleet Met Officer on the staff of CINCFLEET/CINCCHAN. This development led NATO to organise several MILOC surveys in the eastern Atlantic, the Norwegian Sea and the southern Baltic over a number of years. All of these were designed to collect data about the temperature and salinity of the water column and to improve knowledge of the effect on sonar transmissions. Scientific input from the NATO ASW Research Centre in La Spezia, Italy, greatly helped the planning and execution of these surveys.

At the end of 1965, Geoff Fosberry was relieved by Lieutenant Commander David Davidge and sent to Malta in the national post of Fleet Met Officer, Mediterranean Fleet and in the NATO post as Chief Met and Oceanographic Officer to COMNAVSOUTH. This was probably the first METOC appointment. As well as running the Mediterranean Fleet Weather Centre, his task was to establish the complement for the Oceanographic Centre. This took about a year and as a result a US Lieutenant Commander Meteorologist, an Italian Lieutenant Commander Hydrographer and additional RN Met ratings joined the centre.

In early 1966, prior to the withdrawal from Aden, Lieutenant Commander Dick Abram was lent for three months from the UK ASWEPS Unit to the Fleet Headquarters of the Commander, Far East Fleet (COMFEF), in Singapore. Dick Abram's task was to develop ASWEPS charts for the sea areas likely to be used by the units of the Far East Fleet involved in supporting the withdrawal from Aden. This effort was strongly supported by the supply of historical bathythermograph data for the operating area by the Hydrographic Office. As a result of this venture, in January 1967, Dick Abram was appointed to the staff of COMFEF for Meteorological and Oceanographic duties to continue this work for the Far East Fleet, which involved sea time in both national and multi-national exercises.

Also in 1966, David Carter spent about two months in the submarine *Rorqual,* going from Portsmouth to Bahrain via the Cape of Good Hope as arranged by Captain Graham Britton, at that time the Director of the Naval Weather Service (DNWS). The purpose of this assignment was to assess whether submarines could be good platforms for oceanographic observations. Fitted with an electronic sound-speed instrument, the submarine did provide some interesting data down to the maximum diving depth, but ultimately this exercise proved that a submerged 'tin can' is not an ideal platform.

How successful the early days of ASWEPS were in producing useful forecasts of ocean conditions is probably arguable. Rather, its success was in achieving a much wider and better appreciation throughout the Royal Navy of the importance of oceanography to both submarine and anti-submarine operations. By this time, responsibility for operational oceanography lay with DNWS, whereas oceanographic data collection was the primary responsibility of the Hydrographer; this situation remains to this day.

To reflect this changing pattern of demands and to make more effective use of resources, DNWS was once again incorporated into the Hydrographic Department in 1966 with a new title, Director of Meteorology and Oceanographic Services (DMOS) (Naval). This change lasted eight years. In 1974, to reflect the increasing responsibilities of the Directorate in the oceanographic field, the title was again changed to Director of Naval Oceanography and Meteorology (DNOM). This title better withstood the test of time, lasting until the 1990s, after the end of the Cold War.

Met School Becomes the RNSOMO

In the mid-1960s, both RN Met officers and ratings had ASW oceanography added to their training, although the title of the Met sub-specialisation was not replaced by METOC until the 1970s.

In 1967, the ASWEPS title was considered too specific and was altered in the Royal Navy to Oceanographic Forecasting Service (OFS); in 1968, with more developments in ASW Oceanography being added to the course curriculum, the title of the Met School changed to the Royal Navy School of Meteorology and Oceanography (RNSOMO). By this time there were also oceanographic courses for Instructor Officers appointed to submarines and tailored courses for Instructor Officers serving in survey vessels. Additionally, there was a three-week Oceanographic course for foreign students from NATO countries.

During the mid-1980s the METOC forecasters' course was redesigned and extended to nine months, which included a six-week secondment to a naval air station midway through the course. The first part concentrated on aviation meteorology, whilst in the second part students commenced their oceanographic training with the emphasis on maritime operations.

In the early 1990s, an accreditation process for METOC courses was initiated with the National Vocational Qualification (NVQ) Council and the University of Plymouth.

Golden Years of Naval METOC

From the mid-1970s to the early 1980s, a number of elements came together to bring METOC to the forefront. The Royal Navy still had a significant carrier and amphibious force and five major naval air stations, all of which had Met offices. The introduction of new technology in weapons systems made them, almost perversely, more environmentally sensitive than their less sophisticated antecedents.

Oceanography was also increasingly important, as the Soviet submarine threat was a major defence priority. The development of passive sonar in the surface fleet led to a significant demand for additional METOC officers and ratings at sea in the Towed Array frigates.

RNAS Culdrose in 1970s
by permission of Navy News (MOD)

There was an active NATO programme of Military Oceanographic surveys in which the UK played a leading role. Three NATO Oceanographic Centres had been set up, in Norway, Portugal and Italy, all of which had UK Officers-in-Charge and a significant element of UK manning. Then 'out of the blue' came the discovery that there was a range of non-acoustic oceanographic factors that could lead to the detection of submarines. METOC officers were appointed to assist with programmes at the Admiralty Research Laboratory (ARL) and the Admiralty Underwater Weapons Establishment (AUWE) Portland, where Lieutenant Commander Geoff Kelly led a particularly successful METOC cell.

METOC personnel could be found in expected and also unusual places: a large METOC forecasting cell at Fleet Headquarters, exchange appointments in the US and Australia, on the staff of NATO Command Headquarters in the UK (Northwood), the US (Norfolk Virginia) and Belgium (Mons), at the UK Government Communications Centres, ashore in Hong Kong, and last but not least, at the METOC School at RNAS Culdrose.

It is difficult to put an exact number and date on the peak; however, an article in the *Marine Observer* in 1980 estimates that about 90 METOC officers were then in active appointments. That is probably not far off the top of the curve.

Changing Technology

At the end of the Second World War, weather charts were plotted using pens tied together and then dipped into red and black ink. Weather observations were transmitted by Morse code, and fables are told of those skilled enough to plot straight from the signal received via headphones. Balloons released to measure upper winds were tracked by theodolite. By the 1960s, advanced technology gave us red and black biros taped together, teleprinters produced coded observations and charts could be transmitted by fax, balloons were tracked by radar, satellite technology was beginning to revolutionise meteorology and had some esoteric applications in oceanography.

The situation went on like this for some time as, looking back, we were waiting for the development of computer support. In 1975, there was one rudimentary computer at Northwood that belonged to the Operational Research cell, and a Wang computer in the Oceanographic Centre upon which the US Navy exchange officer strove to run a wave forecast model.

Then things changed. Now we have XY plotters and model output being zipped round the globe at a speed that frankly we could not even imagine then. The detail is beyond the scope of this enterprise, but two stories illustrate the flavour of the early days.

In 1976, the Fleet Oceanographic Centre obtained a US Navy deep ocean Acoustic Propagation-Loss model. It arrived in several canvas bags that disgorged reams of punched Hollerith cards. Within a year, Lieutenant Commanders David Fraser and Mike Frost had an operational system running on 'borrowed time' on the Operational Research computer. Two years later, DNOM ran a project to get the Propagation-Loss programme to sea in submarines on Hewlett Packard computers. The specification was simple. The hardware had to fit through a submarine hatch, and the programme run-time had to be as short as the budget would allow. The rate of improvement of the Hewlett Packard computer was such that the system, supplied in less than 12 months from inception, was two or three orders of magnitude better — at the same cost! Mike Frost was again to the fore in that venture.

Satellites allied with computer processing brought another step change in capability, particularly our access to the US Navy programme and the development of techniques to use the data operationally in support of submarine operations.

The External Links

The close relationship between the Royal Navy and the US Navy since the Second World War has been reflected in the enduring ties between their respective METOC organisations. This has been maintained by formal arrangements such as Information Exchange programmes and personnel exchange, and by close personal dealings at senior staff level through bilateral and NATO structures. DNOM played a key role in the earlier mentioned NATO MILOC Group, providing the Officer-in-Charge and staffing for the Regional Centres and a Commander on the staff of the Chairman of the MILOC Group at SACLANT Headquarters in Norfolk, Virginia. For many years, the UK also provided a METOC Captain on the staff of SACEUR in Belgium.

While the Royal Navy provided the lead for the UK on oceanography in the MILOC Group, the Met Office was the lead on the sister NATO organisation for meteorology, the Military Committee Meteorology Group. The Deputy DNOM represented the Royal Navy for the main Group meetings. Within the UK, working closely with the Met Office, the Director of DNOM was an active member of the Met Committee and the Met Research Committee. Operational links were maintained between RAF Strike Command, the Fleet Met Officer and Staff Officer (Met) at DNOM.

Changes after the Cold War

In the 1970s and 1980s, the Cold War had placed oceanography and meteorology high on the list of operational significance and, crucially, funding priority. The end of the Cold War heralded an adverse environment in the 1990s. The collapse of the Soviet Union and the realisation that the Soviet war machine was not as fearsome as we had thought, led our political leaders to look for significant cuts in the Defence budget. The maritime warfare priority moved from deep ocean submarine operations and anti-submarine warfare to littoral operations, mine warfare and surface surveillance. The carrier and amphibious capability has been eroded over a number of years, the Fleet Air Arm reduced to two naval air stations, at Culdrose and Yeovilton, and the Submarine Service is a shadow of its former self.

Overarching all of this, the Royal Navy faced ever-increasing pressure to reduce manpower costs. In five years, the METOC Captain's posts in Brussels and at Northwood were lost, two headline events that caught the spirit of what was afoot. About June 1992, there was a very hostile 'anti-Instructor' sentiment. It was a time of lean resources when, across the board, posts were being cut and staffing levels reduced by rank. The patchwork of piecemeal solutions being bandied about had a common thread, 'ditch the Instructor Specialisation'.

The End

As part of the rationalisation, the Hydrographer's MOD Directorate of Surveying was amalgamated with DNOM in 1995. The first three Directors of the new organisation (Naval Surveying Oceanography and Meteorology) were METOC Commodores: Richard Willis, Steve Auty and Charles Stevenson.

After the demise of the Instructor Specialisation in 1996, existing I(METOC) officers continued doing their normal tasks, but as X(METOC). The RNSOMO became amalgamated with the Hydrographic School, changing its name in 2001 to the Royal Navy Hydrographic, Meteorological and Oceanographic School (Culdrose). In 2003, the School moved to *Drake* as Flag Officer Sea Training (FOST) Hydrographic, Meteorological and Oceanographic (HM) School.

Finally, after another Defence Review, Commodore Charles Stevenson supervised the move of the Directorate out of the Naval Staff into the MOD Central Staff.

Postscript

The Heads of Meteorology and Oceanography; Admiralty and MOD Naval Staff are in Annex 6 and the Officers-in-Charge of the RN School for Meteorology and Oceanography are in Annex 7.

Further information and photographs of Met School staff and students over the years can be found at:

http://cloudobservers.co.uk/comms-room/downloads/

Long Met Course at RNAS Culdrose with Commander Ken Allcock,
Lieutenant Commander Peter Rogers and students in June 1969

ROYAL NAVAL COLLEGE GREENWICH

Ken Cropper

The Royal Naval College, Greenwich was founded with the aim of providing officers with appropriate studies that would have a significant bearing upon their profession. The College opened in 1873 in buildings that, since 1694, had provided a respite for seafarers who 'by reason of age, wounds and other disabilities were incapable of further service'.

Royal Naval College, Greenwich in 1998
by permission of Howard Broadbent

By the 1950s, the academic departments, with an Instructor Captain as Dean, included Mathematics, Physics and Electrical Engineering, Materials and Chemistry, Mechanical Engineering, Marine Engineering, Nuclear Science and Technology, Modern Languages, Navigation, and History and International Affairs.

By the early 1970s, only the Department of Nuclear Science and Technology (the Nuclear Department) and the Department of History and International Affairs (DHIA) remained.

However, at various times, the college was the home of several autonomous units such as:

- The Senior Officers' War course (SOWC).
- The Joint Services Defence College (JSDC).
- The Royal Naval Staff College (RNSC).
- The Lieutenants' Greenwich course (LGC), which later became part of the RNSC.
- The SD Officers' Greenwich course (SDOGC).

The college was also a base for the RN officers attending The City University (TCU).

With what many considered an unwieldy organisational structure, the college survived until its eventual closure as an RN establishment in October 1998.

New Entry Instructor Officers' Courses

In the early 1950s, the Home Fleet Training Squadron came into being with *Indefatigable* and *Implacable,* followed later by *Ocean* and *Theseus;* thus there were no NEIO courses planned at Greenwich. After the demise of the Training Squadron, the Appointers arranged for NEIOs to be accommodated in ships where possible but in 1959 NEIO Training returned to Greenwich.

These Greenwich courses were primarily for those entering the RN who did not hold a teaching qualification and followed their initial training at RN Barracks, Portsmouth (*Victory*/*Nelson*). One of the main aims of the course was to develop their instructional skills and included periods of teaching practice at other RN or RM training establishments. As with earlier NEIO courses, additional lectures were added to cover Service history and traditions together with visits to Parliament and the Law Courts. The Course Officers, who were directly responsible to the Dean, were in turn Lieutenant Commanders Peter Hockley, Gwyn Arthur, David Fowke, Gerry Tordoff and Brian Drinkall.

Even after initial New Entry training for most IOs moved to BRNC from late 1963, those joining in their mid-twenties through RN Barracks, Portsmouth and those from BRNC who did not have a teaching qualification, continued to be sent to Greenwich for training in Instructional Techniques until this task was eventually transferred to the IT School/ RNSETT.

Other Appointments at the College

In 1965, Commander John Bell became the first Instructor officer to be a member of the Directing Staff for the RN Staff Course and, until the closure of the RNSC at Greenwich in 1997, there was usually at least one Instructor Officer on the RNSC staff and one or two Instructor Officers as students on each Staff course. Occasionally Instructor Officers did the LGC.

However, most Instructor Officers within the college were in the Nuclear Department and some were associated with TCU; hence these departments are covered in more detail.

Department of Nuclear Science and Technology

Following the advent of nuclear-propelled submarines in the United States, it became evident that there was a need for nuclear engineering training for the Royal Navy, so in 1959 Professor Jack Edwards from Naval Section Harwell founded the Department of Nuclear Science and Technology (DNST).

The US Navy had already built a handful of submarines, each with a different reactor system from which the best option was to be chosen. The first Royal Navy nuclear submarine, *Dreadnought,* was close to launch. Nuclear power was revolutionary. The absence of a need for an air supply to the propulsion unit meant that submarines could have propulsion the equal of surface ships, with faster speeds submerged and silent running, once hull design and other aspects were improved. Some described these nuclear submarines as the first proper submersibles, and they certainly highlighted the severe limitations that earlier conventional submarines had had to cope with. It was a time of great technical interest and *Dreadnought* was soon to be fitted with a US reactor system of the preferred type.

The concept of carrying ballistic missiles was well advanced, and responsibility for the UK's nuclear deterrent was transferred from the RAF 'V' bombers to Royal Navy nuclear-propelled submarines, which would carry ballistic missiles, SSBNs. Attack nuclear-powered submarines, SSNs, carried torpedoes in keeping with their different role.

Returning to the Nuclear Department, Instructor Officers were involved throughout. Although this article names only some dozen, there were very many more over the years, and they were present in the very first batch of staff, who were mainly civilian, but included Marine and Weapon Electrical Officers. The first Instructor Officers in the Department were Lieutenant Commanders Ted Chittleburgh and Brian Vaughan. The latter came from Royal Naval Engineering College, Manadon, and was known for his prowess as an England rugby forward and was soon to be manager of the British Lions in South Africa.

To provide for the design, operation and maintenance of these nuclear power systems, the very first task was to develop a wide range of courses to suit all the requirements. The most pressing were addressed by the following courses:

- A three-term Nuclear Advanced course aimed at Royal Navy and civilian officers who were destined for design jobs. The first course, which included Lieutenant Commander Terry Carter from Manadon and who returned to the Nuclear Department a few years later as Training Commander, earned the recognition for the award of a Master's degree for all such future courses.
- A two-term Nuclear Reactor course for Engineer Officers who had left Manadon en route to nuclear submarines as watchkeepers. This course was also attended by the early XOs destined for *Dreadnought*; this course earned a postgraduate diploma.

A particularly advantageous early acquisition by the Nuclear Department was that of a low-powered reactor (JASON) that served to illustrate reactor behaviour without the complications and expense of a full-power reactor. JASON served the department well throughout the years in a range of internal tasks and helped in the link with the new Nuclear School for ratings at *Sultan*. At Greenwich, the eventual Reactor Manager was Lieutenant Commander Jerry Highton, who had experience as a submarine watchkeeper and had earlier brought his expertise in materials to cover the chemistry requirements.

The training was split between two divisions: Physics and Reactor Engineering. Metallurgy and Chemistry were part of the latter division and Lieutenant Commanders Bryan Gibson and Trevor Spires were involved in the teaching of these subjects. Despite being a metallurgist, Lieutenant Commander John McGrath found himself in the Physics Division teaching Radiological Protection and Reactor Physics.

Returning to courses, an ever-wider range was to follow, including:

- An introductory two-week course.
- A one-term course for XOs and Dockyard Officers.
- A Nuclear Radiological Protection course covering the effects of radiation on the human body.
- A short course in the Management of Nuclear Accidents.

Many Instructor Officers were employed on lecturing and other duties, including Commanders Peter Smith, Alan Alabaster and Ken Tucker, and Lieutenant Commanders Hamish Wilkie, Jeff Kelly, Ian Purdie and Alan York. It also became necessary to assign an Instructor Officer, responsible directly to the Training Commander, to work on course design.

In the fullness of time, some were re-employed on a permanent basis including, for example, Charles Marchant and Brian Walsh who had served as Lieutenant Commanders during their time in the Royal Navy. This may be the moment to add that Lieutenant Dennis Gibbs joined the department as a Short Service Instructor Officer early in its existence and stayed on in a civilian role, rising through several stages to become head of Physics and Computing and later, the Professor. He was relieved as Professor by Keith Barratt, another retired Instructor Officer, who had served in the department in earlier years as a Lieutenant Commander. Another person to mention is Brian Dear who was awarded his PhD for research carried out while on the staff of the DNST; this must have been one of the earliest, if not the first, in-service award of a doctorate.

Throughout, there were significant working relationships with civilian nuclear-power stations, with Harwell and with RN facilities at Bath, Faslane and Dounreay. Many civilian companies were also involved, notably Rolls Royce and Associates, which had been formed at the outset as an amalgamation of Rolls Royce, Foster Wheeler and Vickers Armstrong, names respected by the US Navy. This did much to placate a certain all-powerful US admiral, rightly regarded as the leading man in the world of nuclear-powered ships, especially submarines. Without his approval and the influence of the First Sea Lord, Admiral Mountbatten, in these matters, progress would have been more difficult; in all this the department's Professor Jack Edwards was a major influence.

Security was, naturally, a very sensitive issue. The UK was looking to the US to share their secrets at a time when there had recently been the embarrassment of several spies: Fuchs and the Portland Pair (Houghton and Gee); others were revealed later. Much effort had to be expended in protecting information provided by the US Navy.

When the college closed in 1998, the Nuclear Department moved to *Sultan*. The nuclear reactor JASON was closed, the fuel moved to Dounreay, with the waste to Aldermaston and Sellafield and the

Greenwich site cleared of material. Once more, the Greenwich Council could live up to its title of a Nuclear Free Borough!

It is rumoured that consideration is again being given for a further move of the Nuclear Department, this time to Shrivenham.

The Royal Navy and The City University

The start of the relationship between the Naval Service and The City University (TCU) is only anecdotal. However, it is believed that it began with Admiral Sir Frank Twiss, Second Sea Lord, meeting Sir James Tait, the Vice Chancellor of the University. Sir James had been describing the formation of TCU from the Northampton College of Advanced Technology and the future development and the range of study to be offered by the new university.

Sir James referred to a proposal made to the Senate by the Professor of Systems Science, Philip M'Pherson, to develop a programme for an inter-disciplinary Bachelor's degree with the aim of bridging the two cultures of the sciences and the humanities. The principle behind the scheme was to study Physics, Mathematics, Economics and International Relations using a systemic approach to each subject.

In the mid-1960s, the Service was re-examining its policy for producing graduates for the Seaman and Supply specialisations. Entrants with good Advanced levels in Mathematics and the Sciences were easily being placed to read the traditional subjects. However, this left out Midshipmen who had taken disparate subjects at school, such as Physics, History, Economics and English, frequently with only modest success at Mathematics.

The TCU proposal, in which the Mathematics Department would design a course to cover sufficient mathematical methods to facilitate a systems approach, offered an interesting curriculum. For example, sets, mappings, logic and computer programming would be included in the syllabus.

Negotiations then began between BRNC Dartmouth and TCU. Liaison with the university was undertaken by Captain Geoffrey Huggett, the Dean of Royal Naval College, Greenwich and a Control Engineer, and Commander Ken Cropper, newly appointed to Greenwich with a Master's degree in Operational Research from Lancaster University.

Professor M'Pherson, who as a Lieutenant Commander had served as an Ordnance Engineer before retiring to follow an academic career, formed a planning committee with members drawn from the constituent departments and Geoffrey Huggett and Ken Cropper as full members. It was two years before all the required external examiners had been appointed, and the university's Senate gave its approval. Obtaining the full cooperation of the various departments had been a delicate business, as they had to adapt and sometimes rewrite their lectures to follow the 'systems' approach.

In September 1972, the first intake of 52 people arrived for the new Bachelor's degree course in Systems and Management; this number included about 30 Midshipmen and Sub Lieutenants. Commander Ken Cropper was made Senior Lecturer and Senior Naval Tutor and led the Systems Science Team of six drawn from the Control Department, with two newly appointed International Relations lecturers and two other RN officers. By this time, Greenwich had also become more involved, and there were visiting lecturers coming to TCU from the Nuclear Department and History and International Affairs Department.

The impact of the RN contingent on the university generated great interest. Most naval undergraduates decided to live in at Finsbury Hall or in digs, but a small number took advantage of living at Greenwich. Soon sports teams were formed and the young men made an excellent impression at the university, in the college and with the civilian students. Most lecturers were surprised to find members of their classes standing when they entered a lecture room.

This situation continued for many years but, by the 1990s, the end was in sight. The degree itself was losing numbers because the title had become confusing. The degree was about systems theory, but tended to be confused with systems as a computer science degree; eventually the degree was subsumed into a generic business degree.

Lieutenant Commander Chris Brady, who had relieved Peter Hamilton, was the last RN lecturer to work with TCU. By the time he arrived in 1990, the role was full time. The deal was that the Royal Navy provided a full-time lecturer from the Department of History and International Affairs, and the RN students attended at no cost. However, by that time, the cohort was only about ten strong. Chris Brady was an international politics specialist and taught that subject on the undergraduate degree, acting also as the Divisional Officer for the group. When the Royal Navy decided to end the relationship as a consequence of another cost-cutting round, he managed the run-down of the last group in 1993.

Throughout the time that the degree was run, officers from Dartmouth made regular visits and a good working relationship developed between TCU and Dartmouth.

ROYAL NAVAL ENGINEERING COLLEGE, MANADON

John McGrath

In 1877, *Marlborough,* an old screw line-of-battle ship, which was no longer required in the fleet and was paid off in 1864, became the home of Engineer Officer students in Portsmouth. Soon afterwards, a new facility was built at Keyham, on the fringes of Devonport Dockyard, and took its first students in 1880.

Plymouth - Keyham College for Engineer Officers circa 1930s
by permission of NMRN

Keyham College continued to be the centre of Engineer Officers' education until the threat of war in the 1930s caused their Lordships to look for a less vulnerable site to accommodate future Engineer Officers. In 1937, the 100-acre Manadon estate on the northern fringes of Plymouth was purchased, and plans were drawn up to relocate the college to its new site. Wartime economies meant that much had to be improvised, and huts for accommodation were built in the grounds. In 1940, Keyham and Manadon became one unit.

In 1947, the college was named *Thunderer;* Keyham finally closed in 1958, leaving engineering training to be carried out only at the Royal Naval Engineering College, Manadon. The Keyham building was used by the Devonport Dockyard Technical College from 1959 until demolished in 1985.

Early Days

Lieutenant John Franklin first went to Manadon in 1952 to teach Applied Mechanics. The Wardroom had not yet been built – the foundation stone was laid by Lord Mountbatten in 1956; therefore, accommodation was variously in the old college buildings at Keyham, in temporary huts at Manadon and in Manadon House. The so-called Recreation Block at Manadon provided mess facilities for those in the huts and for mess dinners generally, whilst those at Keyham were self-contained. Manadon House, which was shared with the Captain, was the most sought after, with small separate cabins on the top floor. Travelling up and down the stairs of that elegant house meant passing through the Captain's quarters on the first floor, which must have been a trial for him and his family. The temporary huts faced across the tarmac from the Recreation Block.

The Instructional Block, which was completed in 1951, was where the academic teaching took place, supplemented by practical work in the well-fitted workshops and the three aircraft hangars, one of which was allocated to private work on motor cars and other pursuits. This very valuable facility was both highly educational and also rewarding, coming at a time when car engines could be taken apart and reassembled without specialist equipment. The other valuable facility was the college's airfield at Roborough, a little way out of Plymouth, where useful flying experience could be gained. Of course, on the sports front, there was plenty of opportunity for team sports, golf on Dartmoor, and sailing from the college boathouse where there were three yachts (*Galahad, Gauntlet* and *Gawaine*) and a fleet of dinghies.

Manadon Diploma and the London External Degree

The teaching functions of the college were broadly divided into two: the Directorate of Naval Engineering, headed by a Commander (Engineer), looked after the more equipment-orientated training, while academic education was the province of the Faculty of Engineering, headed by the Dean, an Instructor Captain.

Until the mid-1960s, education and training were very much focused on delivering the minimum to prepare the young officer to perform in his first few complement billets. At this time, the concept of the Chartered Engineer had not been conceived and the professional overlay was that the Manadon product should be acceptable for membership of a professional institute. For fairly obvious reasons, the professional engineering bodies that the college targeted were the Institute of Marine Engineers, the Institution of Electrical Engineers and the Royal Aeronautical Society.

These bodies were satisfied with a two-year academic component and this was, therefore, what most students received. It was, however, recognised that some officers would benefit from a better academic foundation. This was especially true of those who would go on to complete more advanced studies to fit them for design jobs. These officers studied for the London External BSc degree. The college's staff had no input into the setting or marking of the examinations, and it is a tribute to their dedication and professionalism that a very high pass rate was regularly achieved.

Within this framework, there was little external oversight, and the officers on the faculty staff were free to impose intensively taught programmes. The key requirement was to get the students through their examinations, and there was little emphasis on the freedoms associated with more traditional universities; thus, there were very few periods of private study. Another difference was that students did not complete the type of investigative project leading to a dissertation that is so strongly associated with engineering degrees today. Indeed it is one of the main requirements for the Bachelor and Master of Engineering degrees.

This self-contained model of engineering education was about to change forever, despite the reactionary attitudes of some of the older members of the staff.

Royal Naval Engineering College, Manadon in late 1950s
by permission of Kit Reeve

Council for National Academic Awards and the Engineering Council

Many of the polytechnics and technical colleges that had been teaching to the syllabuses of various London External degrees began to demand greater academic independence, so they could develop a wider range of options to attract more students. The upshot of this was the foundation in 1964 by Royal Charter of the Council for National Academic Awards (CNAA). This did not lead to the immediate demise of the London External degree model, but the writing was clearly on the wall. In parallel with this academic development, the engineering institutions were beginning to flex their muscles, and in 1964 the Joint Council of Engineering Institutions was formed to establish common standards for professional engineers. It became the Engineering Council in 1982 and later, had other name changes. Over the past few decades, it has exerted a great influence on the formation of professional engineers, and, despite the name changes, it has effectively controlled the academic component required for recognition as a professional engineer.

The decision was made that all Manadon students should study for a degree awarded under the auspices of the CNAA and that this should be a suitable qualification for professional recognition. The academic leadership to implement these simple-sounding decisions in an organisation as traditional as the Royal Navy should not be underestimated, and it is a tribute to the senior management of the faculty, led by Captain Brin Morgan, that it was accomplished within the necessarily tight timescale.

The CNAA granted the college the right to design its own BSc course in 1966; the last students studying for the London External BSc degree took their final examinations in 1970.

Validation and Accreditation

The academic staff of the college was heavily involved in validation and accreditation, which are often confused in the eyes of those not familiar with the academic development of professional engineers. So, it is probably appropriate to write a few words about them:

- Validation. This is the process by which a degree programme is assessed by the awarding body (in this case the CNAA) to ensure that it is has the academic worth to qualify it to lead to the award of a degree.

- Accreditation. The fact that a course is deemed suitable for the award of a degree does not, of course, mean that the degree is suitable for the development of any particular profession. It is this latter process that is termed accreditation, which is conducted by the professional institutions themselves. In the case of Manadon, it was the Institute of Marine Engineers, the Institution of Electrical Engineers, and the Royal Aeronautical Society. Passage through this procedure was not always smooth, and one early task of Commander Nic Brown, as Director of Studies, was to unscramble the problems resulting from a particularly difficult accreditation visit in 1990.

CNAA Degree for Engineer Officers

Many changes in the way Instructor Officers on the academic staff had to function came about with this degree validated by the CNAA. No longer were they working to a syllabus set by an external body, but they were responsible for designing the syllabus, convincing the validation panel that it was at the correct academic level, and then delivering it in a manner that would also satisfy the CNAA.

Most obvious was the requirement to lighten the instructional load on the students by giving them an adequate provision of private study. This went much against the pre-existing ethos and led to some memorable exchanges between the old and new guards.

Along with forcing this change through, the staff had to adjust to replacing in the final year much of the formal laboratory work with a major individual project. Starting from scratch, this was no simple matter. Good quality project work that delivers a satisfying challenge to the student is usually the by-product of staff research, which was thin on the ground. There were exceptions, such as Commander

George Emmons, who worked on electron spin resonance and Lieutenant Commander Colin George, who investigated ultrasonic fatigue of aluminium alloys; however, these were rare and could not support the necessary number of student projects.

Setting up research could be a challenge, as Lieutenant John McGrath discovered when he was sent for by the Dean and the conversation went something like: 'You've got a PhD, haven't you? Well, I'm told we need some research in the college – just set it up.'

The Instructor Officers working at the college at the time of these changes also had to make the transition from teacher, albeit one operating at an advanced level, to something more approaching the typical university lecturer. This transformation did not happen overnight and was slowed down by the traditional long appointments to the college. The Instructor Specialisation was a broad church and, as well as embracing those who joined because of the opportunity to work at a high academic level, there were those who wanted just the opposite. This necessitated careful selection and career development of officers who were going to fill staff appointments at Manadon.

Royal Naval Engineering College, Manadon in late 1970s
by permission of Kit Reeve

During Captain Henry Morgan's time as the Dean, Commander John Franklin rejoined the College as his deputy. Coming straight from a sabbatical at the Massachusetts Institute of Technology, he set about creating a modular structure for the degree.

Officers who had adopted a selective methodology to passing their own degrees could be caught out on joining Manadon. Nic Brown's 'gulp' moment came on joining Manadon as a second-job Lieutenant and meeting his boss, Commander John Dobson. While at university approaching his finals, he remembers thinking: 'So, it's five out of eight questions, but for me it will be five out of seven, as I am not going to learn about Maxwell's equations, div grad and curl, etc.' Somehow, the strategy worked until he arrived at Manadon, when John Dobson said, 'Nic, I see you are a specialist in radio communications and I'd like you to take on the final honours lecturing for Maxwell's equations, div, grad and curl, etc.' Nic Brown is sure that he was not alone in finding Manadon a very stretching experience intellectually – challenging yet hugely rewarding.

Another officer faced with teaching an alien subject was Lieutenant Commander Mike Barry, who found himself directed to look after statistics. He was mercifully glad of the Edinburgh University short module in that subject in his undergraduate programme.

Royal Naval Engineering College, Manadon – Academic Dinner

In parallel with these changes, during the late 1960s, there was a shift in emphasis from the academic philosophy of the degree to one based on a systems approach to engineering. Two great enthusiasts for this type of approach were Commanders Jack Howard and David Kenner. However, it must have been a difficult balancing act for the Dean to allow them to implement this important change without, at the same time, destroying some of the important traditional aspects of engineering education. This was really innovative and was emulated some years later by a number of universities elsewhere. At Bristol, for example, ex-Manadon IOs Bob Ditchfield and Mike Barry relied heavily on the unit structures concept established at Manadon by John Franklin and others for the 1980 degree.

With the CNAA seeking to develop its validated degrees by adopting best practices across universities, the goalposts could shift between validation visits, so key players among the academic staff needed to keep in touch with the way that body's thinking was evolving. To add to the confusion, the Engineering Council was also continually redefining the academic requirement for registration as a Chartered Engineer. While they set the standard, its interpretation and application were in the hands of the professional institutions to which it had delegated these functions. These institutions all seemed to view the rules differently, and the teams they sent had their own perspectives as well. However, a combination of good preparation in the form of supporting documentation, quick thinking and copious gin and tonic seemed to get the college through these visitations.

One important by-product of these changes was the adoption of a more traditional academic staff structure. This took the form of an Academic Board, chaired by the Dean, and comprised the heads of the academic departments and other key personnel. Not surprisingly, it took time to develop the collegiate *modus operandi* of a traditional university. It is a tribute to the incumbents of the Dean's office early in this process that it moved rapidly from a body deemed necessary by the CNAA to one that genuinely set long-term academic goals and managed the academic resources.

Bachelor Degree for Seaman Officers

In 1988 and 1989, working closely with the CNAA, the Dean, now Captain Colin George, examined a novel way to capitalise on the educational component of the new entry training that Seaman Officers received at Britannia Royal Navy College Dartmouth.

This meant that the young officers would be given academic credit equivalent to one year at university for their time at Dartmouth, leaving just two years of full-time education to be completed at Manadon for the award of a Bachelor's degree in Maritime Defence, Management and Technology. This was a pioneering scheme and the forerunner of a model now common in relationships between higher education and major employers. The major load resulting from this scheme was to fall on the Liberal Studies department. Like most of the others in the faculty, this department had undergone many changes in name. Possibly the most memorable was Complementary Studies, described irreverently by its head, Commander Clive Lewis, by the phrase in general use in Liberal Studies' circles as 'Cultural Sheep-dip'. This was somewhat unfair because the syllabus had evolved to focus on the requirements of the Institutions for the Engineer in Society, tilted a little to those on a naval career.

The Bachelor's degree saw the Liberal Studies department moving from a peripheral position to become one of the core academic departments within the faculty with a far wider subject content in its portfolio. The first few cohorts through the scheme proved both its viability and attractiveness.

Postgraduate Degrees

In 1971, the Advanced Marine Engineering course (AMEC) was transferred from Royal Naval College, Greenwich to Manadon. The potential of this course to meet both the naval needs and the academic criteria for the award of a Master's degree was apparent. Thanks to the efforts of the faculty's staff, led by the Dean, Captain Henry Morgan, appropriate shifts of emphasis were made, and 1976 saw this become a Master of Science (MSc) course. It supplied officers needing deep engineering expertise, especially for appointments in the Ministry of Defence Procurement at Foxhill, Bath, and Abbeywood, Bristol.

It was clear that the college would, in future, be operating at a higher academic level than before, and it became increasingly necessary for successive Deans to ensure a supply of highly qualified officers on the staff. Some of these Instructor Officers would stay at Manadon for very long spells, developing deep expertise in their subjects and providing an essential component of academic stability, without which it would have been difficult to convince validating and accrediting authorities that the college was up to the task of delivering postgraduate degree education. Other Instructor Officers would spend shorter times but return to the college in increasingly senior positions before, possibly, occupying the Dean's chair.

The development of a proper academic structure was an important factor when a completely new postgraduate venture was initiated in 1985. This was the Advanced Marine Defence Technology course (AMDTC), which aimed to give officers of the Weapon Engineering sub-specialisation an MSc qualification equivalent to that earned by their Marine Engineering colleagues on the AMEC. Naturally, this led to Instructor Officers working in the electrical and electronic disciplines, joining their fellows in the mechanical subjects in educating students at the postgraduate level. While bringing a welcome expansion in student numbers, this new course also increased the challenges of providing sufficiently demanding project work in an environment that did not have a strong research base on which to draw. Following start-up, there was a gradual expansion in numbers as the course became more established and its reputation among its customers increased. An agreement was reached with ENSIETA (Ecole Nationale Supériere des Ingénieurs des Etudes et Techniques d'Armement) in Brest, whereby students from Manadon could undertake the project phase of the course in Brest and vice versa. Several exchanges of this type were made. The Royal Military College of Science at Shrivenham saw the real benefit of all of this groundwork when the course later transferred there.

During this period, under the auspices of the CNAA, the academic experience of the staff grew, and visiting validation and accreditation panels found that they faced a much more difficult task imposing arbitrary changes in the face of strong, well-reasoned arguments advanced by an increasingly self-confident faculty. Other evidence of this growing self-confidence can be seen in the way Instructor Officers integrated into the country's higher education structure by belonging to validation panels and steering committees of various degree courses. Nic Brown remembers thinking, 'I have gone in two years from organising elementary literacy training for Royal Marines recruits to being a member of the Engineering Professors' Council for Britain'. At one stage, the heads of the academic departments debated whether to follow the precedent of Royal Naval College, Greenwich in styling its heads of departments as professors, but this proposal was overwhelmingly rejected.

On appointment as Dean, Captain John McGrath recognised that Manadon would only enjoy full academic credibility in universities with engineering faculties if the academic credentials of its staff could be measured. The college was broadly ahead of the field in two of the 'Big Three' areas:

- Teaching – very good.
- Administration – excellent.
- Research – really astern.

While the college was growing in self-confidence, so were the larger polytechnics operating under the CNAA umbrella, whose aim was for total academic freedom. The result of their lobbying was the creation of a new tier of universities, often referred to as the 'polyversities', and the demise of the CNAA in 1992.

Other Courses

In the 1970s, the Royal Naval Engineering College established a one-term Lieutenants' staff course called the Engineering Management course, which ran for six years. This included foreshortened elements of a Master's programme in Management and included a substantial module in statistics, complete with a project that was taught by Mike Barry during his first appointment on the staff.

On the Closure of the CNAA

It was quite clear to the Dean that without rapid action, the college would have been left without any degree-awarding mechanism. It was too small and specialised to bid for degree-awarding powers in its own right. Failure to transfer the validation of its degree programmes to another body would have undone several decades of academic progress, as the only fall-back position would have been reversion to the awarding of a Manadon diploma, which would not have received the necessary accreditation by the professional engineering institutions for its holders to have become Chartered Engineers.

This led to a 'beauty contest' between several universities to determine which should provide the academic top cover for the college. All had their advantages and disadvantages, which were explored by the Academic Board. After a close vote, the Dean was authorised to complete negotiations with the new University of Plymouth. Proximity was not the main determinant in this choice, but rather the opportunity offered for senior members of the faculty staff to sit on the key committees of the university, thus ensuring that Manadon's interests were heard, understood and protected.

Fortunately, there were few changes to be made to transfer to the new awarding body, and the first Manadon students graduated with a degree from Plymouth University in 1996.

Closure of the College

The future of engineering training in the Royal Navy and, therefore, Manadon, had been studied many times in the past. However, by the early-1990s it was decided to close the college in 1996. This affected several entries:

- Those who joined in the 1992 academic year completed their course as planned in 1995.
- Those who joined in the 1993 academic year completed two years at the college and finished their final (third) year at Plymouth University in 1996.

- Those in the 1994 academic year did not go to the college; instead, those 25 officers went on mainly to Southampton University. However, in the September before going to Southampton, they completed the short mathematical shakedown that had been instituted by Mike Barry.

Subsequent university entrants attended Southampton University, where Commander Peter Hadden, a former head of Materials Technology at Manadon, was the Officer-in-Charge of the RN contingent.

Student Project Work

From the inception of the CNAA degree, it was the Instructor Officers who were responsible for finding and supervising a programme of imaginative, challenging and worthwhile student projects. This required setting up and nurturing the links with the naval research establishments. In a climate of some distrust, where some felt that letting Manadon do anything could undermine their viability, this needed real effort and diplomacy on the part of the staff. Some of these collaborations, such as optical signal processing, led to long-running programmes where students from successive cohorts were able to build on the work of their predecessors, in a similar way to a conventional university. Without the traditional resource of research students, staff members learned to use their undergraduate and postgraduate students to further their own research interests. This led to several students having papers published before they graduated and many more seeing their work appear subsequently in print.

Perhaps the greatest vindication of the Manadon educational system came in 1991, when two students got through the regional round of the national competition for Young Electrical Designer Awards to appear in the final at the Science Museum. The Director of Studies, Nic Brown, and the Dean, John McGrath, were there to support their entrants and were stunned when Peter Hoe-Richardson was awarded second place. They thought this was pretty good for such a small place competing with the big boys, but then the unbelievable happened and Steve Brown gained the first prize. The reader is left to imagine the euphoria that followed.

Research

The pioneering efforts of George Emmons and Colin George have already been mentioned, and, as staff turnover brought a different spectrum of officers to the college, the number who pursued active, long-term research programmes grew. On the mechanical side, Lieutenant Commander Graham Reader investigated the Stirling engine, a mantle that he passed on to Lieutenant Commander Gary Hawley. Lieutenant Commander Peter Whelan's research into propeller design led to the offer of a visiting chair at a Canadian University; an offer he was unable to take up. Over on the electronic side, Lieutenant Commander Kit Reeve worked on his optical signal processing. The control fraternity is not to be left out, and Lieutenant Commanders Bob Sutton and Geoff Roberts both pursued an interest in fuzzy logic, not the post-mess dinner variety! These types of research needed strong mathematical and computing support, and this did much to enhance the status of the Mathematics and Computing Department. From this came a massive two-volume work of undergraduate mathematics, authored by Mike Barry. Another support department that entered enthusiastically into research was Materials Technology, and Lieutenant Commander Ken Trethewey was the principal co-author of a textbook on corrosion.

One problem dogged attempts to fund active research programmes, and that was the insistence that any money generated had to go to the Treasury and could not be retained by the college to improve the research environment. When he was the Dean, Colin George was determined to change this situation, and his efforts bore fruit in the form of a mechanism known as 'appropriation in aid'. This enabled his successor to offer researchers the carrot of retaining all the funds they could raise, which they could then use to fund their equipment and travel to conferences to present papers. This was an immediate spur to activity among some of those who saw the potential benefits, resulting in the research income increasing from nothing to a quarter of a million pounds in just three years.

There is little doubt that had the college not been closed, it could have substantially reduced its annual running costs by this mechanism.

Too late in the day, its research potential was recognised by other players and, in 1992, a centre of research excellence was established that linked the Royal Naval Engineering College with Plymouth Polytechnic and the Plymouth Marine Laboratory. In January 1993, a memorandum of understanding was signed in St Petersburg between the college and the Krylov Shipbuilding Research Institute. John McGrath and Commander Paul Gregory represented Manadon during these negotiations.

Perhaps the clearest indication of the quality of the research being conducted by the staff can be seen in the number of Instructor Officers who went on to be awarded chairs at various universities. Bob Whalley probably started the ball rolling at Bradford, followed by Graham Reader at Calgary and Alan Johns at Sussex. Gary Hawley (Bath), Bob Sutton (Plymouth) and Geoff Roberts (Wales) all became professors; many others joined universities as lecturers and senior lecturers.

Non-Degree Education

It is sometimes forgotten that the faculty also provided the academic foundation for the Special Duty Officers before they went to their first jobs as officers. This led to their acceptance as Technician Engineers by the major engineering institutions. A large element of the Manadon course consisted of engineering mathematics with applications specifically dedicated to their sub-specialisations. The mathematical elements, as well as all the others, were subject to rigorous external moderation by the vocational councils.

Raising the Academic Profile Internally

As the training of Engineering Officers moved increasingly into line with that of other engineers, a problem identified by some members of the specialisation was the lack of understanding that the college was a seat of learning as well as a Royal Naval establishment. This was first addressed by the institution of a Degree Ceremony to be held on the same day as the Passing Out Parade and the Summer Ball. Initially, this was quite low key but, as students increasingly came to see it as an important milestone in their careers, it became more formalised and colourful. Nic Brown remembers the Registrar, Lieutenant Commander Bob Moss, describing it as being like organising 400 simultaneous weddings, since it was attended by the graduands' extended families and consisted of a formal ceremony followed by a 'liquid' celebration on a large scale.

An academic mace was designed and manufactured by the staff in the workshops and carried in the academic procession by the Academic Registrar. To emphasise this component of the college's life, an Academic Dinner was introduced and held a few days before the graduation. Senior members of the faculty attended the dinner where the rig was black tie and academic dress; the dinner was discontinued during Captain Brian Leavey's time as Dean.

Graduation Day was special and became better and better. In 1983, the Queen came and awarded the degrees, perhaps the one and only time she has done this during her long reign. Princess Anne came in 1989 and later wandered through the throng outside the Wardroom in the hot summer afternoon. On meeting Mike Barry and his guest, Professor Sir Hermann Bondi, she asked what they were talking about. When Hermann Bondi replied, 'Mathematics', she told them with some delight that she'd never needed to learn any mathematics.

Cultural and Sporting Contributions

Outside their formal duties, Instructor Officers were important in developing and maintaining strong cultural and sporting traditions. The cultural activity that springs to mind is drama, where officers contributed towards both the productions and their performance. Philip d'Authreau will be remembered as a talented and dedicated producer who was able to stage complex and demanding material in a way that made it enjoyable and accessible. There was also a deep seam of acting talent. Mike Barry's performance of the blind father in 'Voyage around my Father' was absolutely outstanding. This talent in the college achieved many successes in the RN Drama Festival.

On the musical scene, Commander Quintin Des Clayes was noted for his performances as a flautist and Lieutenant Commander David Way as the leader of an impressive string quartet. These two, along with many others, contributed to the very popular Musical Evenings in the Wardroom. Musical talent was varied with Graham Reader and Ken Trethewey running a high-quality pop band called 'Funktion', which played at the college and at charitable events elsewhere. The formation of the Manadon Volunteer Band gave another opportunity for Instructor Officers to shine both as performers and, in the administrative role, as Band Officers. Commander Laurie Redstone and Lieutenant Commander John Davies filled both these roles with distinction. This was another area of competitive success, with the Manadon band regularly winning prizes at the Volunteer Band Festival.

Current affairs were not neglected either. In 1975, Commander Bob Ditchfield established the Fisher Society as an after-dinner seminar in defence and related studies. After his departure, members of the Liberal Studies Department ran the society and they secured a succession of distinguished speakers. Lively debates followed these talks, and many benefited from hearing and discussing the views of prominent people enticed to Manadon.

Royal Naval Engineering College, Manadon – Graduation Tea

Sport was another activity where Instructor Officers made a great contribution. The long-term continuity of the faculty staff meant that they were able to develop on-going coaching programmes. Among the sporting luminaries were rugby internationals Alan Meredith, who was capped for Wales, and Brian Vaughan, capped for England. John McGrath competed for Wales at fencing in the 1970 Commonwealth Games and Alec Wallace played hockey for Scotland. Other activities in which Instructor Officers played prominent roles were the Dartmoor Mountain Rescue Team and Plymouth sailing.

Manadon Closure and the Effects on the Specialisation

The final Graduation Ceremony took place in July 1995. The closure of Manadon had a major impact on the Instructor Specialisation by reducing the upper academic level at which its officers operated and curtailing the rigour of academic thinking and challenge available to them. Also, at one stroke, the requirement for one captain, eight commanders and a large number of lieutenant commanders and lieutenants was eliminated.

This may well have been one of the most important causes of the demise of the Specialisation.

The Instructor Officers who held the role of Dean of the Royal Naval Engineering College, Manadon are listed in Annex 5.

SERVICE AND DOCKYARD SCHOOLS AND COLLEGES

Alan Robertson and Bob Hutchings

Service Schools

Until the Service Children's Education Authority (SCEA) was established in 1969, schools for the children of service families in overseas bases were established and administered by the three Services separately. Later, from 1969 and under SCEA, the schools were administered by the Service having the largest presence in the command area.

There were Royal Naval Children's Schools in Malta, in Singapore, at Johore Bahru, and in Mauritius; and Naval and Dockyard children were taught in the Dockyard Technical Colleges in Gibraltar and Bermuda. Up to 1947, the headmasters of these schools were Naval Schoolmasters; later they were Instructor Officers, and these appointments were some of the most interesting and rewarding appointments undertaken by officers of the branch. The teaching staff were mostly UK qualified teachers on three-year contracts, and many opted to renew their contracts. Other teachers were recruited locally, mainly from Service wives, from the wives of Dockyard employees, or other UK qualified teachers living in the area. They were invaluable, especially in helping the schools to cope when numbers were rising rapidly, largely unpredictable, and as there was an inevitable and substantial time lag before extra teachers could be recruited from the UK.

Gibraltar did not have a Naval Children's School as such, and the children of naval parents and dockyard employees were taught in the Technical and Dockyard School. This was closely associated for a time with the children's education of Gibraltar and later became the Gibraltar and Dockyard Technical College.

The Regulations for Service Children's Schools stated that the education provided was to make up for the loss caused by absence from the educational system of the homeland and, from 1944 for UK children, would conform in type and scope to that provided in England and Wales under the Education Act of 1944. In what they provided, the RN Schools far exceeded these basic requirements and in doing so acquired a high and widely accepted reputation.

This account of the part played by Schoolmaster Officers and Instructor Officers in the work of these schools would not be complete without acknowledging the involvement of many of their wives and other locally entered staff. These undertook salaried posts at local rates, as teachers, secretaries, school nurses and coach escorts; whilst other unpaid volunteers organised innumerable extramural activities enjoyed by the children. The smooth and productive running of the schools owed much to this additional assistance.

Mention should be made of the arrangements for teaching the sons and daughters of the Royal Marines in England. As early as 1784, the Master of the Royal Marines School in Plymouth was appointed, responsible for the education of the sons of NCOs and marines; in 1820, a Royal Marines school for girls was opened.

By 1908, there were separate schools for boys, girls and infants at each of Eastney, Chatham, Gosport, Plymouth and Deal staffed by 23 Royal Marines Schoolmasters and head teachers plus their assistants.

Royal Naval Schools Malta

An article in The Malta Times of 19 October 1858 stated that, 'Arrangements had been made by the Lords Commissioners of the Admiralty for the establishment of a school in Malta for the use of children (boys and girls) of all persons employed in Her Majesty's Dockyard and Naval Establishments in this Island, and an afternoon and evening school for apprentices. An excellent schoolmaster, Mr Sullivan, has been appointed and has already arrived from England, and the school is to be opened on the first of November next. The method of education was to be that adopted by the National Society in their schools and by Her Majesty's Dockyards at home, as nearly as found practicable. The office of examiner will be performed by the Naval Instructor of the Flagship, or the Senior Naval Instructor present.'

The school was originally sited near the Chapel by the Sail Loft in Cospicua, but in 1880, was in a building just inside the Dockyard main gate. In those days, there were few naval families in Malta and the children in the school were mostly Maltese or Anglo-Maltese. They were taught so well that many won their way to good positions in the professions or in Government Offices. By 1904, the school had outgrown its room in the Dockyard and moved to an old prison in Senglea where the number of children (aged 5-14) grew steadily to about 250. The headmaster and his deputy were Naval Schoolmasters; one was Schoolmaster M W Candey who joined the staff in 1902 and was later the headmaster until 1918. His daughter, Miss Lilian Candey, also taught at the school from 1949 for 17 years.

Old records show that up to 1918, most of the children entering the school were Maltese, but from that time the proportion of English children grew appreciably and as their numbers increased, the character of the school changed. By 1925, the school had ceased to cater for the children of locally entered dockyard employees and an 'Oxford Junior' class appears in the records for the first time.

By 1929, there were too many children for the Senglea building and the school moved to Verdala. The records show that in 1932 there were 150 boys and 70 girls in the school. By 1938, there were 530 in three classes of infants, five classes of juniors, and six classes of secondary. On the outbreak of war in 1939, all British wives and their children were evacuated progressively from Malta and, though the school struggled on in yet another home in St George's Barracks, it closed completely in September 1942.

After the war, RN and Dockyard families began to return to Malta and the school was re-opened in May 1946 with 55 children in two requisitioned houses in Ta'Xbiex, and was run by two Instructor Officers and their wives. It very quickly outgrew the accommodation at Ta'Xbiex and in January 1947, as the Dockyard School (Children's Section), moved to a disused Army Barracks at Tal Handaq. The headmaster's report for 1948 said that no more children could be crammed into Tal Handaq; in 1949, when the old school at Verdala was repaired after serious war damage, the transfer of infants and juniors from Tal Handaq to Verdala began. This transfer was not completed until 1956.

Tal Handaq was the secondary school for the children of all three Services and Commander Arthur Miles, who had been on the staff at Verdala before the war and re-opened the school in Ta'Biex, became its first headmaster.

Arthur Miles escorting Princess Elizabeth around the school at Tal Handaq in 1949
by permission of Patricia Bingham

A few other Instructor Officers were appointed to teach mathematics and science, as it was always difficult to recruit civilians to teach these subjects. Commander John Bellamy took over as headmaster in 1951, followed by Commander Brin Morgan in 1954, and during these years, the number of children continued to increase. The school's record year for growth was 1952 when the total at Tal Handaq and Verdala increased by 300 to 1470. During the summer holidays throughout the 1950s, the builders moved in and there was always a frantic race against time to provide the extra classrooms and other facilities needed for the increased numbers expected in September. This was not always achieved and occasionally at Tal Handaq, there were a few 'floating classes' with no rooms of their own. By 1960, there were 1050 pupils at Tal Handaq and 1200 at Verdala and in 1956, the increased responsibilities of the headmaster were recognised and his post became an Instructor Captain's appointment. At the same time, his deputy was recognised as headmaster of Verdala and his post there upgraded to that of Commander, though he continued to be responsible to the headmaster of Tal Handaq. In the 1960s, after the closure of the dockyard and the Services began to withdraw from Malta, numbers started to decline, but never as fast as predicted and in late 1966, there were still nearly 900 pupils at Tal Handaq. Up to 1971, they were still between 700 and 800.

When the Services Children's Education Authority was formed in 1969, the headmaster of Tal Handaq, Captain Henry Malkin, became Officer in Charge of all the Service Children's Schools in Malta, Naples and Tripoli. This post continued to be held by Instructor Captains until the Services Schools in Malta were finally closed in 1979. He was replaced as headmaster at Tal Handaq in January 1970 by Commander Mike Law, and the name of the school was changed from Royal Naval School to Service Children's School. Fortunately, as Mike Law had served in the school before, these changes had comparatively little effect on the running of Tal Handaq.

Things changed dramatically when during the Christmas Holiday 1971, a few days before the new term was due to start, it was announced that all Service dependants were to leave Malta within two weeks and that the schools would not reopen. This is not the place to go into detail, but the effects of this change were little short of catastrophic and are left to the reader's imagination. Staff, pupils and equipment were returned and dispersed to all parts of the UK and the schools were reduced to empty shells.

Even more extraordinary, in September 1972, the schools were reopened, somewhat reduced in size and with about 50% new staff and 75% new pupils. Numbers reached 600 by September 1973 and stayed about this level until early 1977. As part of the planned rundown between 1972 and 1979, Verdala was closed in July 1976 when the remaining staff and children went to the former Army and RAF Schools at St Andrew and Luqa until the rundown was completed in 1979.

Royal Naval Schools Singapore and Johore Bahru

Qualified teachers made the first attempts at children's education in the Naval Base, Singapore in 1948 from the families who were based there. They took small numbers of children into private homes and charged fees. Shortly after that, in 1950–51, a RN Children's School was established with 200 children and a staff of six. Lieutenant Commander A W Singleton was largely responsible for its organisation in the early stages. As more families arrived to accompany service personnel, school numbers increased, and more classroom blocks were built.

An ex-Japanese sail loft was converted into an assembly hall that, with the classroom blocks, enclosed a wide grassy space used for all outdoor activities. The buildings themselves were spacious and airy, and the overall appearance of the School, which was situated among grass and trees, was most attractive.

An Instructor Commander was the head of the school that consisted of junior and infant departments, overseen by a deputy headmaster and deputy headmistress respectively.

Royal Naval School Singapore – main administration building in 1960s

The Malaysian/Indonesian confrontation, which started in 1962, led to an increase in the number of children of RN and RM families. As a result, the enrolment peaked at 1,488 children in 1966, making it the largest primary school in the Commonwealth; at that time, the head was Commander Maurice Johnson who served in that role from 1965 to 1968. The standard of education provided at the school was confirmed by the very favourable comments received at the school in a note following an inspection by Her Majesty's Inspectors from the UK in 1968.

The increased pressure on all aspects of the school led to the establishment of a new primary school in Johore Bahru, which took all the children living on that side of the Singapore/Malaysian causeway. This school was opened in 1966 by Lieutenant Commander Dermot Dorrian, relieved at the end of his appointment by Lieutenant Commander Bert Kinsey. The teaching staff of the RN School Singapore normally numbered about forty, both seconded and locally entered, so some key staff had to be transferred to Johore Bahru to form the basis of the staff at that school.

As a result of the opening of the new school at Johore Bahru, the number in school in Singapore fell to about 1,000.

Withdrawal of British forces from the Far East meant widespread closures. By 1971, the number of children in the RN School had fallen to 700 and the UK teaching staff began returning. Commander Alan Robertson, the last head, had the sad task of closing the school and disposing of its furniture and equipment, an undertaking that was being repeated in Johore Bahru.

The reduction in size of the school in the later stages enabled it to be a good neighbour on two occasions. In the first case, when Commander David Fowke was its head, the Dockyard Technical School was removed to make space for the building of the new dry dock and the RN School was able to provide classrooms for David Fowke's apprentices. Adjustments to timetables meant that apprentices and children's activities did not coincide and the system worked well.

Royal Naval School Singapore – the staff in 1967 led by Alan Robertson

On the second occasion, when the ANZAC forces began to take over the naval base from the British, their education authorities were preparing to take over the RN school buildings. They wished to establish an advance party of some key teaching staff and classes before the main party of their school arrived. Once again classroom blocks were made available. For a term, the British element leaving and the incoming ANZAC group ran in parallel and a very good relationship developed. It was good to know that the school was stirring again.

Royal Naval School Mauritius

In 1915, a RN wireless station was installed on the island of Mauritius, 600 miles east of Madagascar, and this wireless station became an important part of the Royal Navy's worldwide communications network.

After the Second World War, the arrival of naval families meant that it was necessary to establish a school for children of ages from 5 to 13, and so an RN school was opened in 1961. Initially, there were 35 children with an Instructor Officer, Lieutenant Commander Richard Wood, the headmaster and

Station Instructor Officer. He and his successors were responsible both for the school and the educational requirements of the ship's company.

The number of children in infant and junior classes grew to over 100 and there were around 14 of secondary age. There were no other secondary age opportunities for boys on the island, although girls could be accepted into Queen Elizabeth College, the local Girls' Grammar School.

Royal Naval School Mauritius – in the early 1960s

The RN school's UK staff consisted of one man and three women teachers, with the headmaster taking the secondary class. The school itself was in an attractive, wooden single-storey building and the classrooms were surrounded by a wide, covered verandah. It had once been the headquarters of the Army garrison, which left when the Royal Navy took over.

Few schools can claim to have a bishop as its visiting Chaplain, but the school enjoyed this honour. The Bishop of Mauritius, Alan Rogers, a good friend of the school, visited weekly to take the senior classes for religious instruction. In 1965, the Archbishop of Canterbury, Michael Ramsay, included Mauritius in his tour of the Far East region and honoured the school by visiting classrooms, meeting staff and blessing the children gathered in the hall. Later, on a similar tour, Lady Baden-Powell visited the school's scouts and guides.

Until achieving independence in 1968, Mauritius was a Crown Colony and the Governor from 1962 until 1968 was His Excellency Sir John Rennie. He really enjoyed watching films but, by reason of his status, could never visit a public cinema. He was always pleased, therefore, to be invited with Lady Rennie to Sunday evening suppers and films in the Wardroom.

When television was first introduced into Mauritius, the siting of the transmitting aerials meant that all but one of the country's regions could receive programmes. The last one, however, required the aerial to be sited on a peak to which the necessary equipment could not be carried and it was decided that programmes would not begin until the whole network could receive them. The Royal Navy came to the rescue when a frigate called at Port Louis. Her helicopter lifted the gear to the site and, when installed, the island's network opened.

Alan Robertson taking Archbishop Michael Ramsey around the school in 1965

And then there were cyclones. Mauritius is situated in the area in which the northern Indian Ocean cyclones curve southerly; from January until early April, the island is at risk. Near misses bring lowering clouds, high winds, rough seas and heavy rain, but once or twice every few years a cyclone hits with winds of 100 to 120 mph and torrential rain, causing considerable damage to property and crops. The RN's communication aerials on the base needed protection, but structural damage to its comparatively well-built property was generally not too serious. Life on the base was affected in many ways during this weather. Local personnel and others who could be spared from duty returned home. The school had to be closed for one or two days at the worst of each storm.

However, the climate for the rest of the year was delightful, the scenery and beaches were beautiful, and having the opportunity to run an excellent school made Mauritius a most enjoyable appointment for an Instructor Officer.

The School finally closed in 1976 when the RN Communications Station shut down.

Finally, the following text relates to the RN School in Singapore, but it probably represents the general standard of RN Schools overseas. This is the concluding statement by Her Majesty's Inspectors after a visit:

> 'This is a school in which people care for children; care thoughtful, but unsentimental, is seen in every aspect of the life of the school and this provides an atmosphere for children to grow and develop, to prepare for life, yet be happy as children, to work together, yet find themselves as individuals, to experience maturity within the security of order. By any standard this is a first-rate school and, if all primary schools in England were of this calibre, the Plowdon Committee would have few recommendations to make.'

Dockyard Schools and Colleges

In 1841, the Board of Admiralty considered a proposal to build schools in the dockyards, and the following year the decision to proceed was taken in order to *'secure the benefits of both a religious and a professional education to the apprentices'*. The schools were to be supervised by a Committee consisting of the Admiral Superintendent, the Master Shipwright, the Chaplain and any other officer interested in education.

The foundation of the Royal Dockyard Schools was approved by an Order in Council dated 1 February 1843. The first establishments were set up at Chatham, Portsmouth and Pembroke in 1843, at Sheerness in 1844, at Devonport in 1845 and later at Deptford, Woolwich, and Rosyth. The staff consisted of subordinate Dockyard Officers and the clerical staff, in addition to their normal tasks, carried out their teaching duties for the sum of £70 to £100 per annum, plus an allowance for fuel and candles!

It is worth remembering that education in England in the mid-19th Century was available only to those who could pay for it. With that in mind, the academic opportunity provided for apprentices, where no boy was excluded by lack of means, pre-empted by many years, the introduction of mandatory education for all children. The dearth of education for the general population was also underlined when one views the Dockyard School syllabus at the time: arithmetic, grammar, dictation, writing, geography and history, scripture and each day commencing with prayers! The academics were complemented by the various practical skills gained in the dockyard.

Over the following 100 years, the schools developed their curriculum and levels of academic challenge to a point where the completion of four years in the upper school was assessed to be equivalent to at least a Third Class Honours degree in Engineering. Unfortunately, academic awards could not be made, but achievements by apprentices were fully recognized by other organisations including Kings College, the University of Durham and the Professional Engineering Institutions.

In 1952, the Royal Dockyard Schools were re-titled Royal Dockyard Technical Colleges. However, with the development of local Further Education colleges throughout the country, the education of apprentices was transferred to Local Education Authorities in 1970.

Their Administration

The Admiralty, through a local Admiral Superintendent, administered the dockyards overall. The heads or principals of the schools and colleges were accountable to a designated Department of the Admiralty; from 1936, this was the Director of the Education Department and from 1951, the Director of the Naval Education Service.

In 1965, the Director of the Naval Education Service, Rear Admiral John Bellamy, was to see the demise of the dockyard colleges at home, in Singapore and Malta during his term of office. Gibraltar's closure in 1984 marked the end of a system of Further Education that began some 141 years previously.

Dockyard Schools and Colleges and Instructor Officers

The intention here is simply to highlight the role of Instructor Officers in staffing the dockyard schools and colleges in Bermuda, Singapore, Malta and Gibraltar, rather than provide a comprehensive history of the development of dockyard apprentice education overseas.

Although dockyards operated in Hong Kong and Mauritius, no evidence can be found of the existence of apprentice training and education facilities.

In the case of the dockyard in South Africa at Simon's Town, which was established in around 1884, a school for apprentices existed before the First World War. It seems, however, that Trade Officers rather than permanently appointed teachers provided the staffing. After the Second World War, lecturers were recruited from the Cape Technical College. In 1953, one of these lecturers was S C (Chips) Biermann, who later joined the South African Navy (Instructor Branch) and retired as a Rear Admiral.

Bermuda – HMS Malabar

The Bermuda Dockyard initially consisted of a large floating dock that was towed across the Atlantic in 1869.

The Bermuda Government archives contain a couple of volumes of dockyard records. The building which was used as the school was vandalized after closure and this, together with the climatic conditions, decimated any records remaining.

In 1950, the dockyard school was closed and the last 49 apprentices were transferred to the UK dockyards to complete their studies. The penultimate Senior Master, Harry Middleton, became the Colonial Archivist in Bermuda after retiring from the Royal Navy.

The Senior Masters who headed the Dockyard School can be found in Annex 9.

HMS *Malabar* – showing Ireland Island and the north harbour circa 1930

Singapore – HMS Terror

The Singapore Dockyard and Naval Base developed during the 1920s, but finally opened for business in February 1938.

The opening ceremony was conducted by the then Governor of Singapore, Sir Shenton Thomas, who in 1942 was imprisoned by the Japanese in Changi Prison for three years, having refused to leave Singapore.

The dockyard college began in the early 1950s and provided the academic education to support the practical training of the dockyard apprentices, who were mainly Chinese, a few Malays and some sons of UK personnel from the naval base.

HMS *Victorious* departing Singapore Dockyard in 1961
by permission of the Fleet Air Arm Museum

In the early 1960s, over 100 apprentices started training each year, studying mathematics, mechanics, science, engineering drawing and English. They spent two or three days a week in the college and the remainder of the week on practical training in the dockyard. The apprenticeship took four years and their final examinations were set and marked by the City and Guilds Board in the UK, which qualified them for a National Certificate equivalent.

The staff in the college consisted of the principal, who was an Instructor Officer, and five civilian teachers from the UK on three-year contracts.

The UK decided to withdraw from Singapore in 1970, with the dockyard being handed over to the Singapore government. They had engaged Swan Hunter to adapt the dockyard for commercial use and one early decision was that a new dry dock should be built in an area on which the college stood. Fortunately, arrangements could be made with the headmaster of the Service school in the dockyard, Commander Alan Robertson, to use some classrooms to continue providing support to the final apprentices in the pipeline, because the work on the new dry dock began before the college was planned to close.

The life of the college had been relatively short, as it was formally shut down in 1970. Therefore, much of the laboratory and classroom equipment was sent to the Gibraltar Technical College, which was to remain open for several more years.

The Instructor Officers fulfilling the roll of principal can be found in Annex 9

Malta – HMS St Angelo

The story of Malta as an RN ship-repair centre goes back to the mid-19th Century with the building of the first graving dock in 1848, followed by another in 1871.

By 1900, a total of four dry docks were in operation. Undoubtedly, in those early days, the skilled workforce consisted mainly of civilians from the UK and naval engineering personnel.

The school was housed in an old section of the bastion at the city of Senglea overlooking Grand Harbour. In 1948, the Equal Opportunity Scheme was introduced whereby boys who performed well academically during three years in the dockyard school had the opportunity to be transferred to a dockyard school or college in the UK to complete their training and education.

The school in Malta finally closed its doors in the 1960s when the dockyard was privatised.

The officers responsible for the school, then college, from 1936 until closure can be found in Annex 9.

HMS *St Angelo* and Grand Harbour in 1960s
by permission of NMRN

Gibraltar – HMS Cormorant then HMS Rooke

The long-established army garrison in Gibraltar had led to the establishment of Army schools. Then work on the naval dockyard began in 1895 and by 1911, the dockyard had its own school.

The school was established under the headship of Mr W J B Hore to provide an education on a part-time basis for local apprentices to complement the practical trade training received in the dockyard.

This system continued until 1949, when a new Dockyard and Technical School opened as a joint venture between the Admiralty and the Gibraltar Government. This provided for both secondary and further education to be conducted under the same roof, staffed by the same teachers. In essence, the school had two distinct departments: one to provide a grammar school type of education for 12 to 14 year olds and the other to deliver technical education for day-release apprentices. The students included boys from the families of UK personnel.

Gibraltar Dockyard with the combined Fleets visiting in the 1930s
by permission of NMRN

By 1960, the numbers had increased and the head was an Instructor Commander with an Instructor Lieutenant Commander as his deputy. The school operated closely alongside the Gibraltar Government secondary age educational framework, but by the 1960s, there was a desire generally in the education world for a revision of the whole secondary school system. Arising from this was a recommendation that the school should be detached from the main school system. There would be no further intake of school-age pupils, although those already enrolled would be allowed to complete their courses and the school would be renamed the Gibraltar and Dockyard Technical College.

The change to a college occurred in 1964 when Commander Paul Stanley was the head, and he thus became the first principal of the new college, dedicated to providing technical education for dockyard apprentices. The staff included a number of Instructor Officers over the years that followed until, in the 1980s, all the lecturing staff were civilian, mainly Gibraltarian ex-apprentices, save for the principal's post, which was filled by a Commander.

The last RN principal of the college, from 1982 to 1984, was Commander Bob Hutchings who handed the college over to the Gibraltar Education Department. He returned to Gibraltar in 1986 as Officer-in-Charge, Service Schools, under SCEA (Service Children's Education Authority).

The details of the heads of the school and college can be found in Annex 9.

Gibraltar in 1962
by permission of the Fleet Air Arm Museum

WORK STUDY AND MANAGEMENT SERVICES

Mike Moreland and Stewart Burrows

In 1957, through contacts with the company ICI, Lord Mountbatten, then First Sea Lord, was the inspiration behind Work Study in the Royal Navy.

About 50 officers and 50 senior ratings of all branches and specialisations received training to form the headquarters organisation under the Fourth Sea Lord, later Chief of Fleet Support, and 18 teams to operate under various Naval Commands.

An Instructor Officer, Captain 'Steve' Stevenson was one of the initial members and was appointed Deputy Director Fleet Work Study. Another Instructor Officer was Lieutenant Commander Philip d'Authreau whose initial practical field study, arranged outside the Service, covered the sterilisation of hypodermic syringes and needles at Guy's Hospital. The outcome of the study showed that it would be cheaper to introduce disposable needles, which would also give a gain in clinical hygiene. This was accepted at Guy's and may have been a major factor in the practice of disposable needles spreading throughout the National Health Service.

Other early studies included catering in shore establishments. Trials of self-service and multiple-choice proved very popular with sailors; far less food went into the swill-bin and money was saved. The principles were soon adopted throughout the Service. A study of admission procedures to hospital revealed that it was far simpler to be admitted than to be returned to a unit after treatment!

The common day-to-day naval processes were soon covered and, before long, more complex and larger scale processes were studied. For example, in studying a ship refit and questioning 'Where else could it be done?' the answers became clouded by political issues, but the seed was sown that only one major dockyard was required to meet the needs of the Royal Navy. Such studies were often difficult, with some senior officers providing entrenched opposition to change, whilst a minority gave terrific encouragement and support. One establishment Captain had received objections from MOD about work study proposals concerning operations at his base. He had supported the work study proposals and wanted to reply strongly to MOD. He asked the Fleet Work Study team leader to draft a reply and said, 'Go and dip your pen in vitriol!'

Steve Stevenson played a major part in the study of engineering maintenance. Eventually, this lead to the formation of the Naval Maintenance Unit staffed by a few officers and about 20 senior technical ratings with Work Study experience. This unit created job cards for routine maintenance tasks, specifying what was to be done, the skill, tools and equipment required, and the time that should be allocated. Standard planning systems were also produced for various classes of ships. In 1967, the unit commenced its enormous task and was eventually out-sourced by the MOD as a civilian unit under Steve Stevenson.

Fleet Work Study had obviously become involved in 'Management' and the organisation was renamed Directorate of Fleet Work Study and Management Services (DFWMS). Commander Mike Moreland, who joined the organisation in 1961, was promoted to succeed Steve Stevenson as Deputy Director in 1966, and from 1967 to 1970, he became the Director.

Part of his experience in Work Study was in the Ship Department, where they had gained the reputation as 'the team that de-angled the angled flight deck'. Although the design of the particular carrier was delayed, the change would have allowed about a 30% increased capability of operating aircraft. The proposals were effected in later designs.

With the support of Director General Ships, a work study approach to design problems led to short courses being given to Naval Constructors and other design personnel. The idea was to establish the true needs and circumstances of a design problem, rather than first looking at what was done last time and wondering if any changes might be necessary. This was bound to lead to designers challenging aspects of Naval Staff Requirements.

During one of these courses, the question arose, 'Where should the derricks be placed in a new RFA class?' This resulted in a study of principle rather than detail, owing to the vast number of factors involved, but bearing in mind the operational need for safe and fast replenishment of ships at sea. Some members of the work study team had experience of the difficulties of keeping a small ship alongside a larger ship at sea, because of the difference in lateral pressures caused through the hulls movement through the ocean. However, parallel courses were relatively easy to maintain if the neutral points of pressure of both hulls were kept abeam. These neutral points were usually between one-third and halfway down the lengths of the ships from their stems. Hence the simple principle evolved that the major derricks for RFAs and reception points in fighting ships, particularly for fuel, should be as close as possible to the neutral pressure points. It has been satisfying to note that present RFAs appear to conform to this principle.

In discussion between them, the Chief of Fleet Support agreed that control of DFWMS should pass to Vice Chief of the Naval Staff and this took place in 1969. One outcome was that DFWMS was co-opted to assist the working party, under the then Rear Admiral Lewin, with problems being met in introducing the Principal Warfare Officer concept into Ops Rooms in ships. Management in a naval ship always had been more complex than in any other service or in industry where the basic general principle was that each employee should only have one boss. A ship operates in various modes, for example fighting, moving or maintenance, or often a combination of these. Then on top of these, there is watchkeeping. A sailor might have several functional bosses or managers during a working day depending on the ship's operating modes during that day. The authority of each functional manager would have to be clearly defined and understood, and known by the particular crew over whom they had temporary control. The role of the Divisional Officer for each individual sailor would become even more important. Explicit job instructions would be required. The introduction of Warfare Officers, changes in Seaman Specialisation and the reorganisation of training through the study CONSTRAIN (Concentration of Naval Training) all followed.

Commander Paul Stanley was the Staff Officer-in-Charge of CINCFLEET's Work Study Team at the time and this team had an input. The final outcome of CONSTRAIN led to such things as the closures of *Mercury* and *Dryad,* and the transfer of many training activities to *Excellent*, including RNSETT, *Collingwood* taking over much of *Dryad's* work and becoming the School of Maritime Warfare.

About this time, the responsibility for the management of Training was passed from DGNT to Commander in Chief, Naval Home Command and this formed the *raison d'etre* for this new Command. On leaving the post of DFWMS in 1970, Mike Moreland was appointed to the Command Staff as Deputy Chief Staff Officer Training replacing Captain Monty Waller who had been Command Instructor Officer to the Commander in Chief, Portsmouth. Much to the consternation of DNEdS, many of the traditional CIO duties were passed to Commander John Taylor as the Command's Chief Education Officer.

There had been many developments in management techniques and philosophy. In 1966, Steve Stevenson had advised Mike Moreland that it would be a good idea to liaise with the British Institute of Management. The eventual result of this was that Mike Moreland was invited to be the Services representative on the British Institute of Management Membership Committee. This provided a ready means of keeping abreast of management developments in industry and public bodies and comparing notes with their representatives; this lasted from 1967 until 1973. Co-incidentally in 1973, Vice Admiral Sir Terence Lewin, who was by that time VCNS, was invited to accept Fellowship of the British Institute of Management.

A further recognition of an increasing focus on management came with the change of title from Fleet Work Study and Management Services to Naval Management and Organisation (DNMO). An Electrical Captain was first in the post and he was relieved by Captain Paul Stanley. DNMO was one of the Directors on the Naval Staff and was accountable to VCNS. During Paul Stanley's tenure, a Book of Reference (BR 32) was initiated, entitled 'Management in the Royal Navy'.

Paul Stanley was relieved by an Electrical Captain followed by Captains Stewart Burrows and Graham Davis.

Another IO, Commander Geoff Greenhalgh, was Officer-in-Charge of FOSM's Work Study Team at that time.

INFORMATION SYSTEMS

Richard Yeomans

In the mid-1960s, computers were large, cumbersome and expensive machines which were not always reliable and required special temperature and humidity controlled environments, and their use was not very widespread.

Early on, Instructor Officers became involved in the development of these systems where they worked in teams building ship-borne systems, national and NATO command and control systems, operational simulators and trainers. Others were to work on software development in highly-classified areas and in scientific systems such as meteorology and oceanographic forecasting.

Operational Systems

The use of computers to automate the Ops Rooms, the input from sensors and the control of weapon systems in ships, led to the early and significant involvement of Instructor Officers in Operational Systems.

Action Information Systems for the Surface Fleet

By the mid-1950s, it was apparent that supersonic aircraft could overload the operators in the Ops Room who had to deal entirely manually with plotting the air, surface and sub-surface pictures whilst maintaining a huge number of state boards and other information.

The first automation was provided by a Comprehensive Display System (CDS), fitted to the carriers *Hermes* and *Victorious*, but this system was only semi-automatic, requiring operators to input radar data for the air picture and it did not cater for the sub-surface picture. These analogue computers provided assistance with air intercepts and many of the manual state boards in the Ops Room and Air Direction Room were replaced with automatic versions.

With computers becoming relatively smaller and more reliable in the 1960s, the Royal Navy decided to apply computers to the Action Information Systems in ships; the generic name for these systems was Action Data Automation and Weapons Systems (ADAWS). Over the next decades, several classes of ship were fitted with an automated system in the Ops Room, each with a different identification. MOD decided not to fit ADAWS systems into some classes of ships and development started on a smaller, simpler and less costly system called Computer Assisted Action Information System (CAAIS).

The user requirements for these systems were specified by officers in the ADA Rule-Writing Group (ARWG), run by a Commander and with officers from all the warfare specialisations including Instructor Officers. The Group was co-located with the procurement project teams at the Admiralty Surface Weapons Establishment (ASWE) Portsmouth and was later to become the Naval Operational and Command Systems Group headed by a Captain.

Eagle re-commissioned in early 1964 and was fitted with a computer system DAA for the Ops Room. Lieutenant Commander 'Boy' Downer was heavily involved in the development work in ASWE and in setting the system to work in the ship. He was joined for the trials by Lieutenant Commander Tom Berry, who was to spend the rest of his naval career in the development of national and NATO operational systems.

There were eight County class guided-missile destroyers. The first four were fitted with the older CDS, but the second batch of *Fife, Glamorgan, Antrim* and *Norfolk* were fitted with ADAWS1 and computer outfit DAB. In the later stages of development, Lieutenant Commanders Bill Norrie and Tom Berry became members of the project team and went to sea in 1966 for the trials in *Fife* and *Glamorgan* respectively, staying until about halfway through the first commission.

It was decided at that time that a limited number of IOs needed to be operationally experienced and have the necessary technical expertise to be deeply involved in the development of the systems. As a result three IOs, Lieutenants Bob Ayres, Richard Yeomans and Patrick Binks were sent on the specialist Seaman Officers' long course for Direction Officers – those officers who worked at the centre of the ship's Action Information Organisation. At the end of their courses, each went off to sea to gain practical operational experience in a ship before becoming members of the ASWE development project teams. Bob Ayres went to *Fife* on trials in 1966, Richard Yeomans to *Eagle* in 1967 and then to *Glamorgan*, and Patrick Binks joined *Eagle* and briefly *Glamorgan* in the Far East in 1971.

Richard Yeomans was in *Glamorgan* during a major exercise where the strengths and weaknesses of ADAWS1 were clearly shown, a 'Get Well Programme' was initiated and he was appointed to ASWE Portsdown as a member of the project team. After a considerable effort, the improvements were installed in ships in 1972 after successful trials. Richard Yeomans was relieved by Patrick Binks and during his appointment, the major enhancement to ADAWS1 was to implement data links, whereby information could be transferred between the computers of ships over a wide area.

For the computers fitted in *Eagle* and the County class destroyers, RNSS staff carried out the programming in-house and IOs were involved in the analysis, programming and implementation of the facilities being delivered to the Ops Room users. Later, the software development for these and subsequent systems was carried out totally by Ferranti Naval Systems, who continued to do this work for the surface fleet until the late 1980s.

A change then took place in the role of the IOs involved in the ships after the County class guided missile destroyers. The process now was that IOs would work in the ARWG at Portsdown, liaising with the Seamen Officer users and the developers from Ferranti, before going to sea with the first of class for the setting to work, trials and acceptance into service; the IO's work from start to finish would take two to three years.

Type 42 *Sheffield* class destroyer Ops Room model in Cook Building HMS *Dryad*
by permission of Navy News (MOD)

Lieutenant Commander John Davis worked on the ADAWS2 development for *Bristol* which was the trials ship for the new automated 4.5-inch gun and the Sea Dart medium range ant-aircraft missile; Lieutenant Commander Derek Lord dealt with the ADAWS4 derivative for the 12 Type 42 destroyers and he went to sea in *Sheffield;* Lieutenant Commander Stewart Bruce was with the six *Leander* class ships fitted with the Ikara anti-submarine weapon and he went to sea in *Leander* for their ADAWS5 trials and acceptance.

The low-cost CAAIS systems were fitted in the Type 21 class frigates (*Amazon* and seven others); the Hunt class mine-counter measures ships (*Brecon* and 12 others); the Batch 2 *Leanders* (*Penelope* and two others) fitted with the Exocet system; the Batch 3 *Leanders* (*Andromeda* and four others) fitted with Sea Wolf. Lieutenant Mike Piper was part of the development team for CAAIS, which was taking place during the period 1972 to 1975.

Another IO-led initiative for ship-borne systems took place in the late 1970s where successive IOs in the ARWG developed and implemented the Link 14 Autoplot using a Hewlett Packard desktop computer. This system enabled the ships fitted with ADAWS and CAAIS to broadcast the compiled air, surface and sub-surface pictures to the Ops Rooms of the ships without a computer-based Action Information Organisation. A CINCFLEET team led by an IO deployed this system and the Link 14 Autoplot proved itself in the Falklands conflict. The IOs involved in this work included Lieutenant Commanders Phil Pool and Ross Munro.

The Ferranti series of military computers were the mainstay of operational systems and trainers in the Royal Navy for over 20 years. They were a great success in their time, before being overtaken by robust commercial technology driven by the introduction of universal personal computers.

The advent of the new Type 23 frigates in the late 1980s with towed sonar arrays and huge amounts of data required a new approach to computing in the ship. This was the subject of a long competition, eventually won by Dowty-Sema, which became part of BAe Systems.

Type 23 Duke class frigate Ops Room in Cook Building HMS *Dryad*
by permission of Navy News (MOD)

The importance of IOs in the field of operational ship-borne systems cannot be overstated; the Royal Navy was, for a time, the world leader to which the branch was a major contributor. At the end of a major NATO exercise, the US admiral commanding the friendly forces sent a signal to the fleet to say that, '*Eagle* and her new system had improved the air defence of the fleet by an order of magnitude'.

Operational Trainers

To ensure that ships are fought effectively and that best use is made of their weapons and sensors, training must be provided at operator, team and tactical levels.

For many years, the Royal Navy had used fairly primitive analogue technology as training aids, but as the equipment at the Tactical School at Woolwich reached the end of its life, it was decided to move the school to *Dryad* and to provide a state-of-the-art trainer. This trainer, called Combined Tactical Trainer 1 (CTT1), was housed in the new Cunningham Building and IOs were at the forefront of the CTT1 development: working closely with Ferranti on the specifications, setting the system to work, training the Tactical School staff and continuing the programme of improvement.

The first project officer was Lieutenant Commander 'Boy' Downer, but the majority of the development was done under Lieutenant Commander Tom Berry after he returned from setting up the systems in *Glamorgan* and *Fife*; he saw CCT1 through to acceptance in 1970.

Cunningham Building HMS *Dryad* housing the Combined Tactical Trainer (CTT1)
for the Maritime Tactical School

First Officer Julia Simpson then provided technical support to this system, working with Ferranti, before being relieved in 1973 by Lieutenant Commander Steve Fryer, who in turn was replaced after two years by Lieutenant Commander Harry Hellier.

The facilities in the Cunningham Building included a replica model of the Ops Room of the County class guided missile destroyers fitted with ADAWS1. The project officer for this procedural training was Lieutenant Commander Gordon Fairgrieve who provided the link between the users and Ferranti. He was relieved in 1974 by Lieutenant Commander Mike Willcox.

Combined Tactical Trainer – Maritime Tactical School staff in the Control Room running
the games

Whilst the development of CTT1 was going forward, it was decided that two other *Dryad* trainers (Redpole and Harrier) needed to be replaced by better facilities – to train individual users or teams in a realistic operational scenario on their Ops Room equipment before going to sea.

This new trainer, Combined Team Trainer (CTT2), was installed at *Dryad* in the new Cook building which was built in 1971. The project team for CTT2 started in ASWE and the RN members of the team included Lieutenant Commander Guy Warner, an IO, as the Technical Officer. The development was done under contract by Ferranti at their offices in Bracknell, where it was commissioned and then dismantled for shipment to *Dryad*.

Cook Building Trainer HMS *Dryad* housing the Combined Team Trainer (CTT2)

Guy Warner was relieved by Lieutenant Commander Richard Yeomans; by this time, the project had evolved to consist of three Ops Rooms, for the Type 42 *Sheffield* destroyers, the Ikara *Leander* and the CAAIS *Leander* frigates. In addition to the Ops Rooms, Cook Building housed the computer rooms and the main control room from where the games were controlled. A standard *Leander* Ops Room in another building was connected to Cook Building so that up to four ships' teams could take part in linked training.

Working with the contractor, it became clear that there were a number of particular problems for which off-the-shelf solutions were not available. Solutions were provided by mixed teams of RNSS and RN officers, which were then developed further by the contractors and eventually used by them in their trainers for other navies with royalties paid to the Royal Navy.

By the time that Cook Building had been completed and the various Ops Rooms were being equipped, First Officer Julia Simpson had joined. As the ships' delivery dates were slipping and the simulators were well ahead of them, Cook Building was able to offer facilities for the developers of the ships' operational systems. More importantly, this process unearthed a few issues and both Richard Yeomans and Julia Simpson were asked to help with a number of inspections and sea trials.

As CTT2 was nearing completion, Richard Yeomans was relieved by Lieutenant Commander Stewart Bruce and later, Julia Simpson was replaced by Lieutenant Commander Derek Lord.

Over the following years, new classes of ship were ordered together with their Ops Room trainers. The Cook Building enhancements took place to provide these new Ops Rooms and changes were made to the earlier models, so that they were always exactly the same as the ships at sea. The following Ops Rooms were added to Cook Building: the Type 21 frigates (6 ships of the *Amazon* class), the Type 22 frigates (14 ships of the *Broadsword* class) and the Type 23 frigates (16 ships of the *Duke* class)

IOs were there throughout to provide software support as part of the *Dryad* staff. The work comprised carrying out changes, correcting errors and working with the users on proposed improvements. The first incumbent in 1985 was Lieutenant Commander Patrick Binks who was relieved by Harry Hellier, followed in time by other IOs including Lieutenant Commanders Ross Munro, Roger Hockey and Roger Greenwood.

The trainers in *Dryad* were a great success and operated until December 2011.

Technical Training

At the time that *Eagle* was undergoing trials in 1964, Lieutenant Commander Bill Norrie set up the Digital Group in *Collingwood* to provide the facilities to train those going to maintain the computer system in *Eagle*.

Further systems for the maintainers were installed at *Collingwood*, which eventually had every installed ship-system comprising the computer systems (ADAWS, CAAIS) and their weapons: Seaslug, Ikara, 4.5-inch Mark 8 gun, Seawolf and Seadart. The equipments were installed in the Systems Training School, which was normally headed by a WE Commander although one Instructor Officer, Commander Tom Wingate, held the post from 1978 until 1980.

Satellite communications were being developed in the late 1960s and Skynet was deployed in 1969 with a satellite stationed over the Indian Ocean, serving eight earth stations, two of which were at sea in *Fearless* and *Intrepid*. The training was done by the Communications Section at *Collingwood* headed by an IO, Lieutenant Commander Bryan Collins, already a professional communications engineer when he joined the Royal Navy.

Command Systems - OPCON

As the ship and submarine systems were being developed, there was a parallel stream of work for command headquarters where improved communications technology had led to a great increase in the signal traffic, to such an extent that manual distribution, analysis and plotting systems were not able to cope satisfactorily.

An OPCON team was set up at Northwood in 1974 to address the requirement to improve the command and control facilities in the headquarters. The first project manager was Commander Tom Berry who was joined later by Lieutenant Commander Tom Wingate as the Implementation Manager.

Project Observer, the first initiative, successfully operated during a Fleet exercise in early 1975, and it was decided to move ahead to the more extensive system, OPCON Pilot, to deliver signal handling, plotting, ships status and intelligence to a larger number of users. The ICL hardware for this system was installed in the old underground headquarters, which had been built during the Second World War as Coastal Command Headquarters. Tom Berry left in 1976, Tom Wingate was promoted into his job and Lieutenant Commander John Connolly joined the team.

After some delays, the software was delivered by the large team of programmers working in Portakabins in the car park of the headquarters and OPCON Pilot went live in January 1977. The users were satisfied that the system provided the right type of solution, but deeply dissatisfied as it was unreliable, and it did not have all the functions they wanted. However, OPCON Pilot did prove the concept and allowed transition to the main system.

Lieutenant Commander Stewart Bruce joined in 1978 as the Implementation Manager to replace John Connolly. Thereafter, there was a third Director in post, and a WE as the Project Manager. That was the time of Operation Corporate in 1982 and OPCON Pilot proved very useful to the Fleet staff during that very busy period of the retaking of the Falkland Islands.

The OPCON Director by that time had an enormous responsibility. His task was to deliver the new underground headquarters, which would provide secure accommodation for up to 300 RN, RAF and NATO staff during peacetime, exercises and operations. In addition to this challenging construction task, in suburban Northwood, he was responsible for providing all the computer and communications systems for the new underground headquarters. The new Director in late 1982 was a one-star RNSS civilian, Doctor Peter Nutter, who was joined by Lieutenant Commander Phil Pool and later Commander Patrick Binks as the OPCON Project Manager.

The software was still under development by ICL who had a large 100-strong team based nearby at RAF Stanmore Park. Over the next three years, eight more projects were added to the OPCON Programme of inter-related projects. As well as delivering the functions of the OPCON Pilot to all staff and extending the information in the database, these projects were to provide OPCON to the staff in six UK and NATO war headquarters; automate the RN Shore Communications Network comprising six shore communication centres and all establishments around the UK and some abroad, through a project named NSR 7126; and automate the communication centres at Northwood and the MOD for the Intelligence organisations.

The OPCON project manager had a huge planning and logistical task, who with a small project team and several groups of contractors, had to provide special computer rooms, thousands of user facilities and secure communications to protect information up to the level of Top Secret, and involving close coordination with RN and MOD staffs, many contractors and the other Services.

Patrick Binks with Prince Charles at the opening of Northwood underground headquarters in 1986

The project managers over this period were Patrick Binks until 1986, Chief Officer Julia Simpson until 1988 and Commander Derek Lord until 1990.

On the Fleet Staff, Commander Laurie Redstone was the Fleet OPCON Staff Officer who worked with others in planning the occupation of the new underground headquarters and the subordinate war headquarters in Plymouth and Pitreavie, Scotland. His job was to coordinate the training of the Fleet staff, as each section moved into their part of the new underground headquarters.

An additional pressure on the OPCON project was that the new communications facilities needed to work, as savings of more than 300 communicators had been assumed and recruitment had been reduced in anticipation of the success of the new systems.

Over a period of five years, all the facilities were delivered, starting with the new underground headquarters at Northwood which went live in mid-1985.

'It is hard not to sound dramatic,' said Commander Tom Morton, the Fleet Shore Communications Officer, 'but OPCON transformed naval communications and fundamentally changed the conduct of maritime operations'.

Many Instructor Officers worked on the OPCON projects over a period of 15 years and their names are included in Annex 9.

Command Systems at Sea

Laurie Redstone was the coordinator for a trial to get OPCON and two other command systems embarked in *Illustrious* for the exercise Ocean Safari 1986, where he would provide training, resolve problems and document the lessons learned; the main lesson learned was that providing command systems at sea could be done and the trial clearly demonstrated the potential benefits to the command, both afloat and ashore. Subsequently, an OPCON installation was installed for all major exercises in RN and US command ships, including *Invincible* and USS *Mount Whitney*.

Another arrangement at this time was the installation of an OPCON terminal in ships deploying to the Gulf, and Laurie Redstone was responsible for training the ships' staff prior to their departure from the UK.

SACLANT

In the late 1960s, an Information Systems Division was instituted in the United States within the headquarters of the Supreme Allied Commander Atlantic (SACLANT) in Norfolk, Virginia. This was NATO's only headquarters outside Europe. The Division was given responsibility for all the management information systems within the headquarters and for all operational Command, Control and Information Systems (CCIS) across the ACLANT maritime commands.

The Division was headed by an Assistant Chief of Staff (ACOS); eight Captains (I) headed the division and the branches over subsequent years.

In the beginning, the Division was opened with a staff of two – both from the UK. The head was Captain Willie Waddell, who already had US experience from his Dam Neck time on Polaris training and he was joined by Mr Derek Gurney, who came from the Ministry of Defence. In 1971, the staff was doubled by the addition of two IOs, Commander John Locke and Lieutenant Commander Tom Wingate. By 1974, there were other non-Instructor Officer additions to the staff from the US and Norway. As well as the business of starting a new Division, establishing responsibilities within SACLANT and NATO wide, providing representation at NATO Committees, and establishing SACLANT requirements for CCIS, specific immediate help was given to SACLANT staff and NATO generally, including the provision of the first computer support system. Overall operational CCIS support to SACLANT himself, as US National Commander, was still provided by the co-located WMCCIS system, which was off-limits to NATO personnel.

Willie Waddell was relieved by Captain Tony Newing, John Locke by Commander Bill Daniels, and Tom Wingate left to go to OPCON and was replaced by Lieutenant Commander Jock Ambrose.

SACLANT Headquarters in Norfolk Virginia – service personnel and families celebrating a National day
by permission of Navy News (MOD)

The first Director of the Plans and Policy Branch was Tony Newing, who retired from the Royal Navy to take up the post. In 1991, he was relieved by Commander Bob Young, who also retired from the Royal Navy to take up the NATO civilian position, in which he served until the post was realigned during a major command restructuring in 2004.

In the early days of the Division, it was anticipated that the NATO CCIS requirement could be met by using a part of the US World-wide Command and Control System, but after several years of usage it was eventually decided that this did not meet some specific NATO operational requirements; there would need to be a separate development.

In 1979, a new CCIS project was established, headed by Commander Richard Yeomans. The project was tasked to analyse the SACLANT requirement, including essential interoperability with other NATO and national systems, and produce a full specification against which potential suppliers could bid. This phase was completed in about two years and then the technical approvals and funding were obtained.

Over a period of many years thereafter, a succession of Commanders (I) managed the sometimes tortuous design, procurement and implementation processes through NATO, which resulted in the system known today as Maritime CCIS (MCCIS); this is a near real-time Command and Control system, which supports use on both strategic and operational levels.

There were several false starts in the early years of system development and the US Navy Operational Support System (OSS) was eventually selected as the foundation or core system for MCCIS. In 1992, an agreement was signed between SACLANT and the US Navy to provide for the co-operative development of CCIS capabilities. In due course, SACLANT Information Systems Division took over the integration and maintenance responsibilities for the product.

In this transition process, MCCIS was designed and progressively evolved so that it could operate over a wide range of command levels and be interoperable with an expansive set of NATO, national and commercial formats and interfaces. Its operational capabilities included the graphic display of positional data and automatic update, the automatic and user-controlled database update and access, and automatic generation of formatted messages.

During this period of evolution, several Commanders (I) and Lieutenant Commanders (I) served in the Division in key specialist roles involving Program Management, Computer Security, Quality Assurance and System Training; they undoubtedly contributed to the success of a system which became the operational users' chosen platform for managing NATO's maritime data and its display, known as the common operational picture.

The success of the system is evident in its widespread implementation, being in operational use in over 50 NATO and national sites in Canada, Denmark, France, Germany, Greece, Iceland, Italy, Netherlands, Norway, Portugal, Spain, Turkey, United Kingdom and the United States.

A large number of IOs served in the Division and their names are listed in Annex 10.

Administrative Systems

In the administrative area, computers were coming into use in large organisations under the acronym ADP (Automatic Data Processing).

The Royal Navy was not quick to follow this trend, because of the widely dispersed nature of the shore establishments and ships, although in due course major projects were established for the RN Pay and Records Centre and for Naval Stores.

Initially, the development and implementation of some small computer systems was primarily due to a few officers, of all specialisations, persuading a senior officer to provide funding for a particular requirement.

Then in the late 1980s, three things took place that significantly affected the delivery of administrative systems in the Royal Navy: the arrival of mini-computers and later the personal computer; the delegation of financial control under the New Management Strategy (NMS) to establishments and commands, so they were able to fund computer systems from their own budgets; the MOD requirement that the Services adopt a strategic approach to delivering Information Systems which meant that each Service had to carry out Strategy Studies.

Until 1989, the development and implementation of Information Systems in support of administration in the Royal Navy was the responsibility of the Directorate of Naval Management Services (DNManS); the Directorate was also responsible for managing the work described earlier under Management Services. In 1989, this organisation changed and became the Directorate of Naval Information Systems (DNIS).

Many IOs were involved in the Directorate working on Information Systems and Management Services; the Director in the later 1980s was Captain John Watt who was relieved by Glyn Macken. It was during his tenure that DNManS became DNIS and his successor was another IO, Captain John Hart.

Until the Late 1980s

There are many systems where IOs were involved in the early development and use of computer systems for administration; here are a few early examples.

Training Support

These systems were used to support the Training Planning organisations in the RN and RM training establishments in their timetabling: location, class, instructor and equipment.

PINT (Project for the Improvement in Naval Training) was installed in several establishments. Commander Tom Wingate, who was on the staff of CINCNAVHOME, was loaned to FONAC for management and acceptance of the first system at *Daedalus*, then he contract managed the next system at BRNC Dartmouth. Once installed, the officer responsible for running these systems was usually an IO. The commercial company PMSL delivered the system and Lieutenant Commanders Alan Bussey, Derek Moore and Malcolm Kitchen were involved in getting them into service.

Another training management system was TRAP (Training Resource and Administration Programme) which was implemented for the Royal Marines at Lympstone. An IO, Lieutenant Commander Clive Robinson, was instrumental in its development; the whole application was written in a package called LEX which was subsequently chosen by the Royal Navy as its word processing package. LEX was installed later on several systems including OASIS and Clive Robinson subsequently left the Royal Navy to set up his own business to support LEX.

OASIS

OASIS was the On board Administration and Stores Information System which was a Supply Specialisation system for use in ships and an extension of the stores system at Bath. All previous and subsequent heads of Oasis were WE Captains, but one IO, Captain Glyn Macken, led the project for four years. Although the majority of the team were Supply and Engineer Officers and civilians, another IO, Lieutenant Commander Colin Mair, was also on the project.

During Glyn Macken's time, the PC emerged as the way ahead, allowing them to fit smaller less expensive machines; this enabled the project to speed up the fitting programme and to provide several office packages. These cheaper machines with readily available software allowed the project to be implemented in RN establishments and offer general office support.

Manpower Modelling

In 1983 the Naval Manpower Planners did not have computer support to help them define the recruiting targets for Naval Recruiting, but they relied on a group of statisticians using books of tables which took days to answer a question and further days if refinement was needed. The head of Naval Manpower and Training, Rear Admiral Nicholas Hunt obtained funding and tasked Commander Richard Yeomans, who worked for him, to deliver a solution that would give the planners the details of the steady state and an option to carry out predictive modelling, the 'what if questions'. It was decided to carry out the development in-house; Richard Yeomans started the work and another IO was brought in to assist with the programming. At the end of his appointment, he handed over the system to Commander Bob Young. A four-terminal system was delivered to the planners that enabled them to carry out in minutes what previously had taken several days to do manually; the system was still in use many years later.

From the late 1980s

The new Directorate DNIS was formed at a time of great change in administrative information systems. The initial major task was to oversee the work being done by contractors on the strategic studies for the functional areas of the Royal Navy: Personnel, Operations and Logistics.

For the Personnel area, this involved Commander Andy Edouard working with the contractors on the Strategy for Naval Information Systems in Personnel (SNISP); in the study for Operations, the IO on the team was Commander Ross Munro and the study was called Naval Operations Management Information Strategy (NOMIS).

For SNISP, the study defined five business areas; personnel administration, manpower planning, medical/dental, training administration and recruitment. In total, there were 15 projects that would deliver the requirements of the Royal Navy over the timescale from 1992 to 2000, involving 4,000 terminals installed in 250 locations ashore and afloat across the Naval Service. The cost was estimated at £100 million and was expected to deliver benefits over £200 million.

A new Directorate was established at *Centurion*, Gosport, to deliver these systems, with Captain Richard Yeomans as its first head. A number of IOs were on the strategy and planning staff of DSNPS including Commanders Patrick Binks and Andy Edouard, Lieutenant Commanders Paul Stubbs, Chris Parke, Brian Sutton and David Bridger.

Centurion Systems

The mainframe systems at *Centurion*, which had been in service for many years, were key to the implementation of SNISP. However, it is necessary to go back to the development of technology in the 1960s, where the promise of large savings in manpower made it inevitable that there would be computerisation of the Pay and Drafting of Naval and Royal Marines personnel. In 1970, it was decided to move all the personnel associated with these tasks from Bath and Haslemere into a new building in *Centurion* at Gosport; this large three-storey building on land to the north of *Sultan* had a large computer hall for the mainframes that would be needed.

Commanded by a Commodore, *Centurion* was manned by personnel from the Royal Navy (including WRNS), the Royal Marines and the Civil Service and it included the Computer Division, headed jointly by a Principal and a Captain RN. They were responsible for developing, maintaining and running all the computer systems; this Division was manned by a mixture of civil service and RN personnel.

Lieutenant Commander John Robinson joined *Centurion* in early 1974, by which time the computerised Drafting Information System was undergoing extensive trials. With the details of all the jobs in ships and shore establishments to be filled, combined with the programmes of ships and changes to shore establishments over ten years, it was possible to calculate the future RN manpower needs.

A study group, which included an IO, was then set up to determine how best this information could be accessed and distributed. The system was to become known as Naval Manpower Management Information System (NMMIS), but it was not until the mid-1980s that a fully interactive system became available online.

An IO, Captain John McGrath, became the head of Computing (Manpower) in 1987 and during his time, a fully interactive sub-system of NMMIS was implemented for Officers' Appointing, the On Line Assistance to the Naval Secretary (OLANS). This system won the 1989 Technical Innovation in Personnel Award from the Institute of Personnel Management.

John McGrath receiving the Technical Innovation award from the Institute of Personnel Management

Other IOs were involved in the project; among those employed as analysts were Lieutenant Commanders David Cook and Harry Hellyer. Lieutenant Commander Spencer Taylor worked on this system when still a WE, before becoming an IO.

During this period, NMMIS was further developed including a system to provide online assistance to Officer Promotion Boards; the appointing and drafting systems were extended to take on reservists, to deliver an online Mobilisation system and work commenced on the production of the data for the printing of the Navy List and the Retired List.

Many other IOs were appointed to *Centurion* before 1996, including Captain Laurie Redstone, who was the Head of Computing (Manpower).

Small System Groups

A shortened procurement process was set up in the late 1980s and Small Systems Groups were established in the Royal Navy under the overall co-ordination of DNManS and then DNIS. These SSGs were able to develop applications for the various commands: Commander in Chief, Naval Home Command, Commander in Chief, Fleet, the Royal Marines and the Fleet Air Arm.

Many of these SSGs were headed by IOs and the groups included IOs within the team. At the headquarters of Commander in Chief, Naval Home Command in the period 1989 to 1991, Lieutenant Commander Jeff Belcher led the group that included another IO, Lieutenant Elliot Cowton. The group delivered a variety of small systems, including one to manage the car passes for entry to the Portsmouth Naval Base, another to manage all the assets in the RN Trophy Store in *Nelson,* one to help the RN Special Investigation Branch manage their cases, and one for the registry staff in the headquarters.

The End

With the ending of the Instructor Specialisation in 1996, many of those working in Information Systems saw very little difference, except their titles changed from Instructor Officer to Engineer (Information Systems).

RN SCHOOL OF EDUCATIONAL AND TRAINING TECHNOLOGY

Don Cripps

Even before their entry into the Second World War, the US military had commissioned applied psychologists to research methods of human learning. During the next decade, their work was developed, applied in military training and eventually used by astronauts from the National Aeronautical and Space Administration (NASA).

A major need after the US entry into Second World War was to train technicians for their rapidly expanding Army Air Force and their use of new technologies, for example radar. This resulted in the pragmatic development of an electro-mechanical projection device called a teaching machine. This was developed after the war by US Industries and marketed as the Auto-Tutor.

Development of Programmed Learning in the Military

Other types of teaching machines were developed and marketed, but the Auto-Tutor was eventually adopted by the Royal Navy to great effect. The Applied Psychology Units of the three Services monitored the US research, but it was not until the 1960s that any action was taken in the UK. Several factors accelerated this interest:

- Manpower. Demography showed that the UK would suffer a shortage of graduates leaving British universities. Thus, the Instructor Branch would be unable to recruit enough Short Service officers for manning the training establishments, especially *Collingwood,* the RN Weapon Electrical School.

- Sales. US Industries decided to enter the UK market with their Auto-Tutor and opened a branch in Croydon where they assembled a team of programme writers to develop teaching programmes tailored to the UK needs. Their sales staff started a campaign to approach every UK educational authority, both Service and civilian. The story is told that their salesman left an Auto-Tutor in the Admiralty Boardroom fitted with the programme 'Improve your Bridge'. The Auto-Tutor became the Navy's preferred choice.

All three Service Psychology Units decided that their respective Service should investigate the use of Programmed Learning. The results can be found in 'Programmed Instruction in the British Armed Forces', Wallis, Duncan and Knight issued by HMSO in 1966.

The first RN trials in 1961-1962 were held in *St Vincent,* the junior seamen training establishment at Gosport. This showed that the use of Auto-Tutors was feasible and preferable to the same mathematics programme presented in book form and it was as good as the conventional teaching used for the 'control' class.

Trials were then moved to *Collingwood*, which was a better site as it had a larger number of students and also its own technical reprographic department. Thus, valuable experience on the production side would be gained and all stages would be carried out under the authors' eyes.

Instructor Officers wrote the programmes for these trials, which ran from 1963 through 1964 and were then incorporated into the standard training programme. The 1963 trial was disappointing, but when modified to include a degree of tutorial time with an instructor, the results were good. This system was named 'Integrated Programmed Instruction'. Furthermore, it was found perfectly satisfactory for the tutor to be an experienced senior rating rather than an Instructor Officer. The principal gain to the Royal Navy was saving Instructor Officer manpower; a task originally requiring 16 qualified trainers was being carried out with fewer than 8 by the middle of 1967.

The technique of Programmed Instruction was applied to other courses in *Collingwood*, such as fault-finding, and to remedial arithmetic in *Raleigh* for new-entry training.

The results of the *Collingwood* trials and developments in the other Services made the RN Training Directorate realise that there was a need to generate some expertise in the Royal Navy as soon as possible. Dr Goodman in the Computer Sciences department of Brighton Polytechnic had a good reputation in the field of Programmed Instruction. He had recruited as his assistant, Derek Rowntree, who had been employed by US Industries, Croydon, as Editor for their Mathematics Programme, part of which had been used in the *St Vincent* trials.

DGNT organised a two-week course at Brighton, tutored by Dr Goodman and Derek Rowntree, and called for volunteers to attend. Several of the course members had misunderstood the subject; one thought it was to do with entertainment; some, like Commander Gerry Tordoff from *Excellent,* went out of curiosity; only Lieutenant Commander Robin Budgett from *Collingwood* had any pre-knowledge. When in Gibraltar in 1963, serving as assistant to Commander Frank Finch, he had become interested in Programmed Instruction from the training publications.

Dr Goodman sadly died prematurely, but Mr Derek Rowntree went on to be a Professor of Educational Technology at the Open University.

At a NATO Conference on Manpower Planning in Brussels in 1965, Mr Don Wallis, a member of the Applied Psychology Unit, Teddington, gave a paper entitled, 'The Technology of Military Training'. This predicted a systematic approach to training very close to that eventually developed and adopted in the Royal Navy.

Don Wallis was the psychologist in charge of all the RN programmed learning trials and a keen advocate of the need for the Royal Navy to have a unit dedicated to the development of Programmed Instruction. Eventually, he became the Chief Psychologist in the Department of Employment and later Professor of Applied Psychology at University of Wales Institute of Science and Technology, Cardiff, but he kept in touch with his RN colleagues.

Programme Instruction Unit from 1966 to 1971

The PIU was formed on 1 July 1966. Lieutenant Commander Geoffrey Stavert was appointed as Officer-in-Charge, having been in charge of a major part of the Programmed Instruction in *Collingwood*, had written the Basic Electrics programme for the Auto-Tutors and ran the course with the help of three leading hands.

Geoffrey Stavert had an interesting background: an Oxford chemist, a Royal Artillery Major during the Second World War, a prisoner of war escapee, and an Acting Instructor Commander in Trincomalee, Ceylon. He knew that the PIU was being formed some months beforehand and that he was to be Officer-in-Charge. At the same time in *Collingwood*, Robin Budgett had been appointed to help and, between them, they planned for the housing of the PIU and its activities.

From the start, it was made quite clear that the PIU would be tasked by Director General Naval Training and its professional activities were not the responsibility of *Collingwood*. However, the Officer-in-Charge was responsible for the conduct of the staff and the PIU's administration to the Captain of *Collingwood*, who was prepared to provide temporary accommodation for the PIU in Hut 29, on the understanding that they would move from his establishment after six months. Later Captains had different views and Hut 29 was occupied by the PIU for five years.

RN Programme Instruction Unit in Hut 29 HMS *Collingwood* in 1967
Lieutenant Commanders Robin Budgett, Geoffrey Stavert and 'Jack' Hawkins from left to right

It had been hoped that the PIU would be staffed by about five Instructor Officers and a Psychologist from the Applied Psychology Unit. However, the Psychologist was never forthcoming and eventually an Instructor Officer (Lieutenant Rowley Hawketts) was appointed to the Applied Psychology Unit.

In the beginning, Geoffrey Stavert and Robin Budgett were joined by Lieutenant Commander 'Jack' Hawkins together with two technical staff, whose role was to maintain and help evaluate teaching machines and other equipment. It was agreed that the PIU would maintain its own secretariat; Robin Budgett went, therefore, on the Small Ships' Correspondence Officers course at *Pembroke* and a Wren Writer joined the PIU.

By 1967, Instructor Lieutenants John Coley and Derek Moore had joined. Also Lieutenant Commander Stuart Morse had arrived on exchange from the Canadian Navy. Stuart Morse's fortuitous appointment was of great benefit to the development of RN training, as he had studied Programmed Instruction in North America, had worked with the US Air Force and reviewed developments in Europe, which included a visit to *Collingwood* and the PIU, just after its creation. He had requested an exchange appointment specifically to the PIU, where he led the design and development of courses and did much consultancy work in RN training establishments for the next three years. Finally, a Third Officer WRNS (Education) Jo Bradbury joined.

RN Programme Instruction Unit at HMS *Collingwood* in 1967
includes IOs Lieutenants Derek Moore and John Coley, Lieutenant Commanders Stuart Morse,
Robin Budgett, Geoffrey Stavert, 'Jack' Hawkins and Third Officer Jo Bradbury

The PIU's first task was to 'spread the gospel'. Programmed Writing courses were started and Programmed Instruction acquaintance courses were held. Also presentations on 'What is Programmed Learning' were given to several training establishments. Geoffrey Stavert and Robin Budgett toured both RN and RNR establishments from Plymouth to Faslane, via Cardiff and Rosyth. However, it soon became clear that the detailed work of programming would be wasted if the training syllabus was not clear. Fortunately, the RN did not make any bad mistakes and was able to learn from the experiences of others, especially the RAF. Courses in Task Analysis were started and the move towards Objective Training was made.

Captain Philip Watson, the new WE Captain of *Collingwood*, was enthusiastic about the presence of the PIU, as he realised that its successes reflected well, particularly when *Collingwood* was selected for the first trial of objective management in an RN establishment. Civilian management consultants were appointed and worked in the hut next to the PIU. The management consultants, however, were having difficulty in closing the loop in their recommended system for managing training. A meeting between the two neighbours showed that what was being advocated by the PIU, fulfilled their needs. *Collingwood* training was split into Design and Execution; an Assessment Department within Design then closed the loop.

In October 1968, Geoffrey Stavert was awarded the MBE and retired from the Royal Navy. Robin Budgett took over as Officer-in-Charge of the PIU and John Coley became responsible for its administration. Jack Hawkins retired as well and was relieved by Lieutenant Commander Bob Hawkins; Lieutenant Commander Peter Brookman joined to make up the numbers.

Besides running courses, the PIU staff were engaged in developing RN-wide programmes either written in-house (for example NAMET) or by external consultants (for example the Seaman's Guide to the Rule of the Road, and the Seaman's Guide to Basic Chartwork, both created by ESL Bristol).

In all cases, the evaluation of each programme was carried out by the PIU staff. Within 48 hours, NAMET English had been tested by Derek Moore at *Ganges, Raleigh* and the Commando Training Centre Royal Marines, Lympstone. The breadth of the testing impressed civilian academics who were happy to quote the Royal Navy as examples of best practice.

In 1969, Lieutenant Commanders Brian Drinkall and Clive Lewis were sent on a postgraduate course at the Education Department of the University of Sussex. On completion, Clive Lewis joined *Vernon* and Brian Drinkall replaced Peter Brookman in the PIU.

By the end of 1970, it had been decided to form a School of Educational and Training Technology by combining the PIU, with the Instructional Techniques Schools and the RN Television Centre in Portsmouth. It was hoped to house all the groups in one building and a move from *Collingwood* was recognised as inevitable. It was decided, however, that the Instructional Techniques School in Plymouth would remain there.

Commander Ken Harper, who had been the desk officer in Director Naval Education Service (DNEdS) responsible for the PIU, had been relieved by Commander Don Cripps. Robin Budgett had already been serving in *Collingwood* for six years and it was agreed that he would be relieved from the PIU when the *Nelson* accommodation was completed.

In September 1971, Don Cripps was appointed to *Nelson* as Officer-in-Charge RNSETT and the PIU staff started to move to *Nelson*.

In 1970, Captain Geoff Huggett had moved from *Collingwood* to be the Dean at Royal Naval College, Greenwich. He had been at Massachusetts Institute of Technology (MIT) in the United States, working on their computer based training project, which used a large mainframe computer to train one student to fault-find or play chess. On joining *Collingwood*, he was keen to develop computer based training there, using the establishment's mainframe. He suggested that the Auto-Tutors might be linked by computer, but the PIU advised that it would be extremely difficult and not cost effective. *Vernon* had a device called the Bosch AVIT, which integrated a carousel slide projector and tape recorder to train anti-submarine operators in recognising ships from their propeller noise. The AVIT used a small digital control system and might be considered as the RN's first example of computer-controlled training.

In April 1970, Geoff Huggett organised at Greenwich a NATO Advanced Study Institute course on 'Computer Based Learning and Training Systems', with contributions from academic and commercial experts on both sides of the Atlantic. All NATO members were represented in the student body with the Royal Navy being represented by Robin Budgett and Brian Drinkall and the Canadian Navy by Stuart Morse. RNSETT was to spend much time in the following years researching and developing computer based training and this is addressed below.

The importance of the work being done by the PIU was recognised when Robin Budgett was promoted to Acting Commander in February 1970. As a result of the success of Objective Training, the principal courses in the PIU became those in Training Management and the first course was held in January 1971.

The View from DNEdS

On promotion to Commander in 1968, Don Cripps joined DNEdS in the Training chair and with responsibility for RN training establishments. He had previously worked in the US Naval Guided Missile School in Virginia where he became aware of the new developments in training in North America. In DNEdS, he was also responsible for close relations with the Instructional Technique School located in the RN Barracks, Portsmouth, whose main task was to run courses for all RN personnel in how best to teach in a classroom. It was felt necessary to keep in close touch with the development of the new teaching and training techniques, which were being developed at that time outside the Royal Navy, and he attended meetings and conferences on those topics. On one occasion, he obtained approval to attend an international conference in the US and persuaded the MOD to pay for him to stay for a week in the Disneyland Hotel in California where it was being held!

Proposals were developed at this time for the RN training establishments to assess and improve their own management of training. The basis of this work was that all training courses should be focussed firmly on a clear analysis of the skills and knowledge to carry out the job/work/task that the trainee was destined for. Additionally, it was decided that a feedback system should be set up so that the training establishment would be continuously informed of the success of their training courses in providing these skills and keeping the defined aims of their courses constantly up to date with changes, for example in equipment, procedures or responsibilities.

To carry out this approach generally would, of course, need some training in these management requirements for all those RN personnel in training posts so that they would understand and learn how to carry out the Objective System. At that time, the only training being carried out was in the Instructional Technique School in *Nelson,* which was limited to classroom teaching. This clearly would need to be expanded to cover all aspects of training management and given a new more appropriate name.

It was first necessary to get support for this new training system from the authority in charge of all RN training, the Director General of Naval Training (DGNT) and from the Director of Naval Education (DNEdS), Rear Admiral John Bellamy.

A presentation of these proposals was given to DGNT who agreed that the principles of Objective Training should be adopted by all training establishments, and a centre should be established to run Training Management courses for officers and ratings appointed to appropriate posts in all RN training establishments.

Admiral Bellamy proved supportive to the concept and Don Cripps thought out the title for the centre, the 'RN School of Educational and Training Technology', which he hoped would not offend the pure educationalists in the branch. Also, the acronym 'Rensett' would flow easily off the tongue for the practical training staff.

General Changes in Training

In 1969, Director General Naval Manpower and Training (DGNMT) decided to make a film about Programmed Instruction to help in promoting Training Management. Some years earlier, the US Air Force had made a film, but it did not meet the needs of the Royal Navy. Stewart Films were awarded the contract and the PIU staff helped the film director, Richard Need, with the script. The film was launched by DGNT in 1970 in the Admiralty Cinema and it was shown at the opening of the Annual Conference of the Association for Programmed Learning and Educational Technology at Loughborough University in April 1970. The film was well received and was later bought by several institutions both in the UK and abroad.

As a result of the PIU courses and pressure from DGNT, some RN establishments began to reorganise their training, but the major developments only occurred when establishments had specific problems. An early example was at *Condor,* where Naval Air Engineering training was being moved progressively from Scotland to *Daedalus* at Lee-on-Solent. The Training Commander had been on a PIU course and saw that if he packaged/programmed all the training, he would be able to keep control on the quality from afar. This worked as planned after Stuart Morse had visited to initiate the scheme.

Other courses that followed include the following examples:

- In *Ganges*, the RN Recruiters lowered the required educational standards without warning the Seamanship Training Officer. Fortunately, he had been on course at the PIU and phoned for help. Stuart Morse helped them redesign their seamanship tests which had required a considerable number of written answers.
- In *Pembroke,* the PIU helped the Supply and Secretariat School evaluate a commercial system for training a group of typists (Sight and Sound), which was used successfully for some years.
- In *Dauntless,* the PIU helped with the systematic revision of WRNS Basic Training.

Probably the biggest external project was the development of an audio-training programme for auxiliary machinery watchkeepers in the carrier *Bulwark,* and this meant Derek Moore being lent to *Bulwark's* Engineering Department and sailing with her to the Far East and back. The completed programme was eventually transferred to *Sultan* for more general use.

RNSETT from 1971 to 1975

RNSETT was formed on 1 February 1971 with Robin Budgett as Officer-in-Charge and the staffs of PIU, IT Schools and TV Centre transferred to it. By this time, John Coley had been relieved in the PIU by Lieutenant Richard Palmer, Derek Moore by Lieutenant Jeff Bond and Stuart Morse by another Canadian Naval Officer, Lieutenant 'Benno' Botterbusch. John Coley, however, was now in charge of the Television Centre, so came back into the fold.

Since the premises in *Nelson* were not yet available, the RNSETT main office remained in *Collingwood*. This produced the difficulty of split loyalty for the staff in *Nelson*. Neither the Commodore *Nelson*, nor the SIO, had been happy at losing two jewels from their crown, the Instructional Techniques School and the CCTV Section. Some of the courses in Training Management were switched to *Nelson*, but on the whole the travelling was left to the Officer-in-Charge and the Instructional Techniques School in Plymouth was left unchanged.

In early 1971, the office and classroom facilities of the IT School in *Nelson* were expanded to accommodate the new RNSETT with Don Cripps now the Officer-in-Charge. Instructional Technique courses continued but now were added Training Management courses for a proportion of officers and senior ratings appointed to training establishments. Staff were also made available to provide follow-up visits to training establishments and help or advice for those setting up or transferring existing training into the Objective Training system.

In RNSETT, a video facility was set up to train staff who wanted to produce videos of teaching material either for use in the classroom or for programmed learning.

The RN's development of the video for training purposes clearly attracted attention, as Don Cripps was invited by the Royal Television Society to give a presentation at one of their annual conferences on the use of CCTV in RN training. Apart from the facts put across, this generated a couple of points of particular interest. The first was that having recorded the rehearsal to see how it might be received, it was a shock to find out how dull the presentation came over. Some livening up in the manner of delivery was carried out and this made an enormous improvement. At the end of the presentation to the Society, the first question was, 'Do you really mean to say that in the Royal Navy you will use anyone to operate your television equipment?' Without realising that the questioner was a prominent Trade Unionist, the reply was, 'Of course! If a job needs to be done, we get on with it'. This produced a huge round of applause from the floor!

RNSETT on its formation at HMS *Collingwood* in 1971
includes Lieutenants Richard Palmer and Jeff Bond, Lieutenant Commanders Bob Hawkins and Brian Drinkall, Commander Robin Budgett, Third Officer Jo Bradbury and Lieutenant 'Benno' Botterbusch (RCN)

These were interesting days working with a new development across the Service. There were also two interesting visits abroad following invitations to bring a small team of RNSETT staff to give a presentation on the new approach to the management of training in the Royal Navy, one to the Royal Norwegian Navy and another to the Royal Danish Navy.

In 1977, Commander Cripps was relieved by Commander Ken Cropper. RNSETT was by now a busy and influential part of the training scene. Its courses, led by the Training Management Course, which had become part of all Commanding Officers' Courses, were fully booked and highly regarded. The Television Section had excelled itself in responding to a strike of Fire Engine crews by making a training 'film' which was quickly distributed throughout the Naval Home Command. Demonstrations of Holograms led to ideas of their possible uses in simulating three-dimensional models.

At the annual Conferences of APLET (Association of Programmed Learning in Educational Technology) and at the tri-service level, RNSETT was leading the field. Experience in training design from skills training to educational objectives (at Britannia Naval College, Dartmouth) and in training methods from classroom instruction to role playing, simulation and case studies, had established its reputation.

During this period, RNSETT, with help from Fleet staff, embarked upon a survey of the effectiveness of training. Led by Lieutenant Commanders Malcolm Kitchin and Derek Moore, visits were made to ships to obtain data for subsequent analysis.

At this time, Computer Based Training (CBT) had entered the scene. The same two officers spent two weeks at the invitation of the University of Minneapolis acquainting themselves with PLATO (Programmed Logic for Automated Teaching Operations) following a visit to UK by representatives from Control Data Corporation (CDC). Returning to UK, they were able to program and demonstrate a machine loaned by CDC.

It is interesting to note that even in these early days, although the computer was being seen as a teaching aid, its future in computer management of training became apparent.

As mentioned earlier, hard work by Don Cripps had centralised RNSETT at *Nelson*, but as a 'quasi-independent territory in the Barracks' in the words of the Commodore. This untidy situation was clarified, and the significant role being played by RNSETT in the Training Command recognised when Naval Home Command assumed direct responsibility for the School and accountability was made direct to the Commander in Chief, with Ken Cropper now its first Commanding Officer.

Postscript

Later, the role of RNSETT changed to include the Video Production Units (VPUs). These included a full-scale studio, control room, editing suite and duplication bank which enabled RNSETT to provide training courses in video scripting and editing as well as courses in basic camera work and production. Staff expertise rested with senior rates for technical support and cameramen editors, the latter coming from the RN Photographic Branch. Under the guidance of a section officer, RNSETT oversaw the equipment updates and the tasking of productions in the VPUs at Lympstone for the Royal Marines, *Daedalus* for the Fleet Air Arm, *Sultan* and *Raleigh* for the training establishments.

Latterly, the development of better quality VHS tapes and handheld cameras allowed local establishments and ships to shoot and 'crash edit' their own productions. RNSETT responded to this by introducing a camcorder user's course. Civilian Instructors were involved in the Media Interview techniques course, which was set up by Lieutenant Commander Nigel Huxtable in response to a need identified for those officers in the public media spotlight. This provided senior officers with advice and guidance on preparing to appear on the radio or television as well as practice in response to incidents which they might have to deal with. This involved work in the studio and on location within *Nelson*, followed by debriefings to show how words can be edited and casual glances misinterpreted!

The VPUs received a variety of requests for training videos, which included submarine rescue techniques, nuclear accident emergency responses, NATO combined operations with the Royal Marines, sea-time with the ships of the Training Squadron for BRNC, to sports and adventurous training for the RN's Sports and Recreation School at *Temeraire*.

COMPUTER BASED TRAINING

Dennis Dowsett and John Hall

The 1970s were witness to the development of relatively cheap, widely-available microprocessors, which were to provide the basis for a worldwide phenomenon that became known as personal computing. This was eventually to have a significant impact on the way training could be delivered. Thanks to the foresight and expertise of the Instructor Specialisation, the Royal Navy was at the vanguard in applying this new technology to training.

Early Implementation

The 1981 Defence Review called for increased efficiency in training and the need to conduct more training on board ships and submarines. Using computers to support the delivery of training was not new in the Royal Navy; Computer Based Training (CBT) was already being used, albeit in its early form, and this led to the first full-scale classroom implementation of CBT with the Action Data Automated Weapons System (ADAWS) keyboard trainer at *Dryad* near Portsmouth.

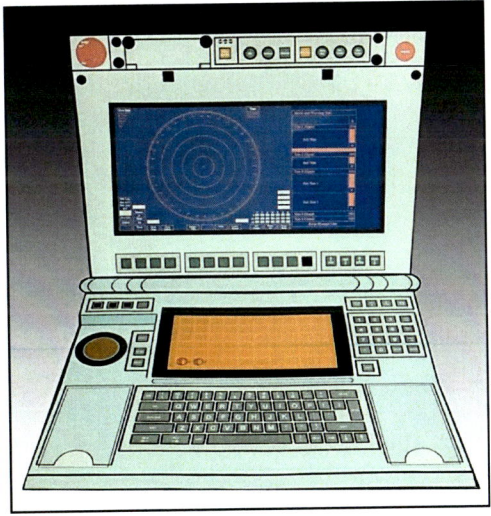

ADAWS Computer Based Training Console
by permission of Flagship Training

The ADAWS system was fitted in the Ops Rooms of several classes of ship. The operator was required to memorise a series of manual injections to input data, gathered from a variety of sensors, to build up and maintain the surface, air and subsurface pictures. When taught by traditional means, there had been a failure rate of 20%. With the introduction of 24 CBT workstations using high-quality courseware, the failure rate was reduced to 3%.

Pilot Studies

In 1984, three years after the advent of the IBM Personal Computer, a CBT Pilot study was set up by the Directorate of Naval Education and Training Support (DNETS) with the aims of:

- Helping Commands and training establishments to get CBT experience.
- Developing means of quantifying the benefits and cost effectiveness of CBT in the RN.
- Testing how CBT courseware could be transferred from shore to ships and submarines.
- Evaluating the methods of buying CBT courseware.

The Royal Naval School of Educational and Training Technology (RNSETT) was tasked with managing the study. Commander Brian Drinkall, who headed RNSETT at that time, was well placed to set up such an undertaking and was well versed in the application of CBT. At a technical and working level, the project was driven by Lieutenant Commander Wally Brown, Staff Officer RNSETT, and Lieutenant Commander George Allen, who later joined the academic staff at Portsmouth University when he left the Royal Navy.

DNETS selected six projects for the study and, with their relevant sponsors, they were:

- Rule of the Road – BRNC Dartmouth.
- Joint Message Handling – Commando Training Centre Royal Marines Lympstone.
- Electronic Warfare Principles – *Dolphin.*
- Passive Sonar Principles – *Dryad.*
- Morse Training – *Mercury.*
- Naval Mathematics and English Test (NAMET) – *Raleigh.*

The setting up of the trial gave a focus for the development of a policy for CBT, which made the Royal Navy a leader in the field, amongst both the other Services and UK industry. However, there were problems with communication failings between the sponsor organisations and the trial's management, throwing doubt on the validity of the data collected. Also, the underpinning methodology of the trial was always chasing the implementation and the 'transfer to sea' aspects never really got off the ground.

Three Particular Successes

However, three of the projects went on to become ground-breaking applications that served the Royal Navy well and generated considerable financial return for the UK defence industry:

- Passive sonar was developed with the assistance of Lieutenant Commander Ian Purdie at *Dryad.* Towed Array sonar was being installed in a range of surface ships and submarines and this led to an increased demand for personnel trained to analyse acoustic signatures of submarines; this subject was difficult to teach in a traditional manner. The project was developed as part of a technology-sharing program with the US Navy over the next decade, with Commanders Robin Stainbank and Robin Hodsdon and Lieutenant Commander John Hall being involved.

- Rule of the Road was another project that was subject to significant further improvement; these enhancements included modelling the view from the bridge of the ship, having the options of day or night, being able to select either good or reduced visibility and incorporating the radar plot. Rediffusion Simulation later marketed this system commercially.

- Electronic Warfare was to prove another success story. Flag Officer Submarines (FOSM) reported that the classification of radar systems on the submarine courses was not well understood by students because of poor visual presentation aids and few experienced instructors. The courseware was used for initial training and for refresher training for submarines going out on patrol; this training became part of an 'alongside the wall' facility.

A later bridge trainer for the officers at Britannia Royal Naval College, Dartmouth
by permission of BRNC

FOSM recognised the potential of low cost CBT simulation in many other areas where individual trainees needed to practise operational tasks. Lieutenant Commander John Hall wrote in a paper, delivered at the International Training Equipment Conference in 1990:

> 'Team training using networked microcomputers is no longer a pipe dream, but only requires development to become reality. Most cost benefit can be obtained where microcomputers provide the same levels of training as conventional simulators. The submarine flotilla is already pursuing real-time training for its tactical personnel'.

The concept of a toolbox was one that put CBT development in the Royal Navy years ahead of others in the commercial and defence markets. Toolbox systems were applied extensively to the development of CBT. Quite properly, it was in the operational areas where CBT implementation was taking place, but the impact that DNETS and RNSETT had on shaping its development within the Royal Navy was very important.

Role of DNETS

DNETS had the responsibility for the development of CBT funding and the foresight to use the funds in a targeted way to influence the Royal Navy's large equipment procurements. DNETS, in effect, put hardware into classrooms to address real, pressing training needs. Captain Richard Yeomans was keen to establish a sound, effective policy for CBT and ensure that the lessons learned found their way back to the larger equipment procurements. Commander Steve Smyth's stewardship of the budget really sharpened the way that funds were spent and the lessons learned were further implemented by the Engineering Desk Officer in DNETS, Commander Bob Duke, who was particularly effective at influencing the financial spends in the operational projects.

The ADAWS trainer and its successors that found their way into the School of Maritime Operations were state of the art in the mid-1990s. The Royal Navy, thanks in no small part to the skills, innovation and expertise of the IOs had come a long way in a relatively short time. However, it is worth reflecting on the sentiments expressed by Commander Jeff Bond in a paper to the Inter-Service/Industry Training, Simulation and Education Conference in 1988, reflecting on the original DNETS Study:

> 'If nothing else, the trial emphasised the fact that the use of CBT must be an instructional issue, not a hardware one. We must focus on the integration of CBT into a total training programme. As with all previous training technology breakthroughs, computers are just a tool and one of a range of possible media for training implementation.'

This is a useful lesson for those grappling to harness today's plethora of new technologies to the education and training cause.

SUBMARINE SERVICE

Guy Warner

More than 50 Instructor Officers served with the Submarine Service during the period 1965 – 1996. They undertook a variety of roles in the mainstream of submarine activity, most of them qualifying as Submariners. They made many noteworthy contributions. How did it all come about and what was accomplished by those who volunteered or were co-opted to serve in a world very remote from normal IO activity?

The submarine environment is a very specialised one with especially demanding engineering, warfare and human requirements. Submarines on regular operations have undertaken some of the most difficult and dangerous tasks over the years – many of them subject to stringent security restrictions. Suffice to say that our submarines were at the leading edge of the Cold War against the Soviets and have been at the forefront of most conflicts – not least in their ability to gather vital covert intelligence, land clandestine forces and fire cruise missiles with great accuracy from afar. Moreover, they have maintained the Strategic Deterrent with great success ever since its first deployment at sea in 1968.

The Submarine Service was always a difficult world to enter and make a worthwhile contribution without substantial training and sea experience. It is, therefore, remarkable that so many IOs were able to operate successfully in the submarines. This then is their story, necessarily limited by my own experience, but assisted hugely by those I have been able to contact and who have made valuable contributions to this account.

The Beginning

In the early 1960s, the Submarine Service consisted of 'T', 'A', 'P' and 'O' class diesel submarines, with squadrons based at Gosport (SM1), Plymouth (SM2), Faslane (SM3), Sydney, Australia (SM4), Halifax, Canada (SM6) and Singapore (SM7).

The depot ships *Forth, Tyne, Adamant* and *Maidstone* were still being used to provide submarine support facilities. FOSM staff was based at Fort Blockhouse Gosport, co-located with SM1 at *Dolphin*.

There were the traditional shore education jobs as squadron Instructor Officers in the submarine bases and the Flotilla Instructor Officer (FIO) on FOSM's staff, but they were always well on the periphery of submarine activity. Of more relevance was a supposedly technical support job in the Submarine Attack Teacher at Rothesay, where Lieutenant Commander Tom Berry, followed by Geoff Greenhalgh and Tony Meechan, made it much more than that. There was also a Director of Studies job in the Submarine School at *Dolphin*, which assumed more importance with the modernisation and expansion of the school. Commanders Joe Merritt and 'Boy' Downer were early occupants.

Tom Berry and Joe Merritt, being far-sighted officers, were mainly responsible for starting the infiltration of IOs into submarines, in addition to those in the MOD who were wrestling with the emerging Polaris requirements.

HMS *Dolphin* with several submarines alongside in 1965
by permission of NMRN

The rapid expansion of the Submarine Service in the 1960s, with the introduction of both the submarines with nuclear propulsion (SSN) and those submarines with nuclear propulsion and ballistic missiles (SSBN), made huge demands on submarine manning, training and expertise. Nuclear power and strategic missile systems were completely new, not only to the Submarine Service, but also the Royal Navy. In addition, it was evident that emerging computer technology would have to be introduced into submarine control rooms at some stage to replace the myriad of manual plots, slide rules, calculators and stop watches. Computers were already at sea in surface ships, notably the carrier *Eagle* and the guided missile destroyers. Nearly all submarine-qualified Engineer Officers (including Weapon Engineers) were sent on nuclear courses at DNST Greenwich and required to man the new submarine engine rooms. General Service officers were appointed to the Polaris Weapon System in SSBNs and to fill specialist Long N (Navigation) and Long TAS (Torpedo and Anti-Submarine) positions required in SSNs. It was into this rapidly developing submarine world that the initial IOs were required to enter.

Instructor Officer Pioneers in the 1960s

It was soon recognised that the Instructor Branch could play a significant role in the new Polaris School at Faslane to supplement the engineers co-opted from General Service. Commander Willie Waddell was selected to be the first Officer-in-Charge of the Polaris School and he led a large team to be trained during 1965 at the US Navy Guided Missile School in Dam Neck, Virginia Beach. This team included several IOs and key members of the two crews destined for the first SSBN, namely *Resolution*. The party included Lieutenant Commander Chris Young who was to lead the Navigation area.

Polaris navigation had to be extremely accurate, as the missile was free-fall under gravity, so any error on launch was magnified many times on arrival at the target, probably several thousand miles away. This entailed the introduction of ship's inertial navigation systems whose accurate alignment had to be continually monitored and frequently updated with external information, and this was prior to the introduction of satellite navigation systems in the mid-1970s. Other components of the Polaris Weapon System were the missile system, hovering system, launching system and corresponding computers. The computer department in the Polaris School was to be manned entirely by IOs with Lieutenant Commander Don Cripps the initial head, followed by Lieutenant Commander Ken Healey.

'O' class submarine passing HMS *Dolphin*
© MOD Crown Copyright by permission of RN Submarine Museum

Meanwhile, the development of the first submarine Action Information Organisation system was looming. It was to be called TDHS (Tactical Data Handling System) with the nomenclature DCA. It was destined for *Swiftsure*, which was the first of a new all-UK class of SSN, following on after *Dreadnought, Valiant, Warspite, Churchill, Conqueror* and *Courageous*.

With this in mind, Lieutenant Bob Young was sent to AUWE Portland to assist in the development and training for the first TDHS. Also Lieutenant Guy Warner was put on the Seaman Officers' submarine training course at *Dolphin* in mid-1966 with a similar mission in mind. He was the first IO to qualify as a submariner, serving in seaman complement billets in *Finwhale* and *Alderney* before being appointed to the newly established Submarine Tactical Development Group, firstly at Rothesay and then Faslane, where it became the Submarine Tactical Weapons Group (STWG), responsible for the analysis of weapon firings and for the development of tactics. Whilst there, Guy Warner made a number of important technical advances, including the tactical exploitation of narrowband sonar frequency used in shadowing Soviet submarines.

HMS *Resolution* at speed
© MOD Crown Copyright by permission of RN Submarine Museum

Due to the shortage of submarine Engineer Officers available for the non-nuclear submarines, Lieutenants John Watt and Derek Feltham qualified as WE SM Officers and Derek Gdanitz as an ME SM. All these IOs went on to successfully occupy complement billets in diesel submarines. Lieutenant Sam Poole followed as a seaman submariner in *Ocelot* where he was able to demonstrate his considerable seamanship experience as an accomplished yachtsman. He then went on to nuclear submarines and served in *Valiant* where he relieved Lieutenant Mike Boyce, who went on to become Chief of the Defence Staff and then Admiral Lord Boyce KG. Following on, Sam Poole was then appointed to the Submarine Command Team Trainer at Faslane, which had superseded the Rothesay Attack Teacher, where he performed a key role. Later, he became the first Instructor Officer to head a Division at Dartmouth and was an integral submarine staff officer there.

The new Command Team Trainer, which was to retain an I(SM) complement billet over many years, was sited adjacent to the new Polaris School, which had at least six IO billets, although most did not need submarine experience. However, Lieutenants Mike Simper and Glyn Macken were sent to sea in

Resolution – initially as Education Officers although there was not really a role at sea for them. Mike Simper duly became the Squadron Education Officer ashore, while Glyn Macken integrated successfully as a seaman and became a specialist Polaris Navigator. When the Navigator of *Repulse*, the second SSBN to deploy, was taken off with an injury, Glyn Macken was appointed to the boat as the PNO (Polaris Navigating Officer) for the missile trial firing in the US. This was a marked success and Glyn Macken subsequently relieved Lieutenant Commander Chris Young as the Navigation Systems Officer in the school.

Consolidation in the 1970s

It was by now apparent that IOs could make key contributions to the submarine world with the right training and experience, but acceptance had to be earned amidst some prejudice against IOs occupying SM positions. Here tribute should be paid to the various IO Appointers over the years who strove to get the right people in submarine-related jobs, put them on the right submarine training courses beforehand and keep the appointments going. The IO Appointers played a major part in the success of the Submarine Rampart.

The full submarine training consisted of the Officers' Training Course at *Dolphin* (for Seamen or Engineers) followed by Continuation Training at sea and a Qualification Board on the submarine. There were then the corresponding nuclear courses at Greenwich and further nuclear submarine qualification at sea. All submarine officers had to be completely familiar with the myriad of systems, tanks, pipes and valves on board, details of the trimming, electrical and propulsion systems, and a host of Standard and Emergency Operating Procedures. Award of the coveted submarine badge was not won without much hard work and formal examinations, although a technical or engineering background made it easier.

It was fortunate that the very able Lieutenants Peter Linstead-Smith and Brian Neville were the next IOs to qualify SM. After sea-time and qualification in *Olympus*, Peter Linstead-Smith joined the SSN *Conqueror*, before eventually relieving Sam Poole in the Command Team Trainer. Brian Neville went on to SSBNs after initial experience in *Opportune*. He completed a missile trial firing and two patrols in *Resolution* before relieving Glyn Macken as the Navigation Systems Officer in the Polaris School, where other IOs continued to fill specialist jobs, albeit without needing to qualify SM. The school staff included Lieutenant Commander Graham Davis, who was a highly successful Polaris Missile Instructor.

Within 18 months in the school, Brian Neville had taken on an additional role as the squadron's Polaris Navigation Sea Trainer involving all work-ups, shakedown operations, sea training and inspections. He then continued in the submarine world in 1976, with an appointment to the SSN OPCON team at Northwood as the first Fleet Operations Analyst. This was a major and vitally important role working under the strictest security caveats and involving joint operations with the US Navy.

HMS *Neptune* submarine base at Faslane
© MOD Crown Copyright by permission of RN Submarine Museum

Other IOs were less fortunate. John Wimpress qualified in *Renown*, but did not enjoy the experience. He then relieved John Watt who had become the Squadron Training Officer and made it a specialist job, tailored to his own expertise and experience. This was a hard act to follow and the job was subsequently discontinued, but not before John Wimpress had captained the Base rugby team to the final of the Navy Cup and advanced a new Diving Trainer project.

With the general shortage of SM engineers, there was also an opportunity to fill some of the nuclear Engineering posts. Lieutenants John Marriott and David Drury were sent for Nuclear Propulsion Officer of the Watch training. John Marriot was the first Schoolie to qualify as an Engineer Officer of the Watch and, subsequently, joined the Canadian Navy where he continued in submarines, later becoming First Lieutenant of the diesel submarine *Onondaga*. After time as an Instructor on the Nuclear Propulsion courses for ratings at *Sultan*, David Drury qualified as the second Schoolie Engineer Officer of the Watch in *Revenge* after time in *Renown* and *Resolution*. Being the CO's bridge partner helped him! He went on to serve very successfully in a complement billet as an Assistant Marine Engineer Officer in *Valiant* after passing the SSN Engineer Officer of the Watch Board. Lieutenant Ian Purdie and others followed him in this technically complex role.

Meanwhile, Bob Young had been three years at AUWE guiding the development of TDHS, but the first submarine, *Swiftsure*, was still building at Barrow. Therefore, he was diverted away from the submarine world to further his career along the METOC route. Fortunately, there was a ready-made relief in Guy Warner, already an experienced submariner, who relieved him in 1972.

Guy Warner brought with him a deep interest in what was known as bearings-only analysis, which was a manual process of deriving a contact's range, course and speed from passive-only information. The new system TDHS was to automate this, but the process then available produced only average results on one contact at a time. Guy Warner derived a new mathematical method, able to be used for every contact; he also designed and wrote the first software for it.

The software would probably have remained in the laboratory at AUWE in 1974 if Glyn Macken had not relieved Guy Warner who went off to fill a seaman complement billet in *Swiftsure*, by then on sea trials with the first system DCA. Glyn Macken got the new software to sea in DCA where it was a marked success, although it needed informed manual interaction. Glyn Macken was the specialist officer at AUWE for system DCB that was to add Fire Control to the existing functions. His next appointment was to Dartmouth before returning later to the Submarine Service.

HMS *Swiftsure*
© MOD Crown Copyright by permission of RN Submarine Museum

Guy Warner was in *Swiftsure* for nearly three years, which included a covert operational patrol in the Mediterranean and several to the Barents Sea. During this time, apart from serving as Communications Officer, he helped to further develop system DCA, which also went into *Sovereign* and *Superb*, before being superseded by system DCB. Among others on board *Swiftsure* at that time were two Lieutenants who were to become Admirals, Sir James Burnell-Nugent and Sir Mark Stanhope, who became the First Sea Lord in 2009.

The concept of IOs serving in submarines prior to shore jobs needing submarine expertise was by now well established. Lieutenant Robin Stainbank went to *Sovereign*, before relieving Peter Linstead-Smith in the Command Team Trainer. Lieutenant John Hart had qualified SM and was undertaking important work in the Submarine Tactical Weapons Group, where he was able to apply his sharp academic mind to such topics as the deep analysis of Soviet submarine operations. Later, Lieutenant Laurie Brokenshire had to take up the post in the group in 1977 prior to SM training, as the planned occupant failed his submarine course; all was not plain sailing.

However, this did not stop Laurie Brokenshire running all the desktop calculator software for the entire Submarine Flotilla and liaising with the Americans on what was provided. Lieutenants Roy Westerman and Nigel Turner also qualified as submariners and went on to fill shore jobs successfully.

Very importantly, the Instructor Branch was also able to retain the prestigious position of Officer-in-Charge of the Polaris School by appointing talented officers; they were often required to carry out this job without formal SM sea experience. This post was held by Commanders Tony Newing, Arthur Baxter, Chris Young and Jack Howard, who all followed Willie Waddell. Other Commander-level posts continued at the Submarine School and on FOSM staff, where Tom Berry was followed by Ken Healey, who played a significant role in increasing the presence of IOs in submarines.

Continuation into the 1980s

Lieutenant Trevor Spires started submarine engineering training in the late 1970s. After passing the shore training courses, he completed his Engineering Officer of the Watch qualification in *Repulse* before joining *Renown* as Assistant Marine Engineering Officer, where he undertook post refit trials, safety and operational work-ups. He subsequently relieved Ian Purdie on the nuclear training staff at DNST Greenwich. Lieutenants Mike Potter (SSNs) and Paul Morris (SSBNs) followed him down the technically demanding path of nuclear propulsion Officer of the Watch.

No less than five selected IOs went down the Seaman Officers submarine qualification route in mid-1979. They were Lieutenants Pat Tyrrell, Alastair Kennaugh, Ron Bramhall, Laurie Brokenshire and Paul Gregory; these latter two IOs took up highly sensitive and very critical intelligence collection submarine sea rider jobs as part of Defence Intelligence (DI8). Pat Tyrrell joined *Resolution* and became a TAS specialist, where he gave a popular brief every day. He found his appointment extremely satisfying, both personally and professionally and went on to relieve Laurie Brokenshire in DI8, where he spent some years in the forefront of submarine operations. Alastair Kennaugh served in a *Swiftsure* class SSN before joining *Renown* and Ron Bramhall also served at sea. Lieutenant Commander Ian Williams was another seaman IO who was very well regarded at the Command Team Trainer and nearly went through for Perisher.

Meanwhile, Guy Warner had taken up a new post in the Polaris Post-Patrol Analysis Group, where he was responsible for monitoring the operational security of Polaris submarines. Among other tasks, he organised and managed the first towed array trials by *Resolution* on the Atlantic Undersea Test and Evaluation Centre (AUTEC) range in the Bahamas. He was relieved by Robin Stainbank and, after promotion in 1980, took over from Chris Young on FOSM Staff.

In that year, Glyn Macken was appointed as the Officer-in-Charge of the Polaris School, a role for which he was very well qualified. The decision to purchase Trident from the Americans was made during his time there. In 1982, Brian Neville was moved from *Collingwood* to become the Project Officer at Bath for the replacement of the school, again a job for which he was an ideal candidate. He was to become the first Officer-in-Charge of the new RN Strategic Systems School, which was to come online successfully in 1990, on time and to budget.

Meanwhile, John Watt had relieved Guy Warner on FOSM staff, with the job now expanded to include responsibility for all the Flotilla Training Requirements. Peter Linstead-Smith also served on FOSM staff as the Flotilla Oceanographic Officer and was eventually relieved by Laurie Brokenshire who increased the job specification to include sonar.

HMS *Vanguard*
© MOD Crown Copyright by permission of RN Submarine Museum

Among others to work in the Submarine Service without being a qualified submariner was Lieutenant Commander Des Malone who did an exceptional job at the Joint Acoustic Analysis Centre at Teddington. Des Malone then, after a period on FOSM's staff and in Polaris Headquarters (CTF 345), relieved another IO Lieutenant Commander Mike Vine who was the first Officer-in-Charge of the Anti-Submarine Warfare Analysis Centre at Farnborough.

The Officer-in-Charge of the Polaris School (later the Strategic Systems School) continued as an IO job and when Glyn Macken was appointed as the Executive Officer, *Dolphin* (a first for the branch there and from which he was promoted to Captain), he was followed at the school by Commanders John Hart, Paul Gregory and Brian Neville, who were all qualified submariners. Other key jobs to continue included those on FOSM staff, in STWG, in the school, at Greenwich, in the Analysis/Intelligence world and in the Command Team Trainers, for there was now a second one at Plymouth, as Devonport had become a major submarine base.

Wind-Down in the 1990s

Their Appointer had earmarked Lieutenants Bryan Newton and Jim Wilson for submarines, but they were suddenly presented with a unique opportunity for prior familiarisation before attending the SM training courses. They were appointed to join *Olympus*, one of the last 'O' class submarines, on her decommissioning tour before being sold to Canada. This tour took seven months and both IOs had a great time – much of it being port visits! They then went on to what had become the SM Basic Warfare course followed by the Nuclear Warfare Officers course at Greenwich. For the final three months of Part 3 training at sea, Jim Wilson was appointed to an SSBN, but Bryan Newton got a plum appointment to *Talent*, which was a brand-new Trafalgar class submarine.

Bryan Newton had an interesting time in *Talent*, including deployment to the first Gulf War, followed by the Devonport Command Team Trainer, where he spent three years before joining the Submarine School in *Dolphin* as the Training Staff Officer and Second-in-Command. The Submarine School now housed much complex equipment including weapon loading and handling equipment, control room simulators and a full Computer Graphics Imagery (CGI) periscope Attack Teacher. Transferring the school later to *Raleigh* was an enormous task.

Other officers continued to follow in the submarine world including Lieutenants Neil Lewis and Chris Rudman (Warfare) and Dave Bridger (Nuclear Engineer). Meanwhile, Laurie Brokenshire was appointed as the Commanding Officer *Warrior* at Northwood where FOSM and the Nuclear Deterrent Task Force (Commander Task Force 345) teams were based. Later, as a Commodore, he became the Commanding Officer at *Raleigh*, which included the Submarine School, although elements remained at Faslane and the Escape Training Tower stayed at *Dolphin*.

In the computer world, the need did not now exist for IOs to the same extent for the work was all being done by Industry and a brand new Command and Fire Control System, SMCS, started to replace DCB in every submarine. This was predominantly the brainchild of Guy Warner who had resigned from the Royal Navy in 1982 to join CAP Scientific; this company, with Gresham Lion, won the competition against Ferranti for the new system.

The key to their winning was their use of Commercial-Off-The-Shelf equipment, Apple Macintosh type manual interaction, and another important facility: this allowed post-event analysis and on board training to take place while keeping the system operational in real time. To provide this entailed writing a special-purpose operating system, as the commercial systems did not need second time base facility.

SMCS went to sea in the first Trident submarine *Vanguard* in 1994. A system with the same philosophy also went into the Type 23 frigates. Many advances have since been incorporated in submarine command systems, now named SMCS NG (New Generation). The latest class of SSN, *Astute*, has an integrated combat system with SMCS NG at its heart.

HMS *Vanguard*
© MOD Crown Copyright under the Open Government Licence

Much of RN training passed to Industry and doubtless former IOs and SM officers were involved in that, but this writer knows no detail except that Peter Linstead-Smith was awarded the OBE for that role. However, the new Trident Training Facility, which superseded the Polaris School, would have required a similar team of IOs some of which were qualified SM.

Brian Neville was relieved, on promotion to Captain, by submariner Commander Mike Worrall. Trident made a new set of demands on the Submarine Service and IOs played a full part in helping to meet those.

And in Conclusion…

The author is conscious of the fact that there are some names and careers that are not mentioned – particularly in the later years – but he has only been able to write about what he knows and what has been contributed. However, Graham Cooper, John England, Peter Gregson, Robin Hodson and Nigel Huxtable also qualified as submariners. In addition, Joe Allen was a respected sonar instructor in the Submarine School for some years and John Coker was in the highly sensitive Strategic Systems targeting group at Bath before joining the Computer Sciences Corporation.

This article has tried to present a picture of the involvement of the Instructor Branch with the submarine world, both afloat and ashore, and how it came about. However, much of the penetration and recognition was achieved by the individual efforts of the officers lucky enough to have the opportunity.

Nothing much was handed out on a plate and those who succeeded often did so by putting in a great deal more work than would normally be expected. Some were much more successful than others in a demanding environment and very good personal qualities, together with an ability to build good relationships, were indispensable. There were some who found it too difficult to cope and were phased out.

It should be clear that many names occur repeatedly in jobs working with the Submarine Service that could not have been foreseen at the onset of their training. It undoubtedly helped greatly in all associated jobs to be able to wear the coveted submarine badge (dolphins). That gave membership to one of the most exclusive clubs in the world, as evidenced by the support given at every submarine funeral! A significant number of IO SMs were given the opportunity to join the Seaman or Engineering specialisations, but it is not known that any did. This was not because the time in submarines was not enjoyable – it was immensely fulfilling for most – but probably people felt those alternative career paths were not for them.

Was it all worthwhile? Well, it gave the IOs involved a great opportunity to serve in the mainstream of the Royal Navy with a high level of job satisfaction. However, most IOs outside the Submarine Service were not aware of the considerable contribution that their peers were making. In career terms, this Rampart produced five Admirals and several Commodores and Captains.

Moreover, the fact remains that at most periods between 1965 and 1995, the Submarine Service could not have functioned so effectively without the assistance of the talented efforts of more than 50 Instructor Officers.

THE ROYAL MARINES

Jim Patrick

The primary fighting elements of the Royal Marines were, at the time of writing, the three battalion-sized Commando units:

- 40 Commando, based at Norton Manor Barracks, Taunton, Somerset.
- 42 Commando, based at Bickleigh Barracks, Plymouth, Devon.
- 45 Commando, based at Condor Barracks, Arbroath, Angus, Scotland.

The headquarters of 3 Commando Brigade is in Stonehouse Barracks, Plymouth and there are RM units located around the country including:

- Commando Logistic Regiment based at Chivenor, Devon.
- Fleet Protection Group Royal Marines (previously Commachio Group) based at Faslane, Helensburgh.
- 1 Assault Group Royal Marines based at Royal Marines Poole, Dorset.

Eastney Barracks was a training centre, but closed in 1991, and the Royal Marines School of Music moved from Royal Marines Deal to the Portsmouth Naval Base in 1996.

Commando Training Centre Royal Marines (CTCRM) is the principal military training centre for the Corps and is based at Lympstone near Exmouth in Devon. CTCRM provides training to new-entry recruits and officers along with specialist trade training and command courses. Royal Marines new entry training is the longest basic infantry training programme of any NATO combat troops, and the Royal Marines is the only Service in which officers and recruits are trained at the same place and undergo the same physical tests.

A Royal Marines Commando Unit can operate independently, or as part of 3 Commando Brigade. To enable each unit to deploy as a self-contained entity, the Corps obtains specialists from elsewhere, including engineers and gunners from the Army, and doctors, dentists, padres and Instructor Officers from the Royal Navy.

Although it is the intention to mention in this article some of the key IO personalities who have served with the Corps over the years, it is inevitable that some worthy characters will have been inadvertently omitted.

Instructor Officers in the Corps

A significant proportion of the RN Instructor billets with the RMs are based at CTCRM include a Commander as the Corps Instructor Officer (CIO), the Senior Instructor Officer (SIO) and others who provide the Education and Training Management expertise for the centre and indeed the RM as a whole.

In addition, there are Unit Education Officers (UEO) who not only provide all the education and resettlement services required, but also carry out a myriad of other roles. These secondary tasks tend to vary from unit to unit, and could include jobs such as watchkeeper in Commando Headquarters, Assistant Intelligence Officer, Public Relations Officer, Non-Public Funds Officer and Rugby Officer.

Royal Marines are masters at maximising their resources, and all assets will be used to the full. Therefore, the Unit Schoolie will invariably be invited to carry out many other key functions. Such duties would vary from hosting a group of potential officer candidates whilst in camp, to acting as a liaison officer to another battle group during an operational deployment.

In the majority of cases, CTCRM would be the IO's first Royal Marines appointment when he would have the chance to attempt the All Arms Commando Course. The details of this course are included at the end of this chapter. Success or failure on this course will determine his future employment with the Corps. As with the other personnel seconded to the Corps, Instructor Officers had to complete the course to gain their Green Beret.

Serving as a Commando Schoolie has always brought fun along with tremendous camaraderie. It has also brought extensive and intensive operational experience, even more so in recent years, and for many has become one of the most successful routes for promotion.

In the Beginning

Two individuals merit special mention immediately. Colin George and Simon Goodall were absolutely pivotal in establishing 'Service with the Corps' as a Rampart in its own right, rather than as a continuing offshoot of education and training support in the Royal Navy.

In January 1974, Lieutenant Simon Goodall was appointed directly from initial training at Dartmouth to CTCRM Lympstone. This was unusual, if not unique, as Instructor Officers were appointed to traditional RN training establishments for their first appointments and not to the Royal Marines. It just so happened, however, that the Junior Officers' Appointer at that time was Lieutenant Commander Colin George, who was one of the very few General List officers who wore a green beret; he completed the Commando Course in the mid-1960s and served with 42 Commando RM in Singapore and Borneo during the Indonesia Confrontation.

Alex Manning with D Company 40 Commando RM in the Falklands in 1983
– a window shutter being used as an improvised training facility

IOs serving with the Corps at the time of Simon Goodall's appointment were invariably Short Service or Medium Career Commission officers on the Supplementary List and none of the senior posts needed the Green Beret qualification. Indeed, service with the Corps was regarded by many IOs as a career backwater!

Colin George went on to become SIO at CTCRM and on promotion to Commander, took over as the CIO, the senior IO appointment with the Royal Marines. These posts had rarely, if ever, been filled by a commando-trained officer and whilst serving in these two key appointments, Colin George used his influence, knowledge and wide experience of the Corps to develop serving with the Corps as a recognised Rampart for IOs. The George Policy thus created real career paths for the benefit of both GL and SL officers, and service in a commando unit was regarded as the equivalent of a sea appointment.

Roles for IOs in the Corps

Simon Goodall was the first of these new appointments. After CTCRM, he went on to become Corps Tutor and then UEO of 40 Commando, a triple sequence of Corps jobs unprecedented for a GL officer; as a result, he became the role model and mentor for young IOs with aspirations to serve with the Corps. Simon Goodall and Colin George were thus in the vanguard of change in taking what had been a set of largely *ad hoc* posts and creating a structured and meaningful career path for Schoolies who wanted to serve with the Corps. Over time, more officers with GL ambitions came forward, thereby building up a succession of commando-trained officers who were able, after commando service, to be appointed to more senior posts with the Royal Marines as their careers developed.

For some time, the skills of IOs have also been used by the Corps in many other areas outside the core roles of Education and Resettlement. Information Technology expertise was provided by a number of individuals, including Lieutenant Commanders Hywel Parry-Jones, Dave Burton, Ian Yuill, Pete Murphy and Pete O'Brien. They commanded and developed the RM Small Systems Group and, along with others, devised a strategy for the training and development of Information Systems throughout the Corps.

Road to Stanley
by permission of Navy News (MOD)

Another important post is that of Corps Tutor, a Defence Studies specialist whose role is to provide academic support to RM Young Officers under training at CTCRM and to all RM officers preparing for staff college entry and promotion exams. This was no small task. Corps Tutors, after Simon Goodall, included Lieutenant Commanders Bob Chapman, Sam Poole, Peter Marley, Greg Kenyon, Locker Madden and, more recently, Andy Plackett, Tris Lovering and Lawrence Kies.

Of these, only Bob Chapman and Lawrence Kies have been green-bereted, because there was no requirement to deploy operationally and performance in the post was more important than the holder's hat colour. The legendary Locker Madden, in particular, was an inspired appointment back in the early 1980s. Never an aspirant commando, Locker Madden simply focused on delivering as the Corps Tutor in his own, some may say, eccentric manner. He was a true character and the Corps took him to their hearts. Sadly, no longer with us, he was one of the best Corps Tutors and is remembered with respect and affection by everyone in the RM and RN with whom he came in contact.

IOs have also made an enormous contribution over the years in the running and development of the Royal Marines Video Production Unit. There has been a long line of Commando Instructor Officers in this role, including Lieutenant Commanders David Roberts, John Coley, Paul Tovey, Tony Miklinski, Chris Woods, Campbell Christie, Paul Hart, Pete Adams, Ian Linderman, Chris McGinley and others. Over the years, these officers have maintained and enhanced the strong reputation of the Royal Marines Video Production Unit, ensuring its survival where the others have closed.

In addition to the IO dedicated billets, some other key RM posts have been filled by green-beret Schoolies. In 1994 Commander Campbell Christie was appointed as Deputy Chief of Staff (Logistics) in HQRM and Commander Jim Patrick had the most fortunate experience to serve as Second-in-Command of the SBS from 1995 to 1997. Jim Patrick and Tony Miklinski also have both been privileged to hold the post of Director of Training at CTCRM. IOs in these appointments, less than 20 years ago, would have been unthinkable.

IOs in Operations

Commando Schoolies have long since become an integral part of the Corps and have seen action alongside their RM colleagues in all the operational campaigns of the last 50 years: Malaya, Borneo, Aden, Northern Ireland, Falklands, Balkans, Sierra Leone and, most recently, Iraq and Afghanistan.

In 1982 in the Falkland, there were several Schoolies serving with the Commando Brigade: Lieutenant Commanders Tony Miklinski and Nic Brown in 42 Commando, Lieutenant Mike Hawkes in 40 Commando and Lieutenant Commander Eddie Bairstow in 45 Commando. Others were down there who had served in the Corps including Lieutenant Commanders Terry Le Manquais (*Penelope*), Tom McCrimmon (*Alacrity*) and Alex Manning (*Intrepid* then later MCM11).

Campbell Christie in the field – displaying the 'comfort' of a one-man bivouac!

Also present, with 2 Para, was Major Mike Beaumont, a Green Beret Schoolie at Lympstone in the early 1970s who had transferred to the Royal Army Education Corps on completion of his Short Service Commission in the Royal Navy.

Minister (Armed Forces) John Stanley meets Jim Patrick
visiting 3 Commando Brigade Norway 1984

A number of Commando Schoolies have found themselves serving with the United Nations in posts and locations where their RM backgrounds and training proved invaluable. One such officer was Lieutenant Commander Peter Adams who was appointed at short notice to serve in the Congo, as an acting Commander, working for a Senegalese General. The job demanded a fluent French speaker and, unfortunately, Peter Adams was given no time to brush up on his French, which he described as rusty. In the early days of the appointment, this resulted in a fractious General rendering frequent and stern b****ckings on his language proficiency. However, as he reported, 'Fortunately he was so angry and spoke so quickly that I couldn't understand a word of it!' Not surprisingly, in this environment, his French improved very quickly and he completed a very successful tour.

Lieutenant Commander Alex Manning, who had previously served with 41 Commando in both Northern Ireland and then Cyprus with the United Nations, and in the Falklands, also saw action in Cambodia while serving there with the United Nations Force in 1992-93. At one point, he had what he describes as a somewhat mind-concentrating experience, when he was taken hostage by the Khmer Rouge. They had reneged on the promise of a safe conduct that he had obtained in order to meet with one of their commanders. He tells the tale that the official story behind his eventual safe release was that it was as a result of prolonged and careful negotiations, aided by the fact that he had secured the agreement for the meeting with the Khmer Rouge in front of a large number of UN and Cambodian witnesses. The truth, he says, was somewhat different. 'What actually happened was that I started to give them one of my history lectures, as a result of which the Khmer Rouge were soon banging on the

UN's door begging them to come and get me! I just can't for the life of me think why it took the UN so long!' On the more serious side, he affirms that the Conduct after Capture training that he received in his Corps days paid absolute dividends and that he also came away with more information than he would have gained from weeks of ordinary meetings, even if possible.

In addition to those appointed as Corps Tutor without completing the Commando Course, a number of other Schoolies served with distinction in various key RM posts wearing blue berets. These include Lieutenant Mike Young, Lieutenant Commanders Bert Kinsey, Ken Newell, John Morris, Jon Wakeling and Bob James, and Commanders Tony Mitchener, Terry Le Manquais and Brian Davies.

Serving with the Corps did not appeal to all IOs, but those who were suited to the ethos and lifestyle could go on to carve out a fascinating and varied career. It was something very special, operating around the world in all environments: arctic, jungle and desert. However, what was really special was the quality of the people with whom you served and the way you were received and accepted. Wearing the iconic Green Beret visually demonstrated that you have earned the right to serve alongside your RM colleagues, while instilling a confidence within yourself in your ability to operate in their environment and make a valuable contribution. You were not pre-judged and would be given every opportunity to prove yourself. The Command would always use the resources at their disposal to the full, including the skills and expertise of all staff. It was incredible how much autonomy and responsibility you acquired as a Lieutenant.

However, it was important that you did not lose sight of your primary function and the best piece of advice a young IO could receive on taking up his appointment was: 'Be a first class Schoolie not a second class Royal Marine!'

Honours and Awards for IOs

During the last 40 years, a fair sprinkling of honours have been forthcoming: MBEs for David Roberts (45 Commando) and Barry Brooking (40 Commando) for their time in Northern Ireland in the early 1970s, Tom McCrimmon (ex-41 Commando) for work in Saudi Arabia and Tristan Lovering (Corps Tutor). CBEs have been awarded to Simon Goodall, Tony Miklinski, Campbell Christie, Mike Farrage and Jim Patrick; Colin George was Mentioned in Dispatches.

Ethos of the Corps

The *esprit de corps* and sense of family that exists within the Royal Marines is incredibly strong and is a fundamental factor in what makes them one of the most formidable fighting forces in the world. There is something called the Commando Spirit, the four tenets of which are courage, determination, unselfishness and cheerfulness in the face of adversity; these seem to define the ethos and culture of the Royal Marines.

A Schoolie serving with the Corps cannot help but become part of this ethos. After his appointment with 42 Commando, which included a seven-month deployment to Afghanistan, Lieutenant Alex Burlingham described it as a kind of Stockholm syndrome. He said, 'The culture of infectious inclusiveness permeates every second of the fortunate Unit Schoolie's tenure. It is not so much that one is expected to get involved with unit business as much as possible; you just very much want to. You want to contribute as much as you can and you also want to extract every ounce of experience from the appointment. Any lingering doubt that I had not participated to the best of my ability would be a source of profound longer term regret.'

This camaraderie also exists amongst those who have enjoyed service with the Corps. Commando Schoolies experience a strong bond and still gather once a year for a black-tie dinner to renew old acquaintances and receive an update on service with the Corps. After-dinner entertainment is provided by some of the talented musicians we have in our number (Captain Pete Adams, Lieutenant Commander Pete Le Gassick, Commander Ian Linderman, Lieutenant Anthony Quinn and others) along with contributions from lesser talented but extremely enthusiastic senior officers!

A gathering of Royal Marines Instructor Officers in 2004

The roots of the dinner might actually lie with the famous, or perhaps infamous, GREMLINS (Green Rugged Educators Meeting Licentiously In Night Spots). This was the name given to an *ad hoc* dining club formed in the early 1980s by Commando Schoolies, who were serving in London at the time. These included Simon Goodall, Chris Woods, Paul Tovey, Tony Miklinski, Phil Whalley, Alex Manning and Jim Patrick. As senior officer, Simon Goodall was voted in as chairman and wrote the club's Charter on a napkin during the first meeting! Thereafter, the Gremlins have met once a month, each Gremlin taking it in turn to identify and recce a restaurant and a suitably adjacent pub, the rule being that it could not be anywhere already visited and that it should represent a different culinary culture each time; this was not difficult in London. The original Gremlins have moved on, but the Club was refreshed with new blood over the years and survived into the mid-1990s.

The relationship between the Royal Marines and our branch is unique and based absolutely on mutual respect. Even the term Schoolie, when delivered by a Royal Marine, is affectionate and not in any way derogatory or patronising.

Captain David Murray (Chief Naval Instructor Officer) and Commander David Bittles (the Appointer) visiting CTCRM Lympstone with Commander Jim Patrick and the team of Royal Marines IOs in 1992

Importance of IOs to the Corps

The serious side to the Commando Schoolies' acceptance by Royal Marines is in the extent to which his contribution to the Unit is appreciated and valued. In the early 1970s, when the plans to develop Instructor Officer career paths through the Corps was in full swing, a Commanding Officers' Conference was held at the RM Barracks at Eastney. As ever, questions of structure and manpower were on the agenda and Colin George attended for one item as the Corps Instructor Officer. He later explained how desolate he felt when one CO addressed the item under discussion. In answer to the question posed, 'Do we need to maintain the post of Unit Schoolie?'

The CO replied, 'No, there is no need to maintain the post'. As he prepared to give an opposing view, Colin was mightily relieved to hear the CO continue, 'providing that I can have at least six junior RM officers in his stead'. All those around the table agreed and Colin George was stood down with no further discussion.

The sheer flexibility of the post was, and I suspect remains, a significant factor for the Commanding Officer. The capacity to task a young, intelligent and highly motivated officer with almost any job from organising a quiz night to assisting in planning a disembarkation procedure, or helping maintain an intelligence picture was pure gold; one would like to think that over the years, all have risen to the challenges of each decade, whilst never forgetting or short-changing their fundamental role as educators.

It is for this reason that I believe that the Royal Marines insisted on keeping their Schoolies' posts in the manpower re-structuring that took place in the mid-1990s when the mainstream Royal Navy abandoned similar posts at sea. Therefore, when the demise of the Instructor Specialisation took place in 1996, those working with the Royal Marines saw very little change apart from Instructor Officer billet titles being replaced by that of Engineer (Training Manager).

Through the efforts of generations of highly effective officers, the bond between the RMs and Schoolies has continually strengthened. However, it is testimony to the vision and efforts of Colin George and Simon Goodall that the process for developing IOs within the Corps that was put in place all those years ago has survived the test of time and delivered the goods required.

Training in Helicopter Drills
by permission of Navy News (MOD)

The All Arms Commando Course

The All Arms Commando Course lasts 9 weeks and is run at the Commando Training Centre Royal Marines, Lympstone.

Following a two-week pre-course period, affectionately known as the 'beat up' to ensure everyone is at a common standard of basic skills and fitness, the course focuses on core military skills, including patrolling, defence, and section and troop level attacks.

The course then covers the following Commando skills: amphibious assault drills, cliff assault drills, helicopter drills and small-unit tactics.

The course concludes with a week-long confirmatory test exercise, followed by the Commando Tests which must be completed on consecutive days during the final test week:

- Endurance Course – 2 miles of cross country and water obstacles followed by a 4.5 mile road run in 72 minutes carrying 21lb fighting order and a personal weapon, followed immediately by a range shoot.
- 9 Mile Speed March – as a formed body in 90 minutes carrying 21lb fighting order and personal weapon.
- Tarzan Assault Course – in less than 12 minutes carrying 21lb fighting order and personal weapon.
- 30 Miler – 30-mile cross-country march over Dartmoor in 8 hours carrying 21lb fighting order and personal weapon.

On successful completion of the course, the candidates are presented with their Green Beret, and earn the right to wear the Commando Dagger on their uniform.

ANNEX 1

Chronology of the Instructor Branch and Specialisation

1702 The Naval Schoolmaster is first mentioned in an Order-of-Council when he was permitted to be paid as a Midshipman and to receive a bounty of £20 per year. Candidates were required to pass a test of ingenuity set by the Master and Brethren of Trinity House.

1729 Naval Academy at Portsmouth opened and the training of young gentlemen at sea abandoned. This was not a success and Schoolmasters continued to be borne in ships.

1806 Naval Academy enlarged and renamed the Royal Naval College.

1812 Bounty increased to £30 per year and a tuition fee of £5 per year stopped from each young gentleman's pay. Honours graduates were exempt from entry examination now set by the Governor of the Royal Naval College. Chaplains could claim bounty and levy if no Schoolmaster was borne.

1837 Seamen Schoolmasters awarded Warrant rank.

1842 Title of Schoolmaster changed to Naval Instructor to avoid confusion with Seamen Schoolmasters.

1842 Royal Naval College closed and training to be given at sea exclusively. Establishment of 39 Naval Instructors of whom 11 were graduates.

1861 Naval Instructors appointed by commission. The blue distinction cloth between gold lace of rank was introduced. Uniform was optional until 1891. New entries appointed as Lieutenants with automatic promotion to Commander after 15 years' service.

1862 Seaman's Schoolmaster given title of Naval Schoolmaster.

1867 Naval Schoolmaster was rated as a Chief Petty Officer, ranking with the Master-at-Arms and drawing the same pay.

1880s From the late 1800s, the Royal Marines recruited their own Schoolmasters. They were dressed as Royal Marines and included in the RM section of the Navy List.

1903 Selborne Scheme introduced with the training of Cadets at Dartmouth and Osborne to the age of 17. Because Instruction at sea would no longer be necessary, the entry for Instructors closed in 1904.

1913 Admiralty was already doubtful of the wisdom of abolishing the Naval Instructor and considerable numbers were entered in the next few years.

1914 The Admiralty undertook to pay the compulsory contribution of Midshipman which had lingered on and become 3d per day. This was finally abolished in 1919.

1917 Rank of Chief Naval Instructor with four stripes instituted.

1918 After the war, recommendations made by the Hood Committee in 1912 that all Naval Schoolmasters be given Warrant Rank were implemented.

1919 Dual appointments as Chaplain and Naval Instructor were terminated.

1919 The Instructor Branch was reconstituted and a system of ranks from Instructor Lieutenant to Instructor Captain introduced. Permanent Commissions were awarded to Temporary officers recommended after a specified period. Schoolmasters were promoted Senior Masters and Headmaster Lieutenant.

1927 First Schoolmaster promoted to Headmaster in the rank of Commander.

1930s Royal Marines no longer recruited Schoolmasters but used RN Schoolmasters on temporary appointments.

1933 First Instructor Officer (Lieutenant Commander W G West) completes the 12-week Met Course.

1936 The first Instructor Officer was appointed Director of the Admiralty Education Department. From 1905 to this date administration had been directed by a civilian Adviser on Education with an Instructor Officer as his deputy.

Numbers were Instructor Officers 78, Schoolmasters 204

1937 Naval Meteorological Service formed. Instructor Officers were among the first to take part.

1941 Chief Naval Instructor Officer becomes an Instructor Rear Admiral.

1945 Both Instructor Officers and Schoolmasters were deeply involved in helping 'Hostilities Only' personnel on their leaving the service. They were the first Education and Resettlement Officers.

1946 Amalgamation of the Instructor and Schoolmaster (RN and RM) branches to form one single Instructor Branch. All serving Schoolmasters gain a commission.

1955 The number of Instructor Officers is at its peak of 773.

1956 Instructor Officers would continue to have the title 'Instructor' in their rank, but would wear the same uniform as the General List Officers without the Blue Stripe between their gold lace.

1960s Instructor Officers begin to be employed in Managements Services, Information Systems, Surveying, the Submarine Service and with the Royal Marines.

1962 Officers not selected for the Permanent List were able to apply for a 16-year Pensionable Commission or have the opportunity to extent their 5-year Short Service Commission for a further 5 years.

1963 First Instructor Officers join the Royal Navy and undergo initial training at BRNC Dartmouth.

1971 Royal Naval School of Educational and Training Technology (RNSETT) formed in *Nelson*.

1978 General List expanded to include the Instructor Specialisation:
- All Instructor Officers on the Permanent List incorporated onto the General List.
- The post of Director Naval Education Service (DNEdS) disbanded and Chief Naval Instructor Officer (CNIO) established.

1985 First WRNS Officers recruited as Instructor Officers pass out of Dartmouth.

1990 Instructor Specialisation numbers 623 officers.

1994 Navy Board endorses the Officers Study Group recommendation to implement a Platform Derived Structure for the Officer Corps and as a result the Instructor Specialisation is to be disbanded.

1996 Instructor Specialisation disbanded 5 July 1996. Instructor Officers reclassified as X(METOC), E(TM) and E(IS).

1997 First direct entry E(TM) Officers join on Short Service Commissions.

ANNEX 2

Number of Instructor Officers in the Royal Navy 1920 to 1995

Year	Rear Admiral	Captain	Cdr	Lieut Cdr	Lieut	Sub Lieut	Total Instructors
			Note 1	Note 2	Note 3	Note 4	
1920		2	36		54		92
1925		4	15	14	37		70
1930		4	5	45	16		70
1935		4	14	45	12		75
1940		5	43	16	55		119
1945	1	5	36	36	136		214
1950		10	44	102	532	35	723
1955	1	12	58	222	447	33	773
1960	1	12	59	297	240	22	631
1965	1	13	64	270	295	5	648
1970	1	15	62	262	330	1	671
1975	1	15	65	276	299	2	658
1980	1	17	70	316	207		611
1985		17	72	281	214	4	588
1990		16	73	267	257	10	623
1995		15	66	223	280	2	586

Note 1	Numbers include Full, Medium Career and Temporary Officers
Note 2	Numbers include Full, Medium, Short Career and Temporary Officers
Note 3	Numbers include Full, Medium, Short Career, Temporary and Hostilities only Officers
Note 4	Numbers include Short Career Officers

ANNEX 3

Heads of Naval Education

1903	1916	Civilian	Sir Alfred Newing	Director of Naval Education Director of Studies RNC Greenwich
1916	1919	Gapped		
1919	1936	Civilian	A McMullen	Adviser on Naval Education
1936	1941	Captain	A E Hall	Director Education Department of the Admiralty
1941	1945	Rear Admiral	Sir Arthur Hall	Director Education Department of the Admiralty
1945	1948	Captain	W I Saxton	Director Education Department of the Admiralty
1948	1951	Captain	W A Bishop	Director Education Department of the Admiralty
1951	1956	Rear Admiral	Sir William Bishop	Director Naval Education Service
1956	1960	Rear Admiral	Sir John Fleming	Director Naval Education Service
1960	1965	Rear Admiral	Sir Charles Darlington	Director Naval Education Service
1965	1970	Rear Admiral	A J Bellamy	Director Naval Education Service
1970	1975	Rear Admiral	B J Morgan	Director Naval Education Service
1975	1978	Rear Admiral	J A Bell	Director Naval Education Service then Chief Naval Instructor Officer
1978	1981	Rear Admiral	W A Waddell	Chief Naval Instructor Officer Flag Officer Admiralty Interview Board
1981	1983	Rear Admiral	T O K Spraggs	Chief Naval Instructor Officer Chief of Staff CINCNAVHOME
1983	1984	Rear Admiral	G A Baxter	Chief Naval Instructor Officer Senior RN Member on Directing Staff RCDS
1984	1987	Captain	J Marsh	Chief Naval Instructor Officer DNOM
1987	1989	Rear Admiral	C J Howard	Chief Naval Instructor Officer Chief of Staff CINCNAVHOME
1989	1991	Captain	G N Davis	Chief Naval Instructor Officer DNOA(I) and DNMT(I)
1991	1994	Rear Admiral	G N Davis	Chief Naval Instructor Officer DG Fleet Support
1994	1996	Captain	D C Murray	Chief Naval Instructor Officer NAAFI HQ

ANNEX 4

Deans of the Royal Naval College, Greenwich

The following Instructor Officers occupied the post of Dean of the Royal Naval College, Greenwich during the period 1955 to 1982, after which time it was discontinued:

1955	1958	Captain	E F Byng
1958	1962	Captain	A E Johnston
1962	1964	Captain	V Lamb
1964	1966	Captain	G B C Button
1966	1969	Captain	W H Watts
1969	1973	Captain	G Huggett
1973	1975	Captain	W A Waddell
1975	1977	Captain	T O K Spraggs
1977	1979	Captain	D C F Watson
1979	1981	Captain	T K Cropper
1981	1982	Captain	G N Davis

ANNEX 5

Deans of the Royal Naval Engineering College, Manadon

1957	1960	Captain	A J Bellamy
1960	1964	Captain	H E Dykes
1964	1964	Captain	D E Mannering
1964	1969	Captain	B E Morgan
1969	1972	Captain	H J Hair
1972	1973	Captain	M Moreland
1973	1975	Captain	P J Poll
1975	1978	Captain	H E Morgan
1978	1979	Captain	J E Franklin
1979	1980	Captain	T O K Spraggs
1980	1982	Captain	C J Howard
1982	1984	Captain	A O Holding
1984	1990	Captain	G C George
1990	1993	Captain	J N McGrath
1993	1994	Captain	B M Leavey

ANNEX 6

Heads of Meteorology & Oceanography

Naval Meteorological Branch
>Captain L G Garbett
>Captain F M Walton

Directors of Naval Weather Service (DNWS)
>Captain P Bracelin
>Captain A E Johnston
>Captain J A Burnett
>Captain G P Britton

Directors of Meteorology and Oceanographic Services (Naval) (DMOS(N))
>Captain G P Britton
>Captain J R Thorpe
>Captain J D Booth
>Captain R R Fotheringham
>Captain J A Bell
>Captain R K Alcock

Directors of Naval Oceanography and Meteorology (DNOM)
>Captain R K Alcock
>Captain F J Edwards
>Captain D Roe
>Captain D C Blacker
>Captain J Marsh
>Captain A M Morrice
>Captain D C Murray
>Captain P J Nicholas
>Captain J P Clarke (X(SM))
>Captain R M V Willis

Directors of Naval Surveying, Oceanography and Meteorology (DNSOM)
>Commodore R M V Willis
>Commodore S J Auty
>Commodore C B H Stevenson

Under Commodore Stevenson, the Directorate transferred from the Naval Staff to MOD Central Staff.

ANNEX 7

Officers-in-Charge of the RN School for Meteorology and Oceanography

Royal Naval School of Meteorology - HMS *Harrier*, Dale, Pembrokeshire

1946	1950	Commander	A R Edwards
1950	1951	Commander	J A Burnett
1951	1954	Commander	E T W Smyth
1954	1957	Commander	J R Thorp
1957	1959	Commander	K A Bowell

Royal Naval School of Meteorology - HMS *Seahawk*, Culdrose, Cornwall

1959	1961	Commander	N F Jenkins
1961	1964	Commander	R R Fotheringham
1964	1967	Commander	W M Evans
1967	1968	Commander	F J Edwards

Royal Naval School of Meteorology & Oceanography – HMS *Seahawk*, Culdrose, Cornwall

1968	1970	Commander	R K Alcock
1970	1971	Commander	S R Burrows
1971	1974	Commander	T A Marshall
1974	1977	Commander	M C Lilly
1977	1979	Commander	J Marsh
1979	1981	Commander	D R M Philpott
1981	1983	Commander	P A Rogers
1983	1986	Commander	J Hartley
1986	1989	Commander	W N Bowman
1989	1992	Commander	M J Channon
1992	1994	Commander	C B H Stevenson

1994	1997	Commander	M J Pickering
1997	1999	Commander	A Robinson
1999	2001	Commander	J R Sephton

Royal Naval HM School (Culdrose) - HMS *Seahawk*, Culdrose, Cornwall

2001	2002	Commander	J R Sephton
2002	2003	A/Commander	C S Davies

ANNEX 8

Royal Naval Training Establishments in 1955

The training establishments that existed in 1955 and their role at the time were as follows:

New Entry Training Establishments		**Closed**
HMS *Dauntless*	WRNS Training, Burghfield, Reading, Berks	1981
BRNC	Officers' Training, Dartmouth, Devon	
HMS *Ganges*	Junior Ratings' Training, Shotley Gate Ipswich, Suffolk	1976
HMS *St Vincent*	Junior Ratings' Training, Gosport, Hampshire	1969
HMS *Fisgard*	Artificers' Training, Torpoint, Cornwall	1983

Part 2 Training Establishments		
HMS *Ariel*	Air Electrical School, Worthy Down, Hampshire	1959
HMS *Ceres*	RN Supply and Secretariat School, Wetherby, Yorkshire	1958
HMS *Caledonia*	RN Engineer Training Establishment, Rosyth, Fife	1985
HMS *Collingwood*	RN Electrical School, Fareham, Hampshire	
HMS *Condor*	RN Air Mechanical Engineering School until 1970 (then RM Establishment)	
HMS *Daedalus*	RN Air Engineering School, Lee-on-Solent, Hampshire	1995
HMS *Dolphin*	RN Submarine School, Gosport, Hampshire	1999
HMS *Dryad*	Navigation and Direction School, Southwick, Hampshire	2004
HMS *Excellent*	RN Gunnery School, Whale Island, Portsmouth, Hampshire	1974
RN College	Initial Officer Training and Staff College, Greenwich, London	1998
HMS *Harrier*	RN School of Aircraft Direction and Met School, Dale, Pembrokeshire	1960
HMS *Mercury*	HM Signal School, Petersfield, Hampshire	1993
HMS *Phoenix*	RN ABCD School, Tipner, Portsmouth, Hampshire	1993
HMS *Raleigh*	Stokers Training Establishment, Torpoint, Cornwall	
HMS *Royal Arthur*	RN Petty Officers' School, Corsham, Wiltshire	1992
HMS *Sultan*	RN Marine Engineering School, Gosport, Hampshire	
HMS *Thunderer*	RN Engineering College, Plymouth, Devon	1995
HMS *Vernon*	RN TAS School, Portsmouth, Hampshire	1996

Naval Air Training Establishments

RNAS ARBROATH	HMS *Condor*, Arbroath, Angus, Scotland	1971
RNAS BRAMCOTE	HMS *Gamecock*, Nuneaton, Warwickshire	1957
RNAS GOSPORT	HMS *Siskin*, Gosport, Hampshire	1956
RNAS ST MERRYN	HMS *Curlew*, Padstow, Cornwall	1956
RNAS WORTHY DOWN	HMS *Ariel*, Winchester, Hampshire	1959

Training Ships

Light Fleet Carrier	HMS *Ocean*
Light Fleet Carrier	HMS *Theseus*

ANNEX 9

Heads of RN Service Schools and RN Dockyard Schools and Colleges

Heads of the RN Secondary School at Mtarfa Malta from end of Second World War

1946	1951	Commander	A H Miles
1951	1954	Commander	A J Bellamy
1954	1959	Captain	B J Morgan
1959	1963	Captain	D E Mannering
1963	1966	Captain	L Broad
1966	1970	Captain	H C Malkin
1970	1974	Commander	M F Law
1974	1978	Commander	G D Stubbs

Bermuda Dockyard School – Headmasters

1934	1939	Lieutenant	J H Mitchell
1939	1944	Lieutenant	A J B Springhall
1944	1948	Lt Commander	H G Middleton
1948	1950	Lieutenant	J A Weightman

Singapore Dockyard College – Principals

1957	1958	Lt Commander	R E Collins
1960	1963	Lt Commander	D C M Branwood
1963	1965	Lt Commander	J H C Horton
1965	1968	Commander	L Blamey
1968	1970	Commander	D V Fowke

Malta Dockyard School/College – Headmasters

1936	1938	Lieutenant	W F Plant
1938	1942	Lieutenant	F J Giles
1942	1943	Lieutenant (A/Head)	F G Foss
1943	1945	Senior Master	T W H Foster

1945	1946	Senior Master	C Watts
1946	1948	Lieutenant	A H Miles
1948	1949	Lt Commander	L W Tucker
1949	1950	Lt Commander	W E J Golding

Malta Dockyard School/College – Principal

| 1957 | 1958 | Commander | G E Thomas |

Gibraltar Dockyard School/College – Senior Masters

1936	1940	Senior Master	C J Pickerill
1940	1944	Senior Master	F W Spry
1944	1945	Senior Master	G N Pask
1945	1947	Lieutenant	F J Hill

Gibraltar Dockyard School/College – Headmasters

1947	1950	Lt Commander	A E Willsteed
1950	1953	Lt Commander	D W Lacey
1953	1956	Lt Commander	E L Jarrold
1956	1961	Commander	T R Smart
1961	1964	Commander	F R Finch

Gibraltar Dockyard School/College – Principals

1964	1966	Commander	P O Stanley
1966	1969	Commander	T Carter
1969	1971	Commander	J W Boughey
1971	1973	Commander	D C F Watson
1973	1976	Commander	L J Stacey
1976	1978	Commander	L A J Bailey
1978	1982	Commander	D J Dacam
1982	1984	Commander	R W Hutchings

ANNEX 10

Instructor Officers in Information Systems (SACLANT and OPCON)

SACLANT – until 1996

Captains	Commanders	Lieutenant Commanders
W A Waddell	J D I Locke	T H Wingate
A Newing	W J Daniels	T Ambrose
G A Baxter	J G Davies	J B Simpson WRNS
C J G Young	R Yeomans	T R Syms
J W Boughey	P F Probert	P L Stubbs
T P Berry	A B Edouard	B M Yaldron
J D Watt	R A Young	K P Grimsley
P W Binks	A J Prosser	P Johnson
	D S Burton	J Risley
		J Melrose

OPCON Programme – until 1980

Commanders	Lieutenant Commanders
T P Berry	R W Sudweeks
T H Wingate	T H Wingate
J G Davies	J G Connolly
P W Binks	S M Bruce
J B Simpson WRNS	P W Pool
D A Lord	

GLOSSARY

ABCD	Atomic, Biological and Chemical Defence
ADAWS	Action Data Automation and Weapon System
AFO	Admiralty Fleet Order
ARE	Admiralty Research Establishment
ARL	Admiralty Research Laboratory
ASWE	Admiralty Surface Weapons Establishment, Portsdown, Portsmouth
ASWEPS	Anti-Submarine Warfare Environmental Prediction System
AUWE	Admiralty Underwater Weapons Establishment, Portland, Dorset
BRNC	Britannia Royal Naval College, Dartmouth, Devon
CAAIS	Computer Assisted Action Information System
CBT	Computer Based Training
CDS	Comprehensive Display System
CINCNAVHOME	Commander-in-Chief, Naval Home Command
CINCFLEET	Commander-in-Chief, Fleet
CO	Commanding Officer
COMFEF	Commander, Far East Fleet
CPO	Chief Petty Officer
CNAA	Council for National Academic Awards
CTCRM	Commando Training Centre, Royal Marines
CTT1 and 2	Combined Tactical/Team Trainer
DAA etc	Computer Systems fitted in surface ships
DCA etc	Computer Systems fitted in submarines
DFWSMS	Director of Fleet Work Study and Management Services
DNEdS	Director Naval Education Service
DNIS	Director Naval Information Systems
DNManS	Director Naval Management Services
DNMO	Director Naval Management and Organisation
DNOM	Director Naval Oceanography and Meteorology
DMOS(N)	Director of Meteorology and Oceanographic Services
DNST	Department of Nuclear Science and Technology
DNWS	Director of Naval Weather Service
E(IS)	Engineering (Information Systems)
E(TM)	Engineering (Training Management)
EMA	Early Morning Activity
EO	Education Officer

FDO	Flight Deck Officer
FOSM	Flag Officer Submarines
HQ1/HQ2	Damage Control Headquarters 1 and 2 in Action Stations
IO	Instructor Officer
IOUT	Instructor Officer Under Training
JAAC	Joint Acoustic Analysis Centre
ME	Marine Engineering
MEO	Marine Engineering Officer
METOC	Meteorology and Oceanography
MILOC	Military Oceanographic Group
MOD	Ministry of Defence
MPA	Maritime Patrol Aircraft
NAMET	Naval Arithmetic and English Test
NATO	North Atlantic Treaty Organisation
NAVOCEANO	Naval Oceanographic Office
NBCD	Nuclear, Biological and Chemical Defence
NEIO	New Entry Instructor Officer
OFS	Oceanographic Forecasting Service
OSG	Officer Study Group
OUT	Officer Under Training
OOW	Officer of the Watch
PDS	Platform Derived Structure
PI	Photographic Interpretation
PIU	Programme Instruction Unit
PO	Petty Officer
PWO	Principal Warfare Officer
RAF	Royal Air Force
RFA	Royal Fleet Auxiliary
RM	Royal Marines
RN	Royal Navy/Royal Naval
RNAS	Royal Naval Air Station
RNC	Royal Naval College, Greenwich, London
RNEC	Royal Naval Engineering College, Manadon, Plymouth
RNR	Royal Naval Reserve
RNSETT	Royal Naval School of Educational and Training Technology
RNSOMO	Royal Naval School of Meteorology and Oceanography
RNVR	Royal Naval Volunteer Reserve

SBS	Special Boat Service
SCEA	Service Schools Education Authority
SIO	Senior Instructor Officer
SM	Submarine
SM1 etc	Submarine Squadron 1 etc
SMCS	Command and Fire Control System in Submarines
SMOPS	School of Maritime Operations
SSBN	Nuclear-powered, Ballistic missile-carrying Submarine
SSN	Nuclear-powered Attack Submarine
STWG	Submarine Tactical Weapons Group
TCU	The City University
TDHS	Tactical Data Handling System
USN	United States Navy
VPU	Video Production Unit
WE	Weapon Engineering
WEO	Weapon Engineering Officer
WRNS	Women's Royal Naval Service
X	Seaman - Executive specialisation